Economic Tsunami
China's Car Industry Will Sweep
Away Western Car Makers

Coming off the boat - Cars streaming off a ferry in Qingdao, China, 2006

Economic Tsunami
China's Car Industry Will Sweep Away Western Car Makers

Kevin Baker

Foreword by Tim Fischer
Former Deputy Prime Minister of Australia

ROSENBERG

Dedication

To colleagues who gave their time generously
and their comment honestly. Also to Jane,
for her exacting and creative assistance in
compiling this book.

First published in Australia in 2007
by Rosenberg Publishing Pty Ltd
PO Box 6125, Dural Delivery Centre NSW 2158
Phone: 61 2 9654 1502 Fax: 61 2 9654 1338
Email: rosenbergpub@smartchat.net.au
Web: www.rosenbergpub.com.au

The National Library of Australia Cataloguing-in-Publication

Baker, K. J. (Kevin James).
Economic tsunami : China's car industry will sweep away
Western car makers.

1st ed.
Bibliography.
Includes index.
ISBN 9781877058561 (pbk.).

1. Automobile industry and trade - Economic aspects - China.
2. Automobile industry and trade - Economic aspects -
Australia. I. Title.

338.476292220951

Cover design with apologies to Katsushika Hokusai for use of his painting *Great Wave*, c. 1831

Set in 12 on 14 point Adobe Jenson Pro

Printed in China by Everbest Printing Co Limited

Contents

Figures and Tables

Abbreviations

CIMS	Court Information Management System
CMRS	Contract Management Responsibility System
FAW	First Automobile Works
FDI	Foreign direct investment
GDP	Gross domestic profit
HRM	Human resource management
ISO	International Standards Organization
PRC	People's Republic of China
SAIC	Shanghai Automotive Industry Corporation
SAW	Second Automotive Works
SDPC	State Development Planning Commission
SME	Small to medium enterprise
SOE	State-Owned Enterprise
SUV	Sports utility vehicle
UAW	United Auto Workers
WOFE	Wholly owned foreign enterprises
WTO	World Trade Organization

Acknowledgments

To the Hon. Tim Fischer for contributing the Foreword. To Angeline Lewis for advice on legal issues and Penelope Baker for assistance with translation. Also to many academic colleagues at the Australian National University in Canberra, Sichuan University in Chengdu, Ocean University in Qingdao and the University of Canberra. Special acknowledgements to the postgraduate students of the Pre-Masters Programs in Chengdu and Qingdao.

Also special acknowledgements to Carl Harrison-Ford for professional and always patient editing.

All figures, photographs and illustrations are by the author.

Foreword

Tim Fischer
*Former Deputy Prime Minister of Australia and Trade Minister,
and Leader of the Federal National Party*

Now is certainly the time to ask if we are on the cusp of another key turning point, if not tipping point, with the Great Australian Automotive Industry and its related supply and distribution industries. Are we about to see the decline and ending of the production of Australian made quality cars?

Are Ford, General Motors Holden, Mitsubishi and Toyota at risk? Or are reports and suggestions of their imminent demise greatly exaggerated, as Oscar Wilde and Mark Twain might observe if they were still around.

This is the question raised by Dr Kevin Baker in this challenging book, where he canvasses all the related subsets of this complex subject. He raises the prospect of a giant wave of cars being launched by China on the world in the next few years.

This he terms an 'economic tsunami' of relatively cheap good-quality motor vehicles being exported from China to Australia in epic numbers. In turn he suggests this will wipe out the four Australian car manufactures, and sooner rather than later.

To this I say, 'Not so fast!' There are always caveats in these propositions, and solutions suggested and available, many of a controversial kind. However, as this book argues, the clock is ticking fast and solutions deserve detailed examination and debate. At the end of the day some of these proposed solutions will be rejected, others adopted fully or in part.

At this time of writing, there are many compelling arguments as to why a huge wave of quality motor vehicles will descend on Australian and New Zealand markets, so the case for highlighting the fact the clock is ticking down to this prospect is real enough.

What are less clear are other known and at this stage unknown factors mitigating the deluge of 'Made in China' cars. As Dr Baker notes, one such factor could be exchange rates, which would be one of the less painful and more practical solutions to the problem of imbalance we face.

Part of the solution is also to provide capable and flexible automotive industry leadership, embracing efficient management practices and utilizing all the tools available as they prepare for the onslaught. This must include the peak industry organizations, principally the Federation of Automotive Product Manufactures and Federal Chamber of Automotive Industries, speaking clearly and sending united messages to governments.

These united messages must engage not just the federal but also the state governments, notably in South Australia and Victoria. They must involve professional research and advice, for example, as available from the key consulting firms such as Deloitte.

This will require a good deal of liaison within and beyond the industry, utilizing various networks to help governments and all elements of the automobile manufacturers and the automotive component manufacturers to step up to the mark.

As part of the mutual responsibility and acceptable dimension of governmental assistance and engagement, by both dries and wets and the WTO, research and development must be elevated to the top of the heap, re-energized and revamped to put Australia at the cutting edge in relation to all aspects of the automotive industry. Equally Austrade and other stakeholders must step up to the mark with export effort and facilitating export drives to Greater Asia, including the Middle East.

The truth of the matter is we live in a global village, a global trading village where alternative chassis bolt supplies can be quickly sourced worldwide, or a spare part for a 100 tonne coal mine giant shovel or dragline can be located through the internet within 60 minutes of a breakdown. In turn this can be brought from the other side of the world to an outback mining location in Australia within 36 hours.

Australia gains many extra jobs from the global trading village, as we have far more iron ore and coal and other commodities than we can ever consume with our 20 million population base. Equally, we find it convenient to buy all sorts of toys and clothes and computers from offshore, including from China, all part of the world trading equation today.

Australia is a fully paid up member of the global trading world of the 21st century because it is to our net benefit and wellbeing, it is in our interests.

The movement of complete factories offshore, from Australia to Asia or even to Oceania, is the price we pay for the benefits arising as a fully paid up member of that globalized trading world. Whilst those benefits are in total a net advantage for Australia, there are many sharp bumps along the pathway of globalization.

Whilst some would contend that the shifting of jobs offshore should be blocked at every stage, as a form of 21st century protection, others would argue that this should be an unfettered, unrestricted process to allow the best comparative advantage to emerge for overall economic efficiency. Treasury Secretary Dr Ken Henry is adamant about this, saying: Do not block off-shoring, but let us be as competitive as possible.

I have to confess I am a qualified economic dry and would strongly argue that governments do have a role to provide transition facilitation and to ensure there are not huge industry collapses overnight, at the end of the day to use legitimate tools to help the creation of a fair competitive trading circumstance for the diverse industries comprising the Australian economy. I also declare a membership of the Deloitte Auto advisory board.

If China is going to maintain a rigidity with its exchange rate which artificially helps its exports and provides *de facto* protection against imports, then the Australian government and other governments have a right not only to highlight these issues but to take what reasonable positive action they can to alleviate the ramification arising.

As a solution to this exchange rate rigidity, the author proposes a

Wages Equalization Theory (WET) as part of his core solution, namely a direct WET charge on the incoming vehicle. It is for readers to reach their own view on this but I for one see problems with that particular solution, most notably with the World Trade Organization.

I do salute the author in opening up the debate on all that lies ahead with the automobile industry, and this book throws a penetrating searchlight onto the troubled waters ahead. As Dr Kevin Baker argues, we must move now to consider possible solutions, and we must do so quickly. Timing is everything in politics, but also in manufacturing, especially with the various economic cycles that are still around.

What this book does very well is elevate the problems involved from a flashing amber circumstance to a flashing red circumstance. After Japanese motorcycle manufacturers wiped out many large non-Asian motorcycle manufacturers over the last three decades, the warnings in this book stack up and are there to behold.

It is a timely book giving forewarning of all that lies ahead and creating a debate over possible solutions to ensure that Australia maintains an automobile manufacturing industry through efficient policy settings, along with an automotive component industry, and in the case of both, hopefully they will be so efficient as to export competitively to the rest of the world.

Prologue
Imagine the Following
(*Sometimes Called a Barbecue Stopper*)

Walshie was short, but as the old saying goes, he was 'two yards of smiles'. This warm weekend afternoon he was turning the snags on the barbecue while the sound system blared the commentary from the Bathurst 1000. His mate from high school, Michael Servetus, was just back from two years working in Asia. Both had a Vic Bitter can in hand. Walshie glanced down the drive at Michael's grey '94 Magna which was parked on the road, then took a sip of his VB and asked the Big Question, 'So tell me, Michael — are you a Holden man or a Ford man?'

Michael shrugged and said, 'Well, in the end it doesn't make any difference, because in maybe five years time, neither the Commodore nor the Falcon will be manufactured in Australia anymore'.

Walshie paused, holding a snag on his fork in mid-air while fat dripped onto the barbecue and sizzled. Then he frowned and said, 'That's a pretty weird thing to say'.

'It may sound weird,' Michael responded, 'but it's true. We're heading for the death of car manufacturing in Australia. No more Aussie-designed icons. We're about to get swamped by a flood — a tsunami really — of cheap, quality cars made in China which will finish off our industry. Bear in mind that the Aussie car industry is already struggling, and couldn't withstand a power hit from overseas. Consider this — in 2005, all the car makers in the United States produced 12 million cars, but that figure is falling now as they try to cut costs to be competitive. In China, they made 6 million vehicles in 2005 and the figure is going up — doubling every five years. Okay, that figure includes trucks and buses, but it indicates how fast they're growing. By 2010, China's production capacity could be more than 12 million cars a year, surpassing the production of the United States. And that's the very time that the Australian government — in all its wisdom — will cut back its protection on our car industry to a new low.'

Walshie still stared. He let the snag fall back onto the grill. 'But how's that going to affect us? Is that important? What'll happen to Ford and Holden here?'

Seeing Walshie's chagrin, the other man felt guilty in explaining further, but nevertheless realized that he had to. His friend had to understand what was coming. The shock would hit sooner or later, and probably sooner, he reckoned. 'Well, in Australia, Mitsubishi will go under first, then maybe Ford within three years, then GM Holden within another five years because their parent companies will be under pressure to cut costs, and my guess is that maybe only Toyota will survive in Australia in an attenuated form assembling imported car kits — mainly because Toyota plants elsewhere in the world are at full capacity and they need to utilize all the facilities they've got to keep up production. The Japanese car industry is healthy, but that's because high levels of protection and other gimmicks generally keep out US and European cars, except for those who can afford the higher costs and inconvenience of getting them. However, Ford and GM are under enormous pressure from market forces to get more efficient, so it seems likely that they'll cut back wherever they can outside the US of A — wherever the cost of the cutbacks is less than the political cost of cutting back in the US itself.

'So, Walshie, at the Bathurst 1000 today, crowds may chant "Hol-den! Hol-den!" or "Fal-con! Fal-con!", but in 2015, or even as early as 2012, they won't have any new Holdens or Falcons to support because there will no longer be brand new Holdens and Falcons designed and manufactured in Australia for Australian conditions.'

'That can't happen,' breathed Walshie, and the heave of his chest stretched the ties of his apron. 'Aussies like Aussie cars and they like to follow their car racing.'

'Oh, they'll still have car races,' Michael told him. 'But maybe they'll have to follow racing sedans made by the big Chinese car makers, and maybe they'll have to learn how to chant "Dong-Feng! Dong-Feng!" or "Hong-Qi! Hong-Qi!" That means, "East Wind!" or "Red Flag!"'

Walshie grimaced. 'Australians have always had good Aussie-designed cars, but.'

'Yes, that's true. Ever since the 1940s. We needed good cars of our own then. You know the Poms sent out Morris Minors and Ford Prefects after the second war, but they were simply no good in most conditions outside the cities. They had tiny petrol tanks — only enough for maybe 300 Ks at a stretch — and were far too slow for long drives. That's one of the reasons why we had Aussie-designed cars. We needed something like the Holden because it was a decent size — with good ground clearance for Outback roads, not to mention a fuel tank that'd go 600 Ks before needing a fill. But we won't get cars for Aussie conditions anymore. We'll get a car designed for conditions in most of the world — the "global car" — but it'll probably be too small and cramped for most Aussie drivers. So, no more Aussie icons.'

'What — no Aussie cars? What'll that mean?'

'Well, we won't get cars or vehicles that Aussies like. For example, it'll be the end of the Great Aussie Ute. Asians and others don't need or want things like utes or pickups for everyday personal use; they just use them as workhorses. They want sedans — maybe SUVs — but utes are out. So the range of global cars won't include the ute as we know it. Out in the country, and sooner than you'd think, people who go to B&S Balls will have to trundle down in their Ford Fiesta, not their Ford Falcon ute, unless they've got a vintage model.'

His friend clutched at a straw. 'Gees — I don't know about all that.'

Michael crumpled his beer can, tossed it into the yawning otto bin overflowing with cans in the corner of the yard, and accepted another can from the cook.

'So, Walshie, it'll be the end of the Great Aussie Ute. Buy one while you can.'

'D'you know what you're talking about? It sounds like stuff on stilts to me. What's the evidence for all that?'

'Research into the Chinese car industry. Their factories are expanding rapidly with a huge increase in output. That's an undeniable fact. Some Western analysts forecast that a huge increase in Chinese demand will soak this up, but research I was involved in shows that there are strong restraints on demand — for example, servicing (the system doesn't support small garages and repair shops, etc.), second-hand car markets (buyers can't get expert advice), parking (there's just no room; there's hardly room to park bicycles in many places, let alone cars) and so on and so on. The big cities such as Beijing are at the limits of pollution now and can't accept many more cars on their roads. Some cities are already bringing in measures such as extra taxes to make cars more expensive and restrict ownership. Don't forget, the Chinese have commitments to keep the air clean for the Beijing Olympics, and they want to breathe in the years after that, so they just can't allow the number of vehicles on their roads to double or treble indefinitely. But they can't afford to cut back production levels either. So there'll be a growing number of cars in inventory — a massive surplus of good quality vehicles. The Chinese will export that surplus, and it will be a big quantity: around 4 million cars annually by as early as 2010 and millions more each year after that. Imagine maybe an additional 200,000 good cheap cars hitting Australian markets each year.

'In the US, the Big Three car makers — GM, Ford and DaimlerChrysler — are all cutting back production and there are suggestions that GM and Ford are under threat of bankruptcy. There have been mergers all over the place, but that hasn't solved the underlying problem of excess world capacity. Big names like Jaguar and Volvo have been taken over by Ford, but they're sinking into the red as fast as the *Titanic* went down. GM's profitability is even worse than Ford's, despite its size.'

Michael took a prawn off a plate near the barbie. 'Hey Walshie,' he said, 'I'll show you the prawn test to illustrate how the big car makers of the world are performing — at least in comparison to Toyota, which is the most profitable big car maker in the world. This prawn represents the operating profit margins of the ten largest auto making groups.'

He drew lines on the wooden table with a knife dipped in fat and lay the prawn across the lines.

'Now the top prawn is Toyota, the third largest auto maker in 2004, but the most profitable with an operating margin of nearly 10 per cent. It's a whole prawn. Now watch while I cut pieces off the prawn to represent the proportion of profit of each auto maker compared to Toyota.' He sliced pieces off the prawn with the knife.

'I'm cutting off a piece to represent BMW's operating margin as a proportion of Toyota's. BMW is the ninth biggest but second most profitable auto maker in the world, partly because the cashed-up crowd are now buying BMW limousines instead of Mercedes — and also BMW-made Minis of course.' He cut off a piece of antenna. 'There you are. Still lots of prawn left. BMW isn't doing too badly.'

'Next Renault/Nissan and Honda, also not too bad at 7 to 8 per cent operating margins — although Renault/Nissan does reasonably well because of the level of French government involvement in its operations.' Chunks of antenna were removed down to the head.

'Now, the next two cuts represent the performances of Daimler Chrysler (the fourth biggest auto maker) and Peugeot, and now the prawn loses its head and a piece of body because their profit margin is down to 4 per cent, so there's still a fair return off the prawn, but not as much as the more profitable groups.' Michael made more slices and swept the cut pieces off the table. Walshie's cat sauntered over to inspect, then eat the pieces. He was about to get a bigger feed.

'Volkswagen — remember the red Veedub you used to drive, Walshie? — is the world's sixth biggest auto maker, and the seventh most profitable, but its operating margin was less than 2 per cent in 2004. Not much of a prawn feed on the VW piece. That's despite the fact that VW has been expanding like crazy in recent years, picking up Bentley, Bugatti, SEAT, Skoda and Lamborghini. Funny to think that VW, once the symbol of the basic car, now owns a swag of luxury brands.' The prawn lost its body and part of the tail. The cat pounced on the discard.

'This is where it gets interesting, because now we come to Ford. It's the world's second biggest auto maker, manufacturing eight of the best known car brands such as Land Rover and Aston Martin and part of Mazda, as well as Jaguar and Volvo which I mentioned.'

Michael brought the knife down and left only a small part of the tail.

'That tiny piece represents Ford's operating margin as a proportion of

Toyota's. The world's second biggest auto maker ranks number eight on the scale of profitability, making barely a one per cent operating margin in 2004.'

The Prawn Test: Comparative Operating Margins of the World's Ten Largest Auto Making Groups

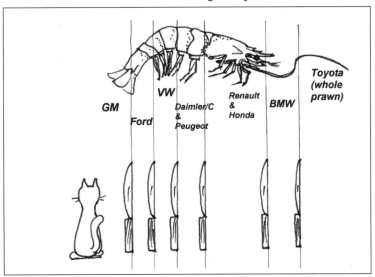

The comparison is of operating margins. Put simply, this means the profits just on the vehicle manufacturing process. The overall profit or loss of the groups will be dependent upon other non-operating factors. So, for example, in this illustration, GM is profitable, whereas it made overall losses in 2005. The illustration cannot be compared with the *Fortune 500* listing in a later chapter. Note: Fiat is off the picture to the left.

Walshie looked glum — but maybe that was because his mate was shedding too many pieces of prawn onto the ground.

'Let's take the world's biggest auto maker, GM of course.' Now Michael cut away almost all of the prawn leaving only a small piece of flipper. 'The world's biggest comes in at number nine on the list of operating margins, barely scraping into the black during 2004. This tiny bit of flipper illustrates the profitability of GM with Toyota.

'And number ten? Worst operating margin of the lot? In fact, operating in negative territory was Fiat. We can't even include it in the picture — it's a minus part of the prawn.' With that, he scooped up the last bit of prawn and dangled it over the cat, which leapt for it and took it away to eat slowly while it was lying under a rose bush.

'What's the point of the comparison? Simply to emphasize that GM and Ford are not performing at all well in the world automotive industry. There are a number of reasons for that. Their chief disadvantages are what are called legacy costs — high wages and benefits negotiated years ago when auto workers had the clout to get good wages and the auto makers were riding high and could afford to pay them. Other long-established car makers, for example UK, French and German operators, have the same problem with these legacy costs.

'Now let's look at China, where there are ten major auto makers, and all of them are expanding rapidly. Most have links to Western or Japanese companies and are drawing on them for the best and most up-to-date technology. Chinese annual production is 6 million vehicles now, but just ten years ago production was 1.5 million. By 2010, they will probably produce 12 million a year — more than the US.

'Few Australians have heard of the Chinese city of Chongqing, yet it has more people than all of Australia and its factories are producing more vehicles than the whole of Australia's auto industry. Just ten years ago, it only turned out trucks, three-wheelers and vans of an obsolete design. The car factories of Shanghai alone are now making twice as many cars as Australia does.'

Walshie broke in. 'What sort of cars?'

'Just like those made in the West. The Chinese are turning away from the "cute" three-wheeler or the basic tin-can to demand the equivalent of Buicks and Camrys. It won't be long before these will be developed and exported to Australia and the West, as well as a flood of car components. Well, we're getting the first wave of Chinese components now, and it's already starting to hurt.'

Walshie was pondering all this while the sausages were burning black on the grill. 'But Chinese cars will be cheap and nasty!'

'No, they won't,' Michael replied. 'That's what a lot of people say, but they're wrong. They're badly underestimating what the Chinese are capable of. The factories in China are modern and set up with Western knowledge and technology. In fact many are more modern than Australian assembly lines. A similar comment was made about the first Japanese motorbikes to hit the West in the 1960s — that they'd be cheap and nasty. They went on to take over virtually the whole motorbike market. I believe that Ford and Chrysler could go the way of the big motorbike makers like BSA and Norton. Remember them?'

'Why can't we compete?'

His mate shrugged again. 'A Chinese car worker now uses the most modern technology, is well-educated, highly motivated — and gets paid $100 a week. Australian car workers get paid $1,000 a week. They just can't compete. It's not a level playing field.'

Michael decided to widen the discussion.

'Chinese manufactured goods are already dominant in many sectors of the marketplace. Check it out at the nearest shopping centre. "Textiles and footwear" is the term used to describe that sector of the economy which involves clothing, shoes, fabrics such as curtains and sheets, hats and sportswear such as the strips of favourite football teams. Most are of Chinese origin — especially since recent changes in WTO rules meant that the more efficient Chinese textile companies have swamped those of Bangladesh and Indonesia. Chinese manufacturers are also dominant across a range of other manufactures, such as tools and hardware. Visit a home and garden centre and examine where the products are made. The tools designed for general use, such as hammers and pliers, will be Chinese-made. So well the pots and pans and other commodity products.

'Then there's toys. Again, Chinese manufacturers have seized the bulk of the market. The world's largest distributor of toys is McDonald's, which is continually offering small cheap toys as part of its promotions. Almost all of them are made in China. The small toy that comes with a cheeseburger may have travelled halfway around the world. Chinese manufacturers are gradually establishing dominance across a range of sectors.

'And why are they dominant? It's not just cheap wages — it's the way they control their currency so it's undervalued compared to the US dollar, and to ours. Ever noticed, Walshie, that you can go to a bank, even some travel agents, and change currency, swapping our money for the money of other countries. You could get US dollars, Pommie pounds, euros, Thai baht, even Fijian dollars — but d'you think you could get Chinese yuan? Or Indian rupees for that matter? Not a chance. They control their currencies as tight as a bee's bum. China is the world's fourth biggest economy now, and India isn't far behind — so have you ever thought it strange that you never hear about people trading in yuan or rupees? Their governments make sure foreigners can't speculate in their money — but the whole world can meanwhile speculate in other currencies like Aussie dollars. Doesn't seem quite fair, does it? That's the open market — but it's not open for everybody, just some.'

Walshie looked a bit despondent, but he was nothing if not cluey. He clutched at what he thought was a strong point. 'But Australian firms can get around all these problems by playing the Chinese at their own game, outsourcing their operations and setting up in China to take advantage of the cheap wages. That's what globalization is all about — going where costs are cheapest.'

Michael nodded at that. 'A lot of boards and executives think that that's the way out,' he said. 'But there's a huge risk. The legal environment in China is not a level playing field, no more so than the economic environment. The legal system is complicated and operates on many levels. Judges are appointed by the Communist Party and it's said that no court will find against local officials in favour of a foreigner. Where foreigners do get judgments against local businesses, they find they can't enforce the court order. Foreign companies risk getting their fingers burnt by expanding in China without a thorough knowledge of what they're doing. A lot of big corporations have lost a lot of money.'

It was Walshie's turn to stare at a blackened sausage.

'So when'll all this happen?'

'Maybe sooner than you think. There are plans to show Chinese-made cars at the Sydney Motor Show in October 2007.'

Washie sighed. 'Is there any bright side to all this?'

'Oh yes, of course,' his mate responded. 'We'll be able to choose from cheap cars. But they'll be made in Shanghai or Beijing. Instead of Holdens, we can buy cheap Cherys, and instead of Falcons we can buy Geelys. That's why I said that there will be no more chants of "Holden" or "Fal-con" at Bathurst in three to five years — unless they're for vintage car races! That's why up on the Hill at Panorama, the fans will chant, "East Wind! East Wind!" or "Red Flag! Red Flag!" It could catch on … if there's nothing else. And by the way, they're unlikely to be V8s. Large Chinese cars are usually powered by six-cylinder engines, and the great global car will probably only be a four-cylinder or a six. The Great Aussie V8 will go into the sump of history just like the Great Aussie Ute. It'll be no more than that puff of smoke from a drop of grease on the barbie.

'In Australia, the car market will become such a small proportion of the global car market that we'll be unlikely to have cars designed for our particular preferences. We'll have to accept the global car, which will be designed to meet the needs of most of the rest of the global market. There's been a lot of planning research done and the resulting designs are generally smaller than what we've been used to, mainly because smaller cars are more suitable to cramped mega cities, and of course fuel economy is becoming even more important — hence the trend towards smaller engines of around 1.6 litres. So V8s will become an expensive rarity!'

There was silence. Both Walshie and Michael found another Vic Bitter each. It looked like they would have to just drink beer as the sausages were well and truly burnt and the cat had found the other prawns while they were talking.

Walshie turned to his friend, sucked his teeth and shook his head. 'Nah — I don't believe all that,' he said. 'No more Holdens? No more Ford Falcons? It's impossible! They're Aussie icons!'

'Yeah, well once we had Chrysler Valiants. They were good cars. Now they're mostly bush-bashers.'

'Yeah, but no, but yeah … but they're … Valiants!'

'Well Walshie, let me make one last point. In the UK they have a new car market more than twice the size of ours — 2.2 million new cars sold every year, against our market of less than one million. How many car makers in the UK are doing well? Not many. Ford stopped making cars there in 2001. GM is losing heaps at Vauxhall and is looking to cut back or close it. Rover's gone to China. Jaguar's losing a poultice of Ford's money. Peugeot closed its plant at Coventry in 2006. Only one UK car maker is doing well, and you know which one?'

Walshie shrugged.

'Mini — and that's managed by the Germans, by BMW. I tell you, Walshie, a lot of car makers around the world are cactussed. We're not Robinson Crusoe. But if times are tough now, what'll they be like when the Chinese arrive? If the UK's down to one profitable car maker. D'you think we can possibly hold on to four?'

Walshie still held the fork with its black, crisp sausage and he waved it in the air. 'But why don't we hear about all this stuff in the papers, or on tellie?'

It was the turn of his friend to shrug. 'Well, some experts do talk about globalization and point out the shift from manufacturing to the services industries, and analyse how jobs will move away from the factory assembly line into, say, tourism. But not many of them have the ticker to talk about the implications of all that — namely, the end of Australian-designed and made cars like the Commodore and the Falcon, and the end of the Great Aussie Ute and the Great Aussie V8.'

Washie sighed, 'Gimme another beer.'

He slammed shut the barbie lid on the burnt sausages. A splash of fat caught fire and fell on Michael Servetus' T-shirt, burning a small hole.

'Oops, sorry,' blurted out Walshie. 'It looks like I'm trying to set you on fire!'

Note: Michael Servetus (the name of the fictional character featured in the Prologue) was a real person. A Spaniard who lived between 1511 and 1553. He was a spiritual writer but he had wide interests and on one occasion, almost casually, he commented that he had discovered the way blood circulates in the human body, pumped around the system of arteries and veins. His account of pulmonary circulation achieved for him the rare feat of being condemned as a heretic by both Protestants and Roman Catholics and he was burned alive for his heresy. This was done in Geneva, on the orders of the so-called reformer John Calvin. Michael Servetus told the truth, but in doing so he managed to upset everyone because what he told them did not accord with their own ideas.

Part One
The Automotive Industry and its Environment

1 Introduction

I've seen the Chinese vehicles in China from various, various brands, and I've said it's a threat that will come to the US, I think, by the end of the decade.
— Thomas W. LaSorda, Chief Executive of Chrysler, 2006.[1]

If an Industry Struggles in Good Times, What Will it Do in the Bad?
The scenario outlined in the barbecue stopper of the Prologue is both real and imminent. The struggling car makers of Australia, and indeed car makers around the world, will have to deal with a large quantity of cheap, quality, new cars and car components hitting world auto markets, and the impact of those cars on the industry will be as sudden and as forceful as a tsunami.[2] It is a characteristic of a tsunami that it comes out of a clear sky and a calm day, but with overwhelming strength it sweeps everything before it until its force spends itself on high ground. It seems that car makers in the West are as heedless as holidaymakers on a beach, watching waves lap the shore (i.e., with their gaze fixed inwards concentrating on current problems in the industry), and not recognizing the risk of a much more powerful wave on the way. Like beachgoers, they are content to do as they have done in past years. Like relaxed and dreaming beachgoers in the sun, it seems that some wish to put the thought of a looming threat out of their minds and find reasons to discount the approaching inundation.

In fact the motor vehicle manufacturing industry in Australia has been faltering in recent years. Senior executives of Mitsubishi and Ford have been put on the spot by questions about the future of the industry and have made pledges that Australian-based manufacturing operations will continue in the foreseeable future.[3] However, the Australian industry has been under enormous pressure even in current world trading conditions — that is, even before the impact of Chinese cars. It is the thesis of this book that the world motor vehicle manufacturing industry is about to be hit by a surge of competition that will be a result of the continuously accelerating development of the Chinese motor vehicle manufacturers. Those manufacturers were still comparatively small and technologically inferior during the latter part of the 20th century, but in the new millennium they have developed with surprising speed. As noted in the barbecue scenario above, they have doubled their output around every five years and in the very near future they will be dominant not only in China but they will also be major players on the world stage.

What will the Australian motor vehicle industry — and its overseas group management — do when this economic tidal wave hits? If the local industry has been struggling to date, and major operators have been forced to deny rumours that they will close, what will happen when a huge number of quality, competitive vehicles roll into the world markets?

To use an agricultural metaphor, it is as if a small group of farmers have struggled to develop their farms during fine and clement weather, while the rain falls and the sun gently shines. What will they do when they are hit by drought?

Or to use a biblical metaphor — and this may be appropriate for what will be an apocalyptic situation — 'If this is what they do to the green wood, what will they do to the dry?' (Luke, 23:31).

There has been much research into the economic development of China, and on aspects of the deregulation of world trade often referred to as globalization. However, there has only been limited research into the development of car industry infrastructure in China and the implications of increasing efficiency in its auto manufacturing industries, particularly on the impact of the Chinese industry on Australia's small manufacturing industry and markets. In this book, the word 'auto' is used to denote all automobiles — cars and trucks and buses. When the term 'car industry' is used, it is intended only to refer to cars.

The author is in a unique position to analyse and comment on these issues, for he has held professorial positions in European and Chinese universities. He has held senior positions in Chinese universities from Shanghai to Chengdu over the past fourteen years, and as part of his duties has supervised over 100 postgraduate students completing dissertations on management and economics, including research into varied aspects of the car industry. Drawing on that experience, he has developed the thesis that an influx of cheap, quality cars and car components will soon transform the world car making industry, just as a flood of cheap, quality motorcycles brought about the virtual demise of Western motorcycle manufacturers a generation ago.

Australia stands to lose most of its car making capacity, and with it the centrepiece of its manufacturing industry. Then, in the words of a commentator, the result will be an 'economy dangerously dependent on what we can dig out of the ground and sell overseas.'[4]

Economic Factors Behind the Impact of Chinese Cars

The storm, or flood of cars of tsunami-like proportions, will come about as a result of two earthquake surges. One is related to relative wage costs in China compared to the West, and the other is related to the supply and demand factors of the car industry in China.

The first factor behind the tsunami surge has been simply stated — a car industry worker in China, achieving around the same productivity as a worker in the West, using equivalent (or even more advanced) technology and plant, earns around A$100 for a week's work. An auto worker in Australia, doing the same work, earns around A$1,000. A simple, iron law of economics dictates that where labour is fungible, that is, where it is possible to transfer the process requiring the labour, the available employment will go to the lower paid worker.

The globalization of manufacturing has effectively made labour fungible, for global corporations have by and large set up in China (and other low-wage countries) manufacturing lines identical to those in Western countries. This means that is now possible for processes to go in search of the cheapest labour for completing a near-identical process.

To date, Western manufacturing operations have had an edge in regard to quality and high-tech processes, but they are rapidly exporting those to China as well. In some cases, indigenous Chinese companies are buying the technology with the manufacturing equipment when they take over ailing Western enterprises — as Nanjing Auto did when it bought MG Rover. William Clay Ford has stated that Australia can become an intellectual capital for Asia, but what happens when Asian professionals become more skilled and adept than Australians ... and are prepared to work for one tenth of the salary? And do we really have an edge in advance technology and innovation?[5]

The lower wage in China is a result of two things — a much lower pay and conditions structure (enforced strictly by the Communist government, ironically a socialist government based on the rights of workers), and the undervalued currency (which is only allowed to move within a very narrow range against other world currencies).[6]

Putting it simply, no worker earning $1,000 per week can keep his or her job when there is someone else who will do the same job for $100.

The result of this inequitable situation is that there are trade imbalances between China and many of its trading partners. As an example, in 2005, more than US$243 billion worth of Chinese goods were sold in the US, but only about US$42 billion worth of US goods were sold in China, and the trade deficit for 2006 was even wider.[7] China holds more than a trillion US dollars in reserves. Its current account surplus (a measure of the excess of exports over imports overall) is larger even than Japan's, and Japan is the world's second largest economy with a 2006 GDP around twice that of China.

This distortion in the operation of world markets, especially in regard to comparative labour costs, has been estimated to have cost the United States nearly 3 million jobs in the manufacturing sector since President George W. Bush took office in 2001.[8] The problem is that the currency distortion makes Chinese goods much cheaper for American consumers and conversely, American products are made much more expensive for Chinese consumers — so clearly consumers will buy Chinese products.

In a world where there were perfect free markets and economic principles could be fairly applied, China's currency should be moving significantly upward against its partners', and this currency movement would reduce the great advantage China's producers have in their lower wage structures. One estimate is that the Chinese currency is effectively undervalued by 40 per cent.[9] However, it seems unlikely that the Chinese government will move quickly — if at all — to revalue their currency by, say, even 20 per cent or 30 per cent or more to enable Western manufacturers to be more competitive.[10] This issue will be discussed again in another context, and a comparison of auto workers' wages suggests that the Chinese yuan should be revalued by much more than 40 per cent.

The United States administration is reluctant to push the issue too hard on the diplomatic level, for if there was an official assessment that China was a 'currency manipulator', this would constitute a major escalation of the matter and the US government would invoke trade sanctions under its domestic law — possibly leading to a mutually damaging trade war with China.

The second factor behind the tsunami surge concerns supply and demand — namely, the rate of increase of demand for cars in China, and the supply of cars by domestic producers, both joint ventures and wholly Chinese-owned corporations. This book describes how China's car industry has developed to the point where car making facilities are nearly as advanced as those in the West and are becoming as efficient, and where consumers' demands have become sophisticated so that they demand cars with features and quality equal to those of cars designed and manufactured in the West. There will be no shortage of Chinese motor vehicle manufacturers able to meet the demand. Most of the very big auto corporations have links with foreign firms, and can draw on their expertise and technological ability.

The conversation around the barbecue that introduced this book is fictional, but it trades in facts. In the US, the Big Three car makers — GM, Ford and DaimlerChrysler — are all cutting back production and some analysts consider that GM and Ford are under threat of bankruptcy. In China, on the other hand, the ten major auto makers are rapidly building up their productive capacity. Chinese annual production has grown from 0.32 million in 1984 to 0.75 million in 1991, 1.5 million

Table 1.1: Large Chinese Motor Vehicle Manufacturers and Their Links to Global Enterprises

Beijing Automotive Industry Corporation (BAIC), Beijing
   Global Links: DaimlerChrysler, Hyundai
Chang'an, Chongqing
   Global Links: Ford, Suzuki
Dong Feng, Wuhan
   Global Links: Honda, Nissan, Kia
First Automobile Works (FAW), Changchun
   Global Links: Mazda, Volkswagen, Toyota
Guangzhou Automobile Industry Group (GAIG), Guangzhou
   Global Links: Honda, Toyota
Harbin Hafei Motor Corporation, Harbin
Jinbei Automobile Corporation,
Nanjing Auto, Nanjing
   Global Links: Rover, Fiat
Shanghai Automotive Industry Corporation (SAIC), Shanghai
   Global Links: GM, SsangYong, Volkswagen

in 1996, 3 million in 2001, and to 5.7 million in 2005. By 2010, if these trends continue, and there is no reason why they should not, they could produce 12 million cars a year — more than the US.

As noted also in the barbecue stopper conversation, the Chinese city of Chongqing is indeed producing more vehicles than the whole of Australia's auto industry. Chang'an Ford, the joint-venture company between the big Chinese producer Chang'an and Ford Motor Company, founded in 2001 in Chongqing, is producing Fiestas and Mondeos to world quality standards and there are plans to produce at least one new car model every year in China — and this is just after five years. The car factories of the city of Shanghai are as big as some of those in Detroit and are still expanding. There are new auto factories being established from the north of the huge country to the south.

Nor can it be said anymore that the Chinese manufacturers are not up to world standard. The factories in China are modern, they are set up with Western knowledge and technology, and in fact many are more modern than Australian assembly lines which were established decades ago. The cars that are now being produced in China, such as those on the assembly lines of Chongqing, are similar to those made in the West, and this reflects Chinese consumer demand. The research conducted by the author in Chengdu and Qingdao shows that Chinese consumers are not only demanding the equivalent of top-quality contemporary-designed Western models such as Buicks and Camrys, but wholly Chinese-owned firms are developing their own designs that will match these models (although in more than one case there are claims that such designs are illicit copies of Western cars).

Chinese auto workers will soon be capable of achieving the highest quality standards, although admittedly they will have substantial obstacles to overcome. Chairman of DaimlerChrysler, Dieter Zetsche, has said that Mercedes and Chrysler models made in China will be identical to models sold abroad: 'The only difference ought to be the country of origin. As far as quality is concerned, there can only be one quality we are striving for with Mercedes or with Chrysler products around the globe.'[11]

At the same time, senior industry figures and analysts profess not to be concerned about the rising capability of the Chinese car makers, because a rapidly increasing supply of cars in China will simply be absorbed by a rapidly increasing domestic Chinese demand.

However, the research conducted by the author and under his auspices indicates that this may not be so. There are critical restraints, at least in the short to medium term, on the ability of Chinese society to absorb literally millions of cars. No matter how big a population may be, there are limits to growth, especially in all the infrastructure aspects necessary to cater to private car ownership. Critical factors such as the expansion of small businesses to service and repair cars, the expansion and acceptance of insurance principles, even finding room to park private cars, are among the factors which must severely limit the growth of private car ownership in China, and result in a proportion of production being exported. Pollution is also a major problem, and too many vehicles must add to the polluted environment.

Supply/Demand Factors of the Car Industry in China

Not only is the Chinese car industry growing rapidly but it will continue to do so. Between 2006 and 2010 and beyond, the supply of cars is likely to increase exponentially. Hence the supply curve for the supply of cars in China has an ever increasing slope (although the slope for the supply of cars by wholly Chinese-owned companies is steeper than the slope for cars manufactured by joint ventures). It can be illustrated as follows in Figure 1.2 (note that the y-axis is not precisely defined, for the graph is illustrative of trends only).

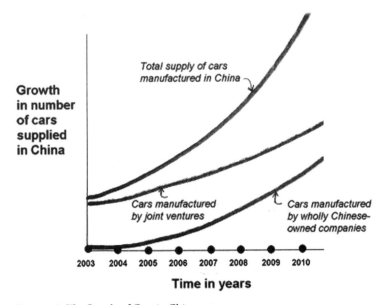

Figure 1.2: The Supply of Cars in China

A commonly accepted scenario is that the supply and demand curves of motor vehicles in China will advance at around the same rate, and the increased production of Chinese factories will be absorbed by the Chinese market.

It is certainly true that the demand for cars in China has taken off in urban areas as increasing real wages have brought increased demand for the private ownership of cars and the burgeoning business sector has brought about increased demand as well.

However, the research in this book suggests that the slope of the demand curve must decline as limits to growth are reached.

There will be a point at which the quantity of cars and car components produced in China cannot be absorbed by the domestic demand, and from that point on there will be ever-increasing exports — a flood of cheap, quality cars and car components.

Already, Chinese vehicle production is on the point of exceeding local demand. It is likely that the Chinese manufacturers will export a yearly surplus production of around 4 million cars — sufficient to pose a challenge to the leaders in the world market — as early as 2010. How many of these cars will come to Australia? If only 5 per cent of this total — that is, 200,000 vehicles — hits Australia's markets in 2010, they will have a major impact. Australia's domestic market for new vehicle sales was around 950,000 units in 2006, and although it will have expanded by 2010 it is unlikely to expand sufficiently to absorb such a large number of new products.

The research detailed later in this book delves into some less appreciated areas of study regarding the auto industry of China, such as the service network (4S system and others) and the growth of second-hand car markets, as well as the demands upon the insurance and legal systems, and this research bears out the likelihood that domestic growth will be impeded until such time as the support systems and networks develop.

Figure 1.3, which illustrates the demand for cars in China, reflects the assumption that demand must tail off within three to five years as the country's infrastructure becomes unable to cope with continuing very high rates of growth, and the aging vehicles create a demand for services/repairs that lags three years or so behind the sale of these vehicles as new.

When the research conclusions relating to supply and demand are put together, they reveal the likelihood that an ever-increasing supply of cars and a stalling demand mean that Chinese car manufacturers will look to exports to continue their high rates of growth. This view is supported by analysts. One comments that: 'The number of passenger cars in China will certainly increase in the near future, but it is questionable whether current growth trends can be sustained for more than a few years. ... with

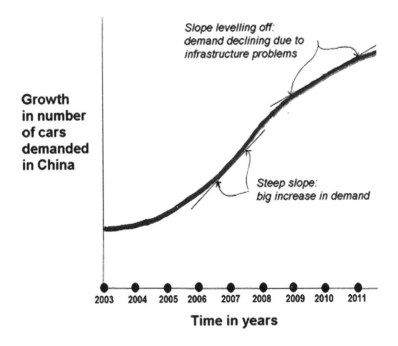

Figure 1.3: The Demand for Cars in China

most industry watchers such as KPMG warning of a plateau and excess capacity as soon as 2005.'[12]

It is likely anyway that the manufacturers, especially the wholly Chinese-owned enterprises, would look to increase exports because they are a source of foreign currency, and income in US dollars and euros dilutes the risk of currency movements. While the yuan remains undervalued, not only does it make Chinese manufactures attractive on overseas markets, but it makes it appealing for business people to earn income in dollars and euros so that they can then invest these proceeds advantageously within China.

In China in the early 21st century, there are high levels of very conspicuous consumption of expensive luxury goods made in the USA and Europe, and this consumption is fuelled by the distorted exchange rate. Those businesses that can earn income outside the country — income denominated in foreign currencies — have a very great advantage

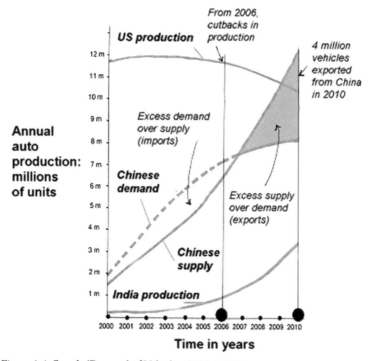

Figure 1.4: Supply/Demand of Vehicles, 2000–2010

over businesses that earn their income domestically.

Figure 1.4 brings the above discussion together by combining the assumptions about greatly increasing production (supply) with a falling-off in demand. It assumes that the yuan will continue to be undervalued to some extent in the foreseeable future and that the Chinese government will resist international pressure to make it freely convertible in the world currency trading system.

The shaded area represents the situation where falling demand and greatly increasing production (supply) means that Chinese cars and car components will flood the world markets with a production surplus of around 4 million cars a year.

The figure is not intended to be an exact representation, but is illustrative of the principles of supply and demand pertaining to the car industry in China. The figure adds a curve for the US production (which is falling and assumed to continue falling). It also adds a curve for Indian vehicle production, which is starting from a much lower base than the Chinese industry and, as in the Chinese situation, will be applied first to a rapidly growing domestic demand.

While the figure indicates the large number of cars that will be exported from China based on analysis of supply and demand, common sense also tells us that as the car industry in China develops and as its manufacturers have the capacity to export cars, they will do so in quantity. Later in this book, the pattern of development of various national industries will be discussed. Every nation — sooner or later but mostly sooner — moves towards expanding the proportion of domestic production that is exported. They do this for various reasons, chief among which are the desire to bring in export income in foreign currency, and to achieve a greater economy of scale by attaining greater quantities of production than could be absorbed by local markets.

Every single national auto industry, from that of Germany in the 1950s to that of South Korea in the 1970s and to that of Brazil in the 1990s, established a target for exports. Sometimes that target, as a proportion of the national production, was set quite high. For example, South Korea aimed at exporting 70 per cent of its national vehicle production, and in the 1960s Germany exported more than half — 55 per cent — of its production. The UK manufacturers of the early post-war period exported more than 40 per cent of the vehicles they made, mostly to Commonwealth countries where a nostalgia for things British lingered. Brazil aimed at 40 per cent exports, and fell far short at its first attempt, but achieved its targets ten years later, in the early 2000s.

Most of those countries developed their industries and set about achieving export targets behind very high tariff and quota walls that protected their own markets while they set about entering others, but that is another issue (which will also be discussed in a later chapter). To those who seriously suggest that China will be an exception to the general pattern of development of every other auto manufacturing country in the world and not aim to export 30, or 40, or 50 per cent of its car production or more, there is only one response. It is the same very brief response that Mr Spock, on the bridge of the starship *Enterprise*, sometimes made when Captain Kirk made an ill-founded proposition — 'Illogical, Captain'.

It is indeed illogical to make the proposition that China's motor vehicle manufacturers will not aim at exporting and capturing a slice of world markets. The flood of cars will come, it is just a matter of when. The time when the flood hits may not be convenient for other nations, or global automotive operations overall, for the timing will be at the discretion of Chinese managers and no one else.

In Response to the Challenge of Chinese Manufacturers

In response to the tsunami-like threat of a flood of imports, many company executives in the West see an advantage for their businesses in deserting their home countries and re-locating to China. This option would see workers in the West lose their jobs, but managers and owners continuing to prosper. This book also includes a discussion of the innate difficulties of setting up an operation in China — namely the inequitable legal environment and pervasive corruption, as well as the risk of losing intellectual property. It also lists a number of cases where foreign parties have been unable to enforce their rights under the law.

In China, the legal system is complicated and operates on many levels, and there have been instances where foreigners have clearly been disadvantaged by judgments that appeared to be contrary to Chinese law. The book judges that the idea that Western businesses can continue profitable operations in the long term by outsourcing more and more of their production to China, using a cheap labour pool while protecting their technology and management practices, is largely illusory.

The research in this book suggests that in the next five to ten years, the world will see either substantial decline of car manufacturers in the West in the face of Chinese competition, or the death of theories of world free trade that are bundled under the heading of globalization as Western governments resort to protecting their domestic markets. The principles of the WTO will be jettisoned as governments respond to a nationalistic backlash against Chinese products bringing about the ruin of local producers.

What is the point of this book, it may be asked, when there are numerous government and private bodies analysing and reviewing the car industry and manufacturing generally? What is different in this book?

The answer is very simple. No Australian studies have been conducted of aspects of supply and demand relating to the car industry in China, and especially of China's industry infrastructure. Consequently, study of Australia's industry has been focused in the wrong place. It is as if people are on a beach examining the sand and the seafront, with their backs to the tsunami which is just appearing on the horizon.

Twenty years ago, an author wrote of the impact of Japanese cars on the Western car industry and commented, 'A smug dismissal of Japanese talent left Europe and America vulnerable'.[13] In 2007, there appears to be a smug dismissal of what Chinese car makers can do. The car industry of the West ignores them at their peril. The next chapters discuss the environment of the car industries in Australia and other countries, before moving towards a more detailed discussion of the Chinese industry.

2 The Australian Car Industry

Background

A thumbnail sketch of the history of car making in Australia is also a history of various protection measures.[14] At first, Australia's first car makers were makers of small engines or motor vehicle body manufacturers. Among the more notable of these were pioneers in Victoria and South Australia. In South Australia, David Shearer built a four-wheeled steam carriage that first trundled down the streets of Mannum in 1896, at no less than 25 kilometres an hour. The following year, the first Australian-made car powered by an internal combustion engine appeared in Melbourne. Victorian Harley Tarrant also deserves mention for setting up a manufacturing line for internal combustion engines in 1898, and developing an Australian-made car for public sale in 1903.[15] The nascent industry was protected by tariffs on car bodies dating from 1902. Imported cars, mainly Ford Model Ts, began selling widely from 1909. In 1917, a firm in Adelaide named Holden and Frost established Holden's Motor Body Builders to make car bodies for Chevrolet chassis. The firm had its origins in a saddlery shop established in the middle of the nineteenth century by James Alexander Holden and James Frost, but Jim Holden never lived to see the first Holden cars roll off the assembly line.

By the 1920s, local assembly became well-established, but only under the shelter of additional high tariffs on assembled car chassis and lower tariffs on unassembled chassis. Around this time, there were a number of Australian-designed and made cars. An example was the Australian Six, designed by Louis Chevrolet, which had an American engine in an Australian-built chassis and body. Another was the Lincoln Motor Car, built in Sydney and using a European engine. Two hundred Lincolns were built between 1919 and 1926. The famous aviator Charles Kingsford Smith lent his name to a venture that produced the Southern Cross — a car with an Australian-made engine and a locally built wooden body. However, the new venture did not long survive Smithy's death in 1935.

The tariff and other protective measures had been brought in because indigenous Australian cars could not compete with the mass-produced American imports, which were far cheaper, despite the high costs of transporting products halfway around the world. In a move to adjust to Australian tariffs on car bodies, Ford set up an assembly operation in Victoria in 1921 and began manufacturing Model Ts in Geelong in 1926. GM (USA) granted Holden's Motor Body Builders a licence to build bodies for GM chassis in 1924, and Holden/GM cars captured about half the local auto market — around 45,000 cars at the end of the 1920s. In 1933, in the absence of regulations excluding foreign ownership, GM took over Holden completely and with Ford dominated the local market. Import duties were increased again in 1930, and by the Second World War Australia could supply 40 per cent of the domestic market for car components, mainly car bodies. There was additional protection for the local industry in the form of a bounty for each engine locally produced. Protection measures of this sort are generally meant to underpin 'import substitution' policies — whereby local manufacturers were supported in building products in home countries instead of importing them ready-made. The advantages were that local employment was created and locals obtained skills and expertise in the protected industry.

In 1944, the Australian government sought to develop a firm base for manufacturing in Australia, with motor vehicle manufacturing at its centre. John Curtin's Labor administration announced it would set up a government-run car manufacturer unless one of the existing businesses proposed to develop a plan to make complete cars in Australia. GM made such a proposal, despite Alfred Sloane's distrust of the 'dangerously socialist' Labor government,[16] and what was claimed to be Australia's first car — the Holden 48/215 — appeared on 29 November 1948. Like the Australian Six, it was a Chevrolet design, based on a prototype that was, in the words of one author, a 'cheap, somewhat primitive, slab-sided car for the masses'.[17]

The prototype Holden, in fact the first three prototypes, had been imported from Detroit. The head of GM in Australia, Englishman Laurence Hartnett (later Sir Laurence), had travelled to GM's American headquarters to persuade Sloane to get behind the idea of an Australian car. Sloane agreed only grudgingly, and insisted that GM would not provide funds — the funding for the new car would have to come from the Australian government (this despite Sloane's expressed contempt for 'socialist' governments). Moreover, Sloane told Hartnett that the car that was to be an Aussie icon would be based on a prototype car already sitting in one of GM's backlots. Hence the model for the 48/215 was American.

There are strong parallels between the events surrounding the evolution of the Holden and the development of new Chinese cars in the 21st century. In both cases, foreign management and foreign expertise and technology were used to develop the cars, which were close copies of foreign designs. Also in both cases, government protection and support — even to extensive venture funding — made the development possible.

Hartnett left GM Holden in 1948 and went on to design what he thought was a better car for Australian conditions, and in time a few Hartnett cars were built … but they did not set the market on fire.

It is sometimes said that the government recognized the need for a car designed for Australian conditions because the English cars that were imported post-war were manifestly inadequate. They were useful in the cities and city suburbs, but they were not suited to develop the wide brown land. For a start, the fuel tank capacity of a typical UK-designed small car took it barely 200 miles, which was not sufficient range for a car to drive Australia's Outback roads. An Australian car needed a range of around 400 miles at least, with good ground clearance, and beefed-up shocks and suspension to cope with dirt roads. Moreover, the UK cars offered 'quaint, clunky four-cylinder English motors,'[18] whereas the

Holden had a six-cylinder engine that coped better with driving long distances.

The Holden delivered what Australians wanted. It coped with country conditions and appealed to nationalistic sentiment in the cities. It helped make Australians feel good, because their country had a car of its own, designed for their sprawling continent. This feel-good attitude should not be underestimated, for it contributed to a widespread feeling of optimism during those times, and this optimism led to a self-confidence, and the self-confidence of knowing that one's nation had its place in the ranks of the world led to the encouragement of immigration and growth. In short, the production of the Holden meant more than just the design of a local machine. The Holden was more than a package of nuts and bolts and plate that transported people from A to B. It made a niche of its own in the national psyche, like a blue heeler finding an accustomed place at the door of the farmer's home.

However, it was a popular myth to describe that first Holden as a car for the masses, because at a price of £733 it was beyond the means of most ordinary workers.

Despite its price, the Holden rapidly became Australia's most popular car, and GM had a 30 per cent market share by 1952. Ford and Chrysler (which also had a plant in Australia) responded by increasing local content, and the Ford Falcon was brought out in September 1960 as a direct competitor to the Holden (and a candidate to become another icon of a down-to-earth tough Aussie for down-to-earth tough Aussies). European manufacturers also set up Australian operations — British Motor Corporation (later to be known as British Leyland) came in 1951 and Volkswagen in 1961. By the late 1950s and early '60s, some 70 per cent of the content of the cars made by the Big Three in Australia was made up of local components.

The government continued to recognize the importance of the local industry and throughout the 1950s and '60s supported its growth through regulated minimum levels of content, import restrictions (quotas and tariffs) and tax incentives detailed in one Motor Vehicle Plan after another. In the early '60s, the industry was booming and a million Holdens were sold between 1960 and 1966 as the Golden

Holden became more affordable.

In 1976, there were five major car makers in Australia, as Toyota (1963) and Nissan-Datsun (1966) had joined the Big Three,[19] and the government supported them to the extent of guaranteeing that local manufacturers would have 80 per cent of the local market. In 1976, a coalition government took steps to enhance protection. The existing rate for tariffs on imported cars (35 per cent) would rise by 10 per cent if imported vehicles took more than a one-fifth share of the domestic market. With the assurance of these levels of protection, four of the car makers — GM, Toyota, Chrysler and Nissan — built new manufacturing facilities in South Australia. In 1977, Datsun produced an Australian-designed car, the 200B, but despite the protection from imports, the company suffered financial losses and closed down its manufacturing operations in Australia in the 1980s. The manufacture of the Chrysler Valiant also ceased, and Mitsubishi took over Chrysler's name in Australia, so there were four car makers vying for Australia's comparatively small market.

In that decade of the 1980s, with the general de-regulation of Australia's markets and the floating of its currency in response to the dictates of globalization, there was still the feeling that the local car industry could not be entirely laid open to world market forces, or not all at once, anyway. Senator John Button's car plan was intended to give a degree of protection while allowing an orderly transition to a completely open market. Under the plan, import quotas declined from 20 per cent in 1984 to be abolished in 1988. Tariffs, some of which were 57 per cent in 1984, were to decline by 2.5 per cent a year to 15 per cent in 2000.

The Button car plan was the brainchild of a new Labor government, which meant that there was an irony in the fact that while in 1944 a Labor government mandated the development of a protected car manufacturing industry it was a Labor government that took steps to wind back its protection 40 years later.

Then in 2001 the Automotive Competitiveness and Investment Scheme was brought in by the Howard Government and offered subsidies to manufacturers while the tariff protection was reduced to 10 per cent in 2005 and would be further reduced to 5 per cent in 2010. The tariff level of 10 per cent cost Australian taxpayers about $600 million in 2006. This equated to about $3,500 for every vehicle manufactured in Australia.

Patterns of Development

There are similarities in the way the motor vehicle manufacturing of various countries have developed. In most cases, there was the birth of the industry around 1900 when local inventors tinkered in their workshops and wheeled out their weird or wonderful version of a motorized conveyance. Then business people got involved and there were numerous small scale manufacturing lines that gradually merged. Then international companies, most often the giants — Ford and GM — entered the scene with plans for local assembly of parts manufactured elsewhere, but the local governments respond by bringing in protective measures to help their domestic industries grow. The local industries expanded and exported over the years, and the US, UK and European auto firms developed their fiefdoms, despite but sometimes because of protection.

Over the past 20 years, most countries' vehicle manufacturing industries have become interlinked with global operations, and their workers have felt the cooling wind of deregulation on a sweaty brow. There are exceptions to this pattern, for example in South Korea, where their industry has grown very quickly in the last 40 years, but with very high levels of government finance and strong protective measures.

The pattern of development of the car industry in Australia can be divided into the four broad periods represented in Figure 2.1. This format will be used again to illustrate the periods of development of the Japanese car industry (Figure 6.1), and then the periods of development of the Chinese car industry (Figure 9.5), to emphasize that the industries in Japan and China have followed patterns of development broadly similar to each other. There were long periods of isolation, but the Japanese and Chinese experiences of motoring expansion were different from those of other countries. Note that although there are bars to indicate the passing from one phase to another, this does not suggest an abrupt transformation. The industry generally slid from one phase to another across a somewhat fuzzy division, but the phases are distinct from each other nonetheless. The two first phases of development have been common to the growth of many national auto manufacturing industries.

- Common First Phase (1): Industry in infancy; many local

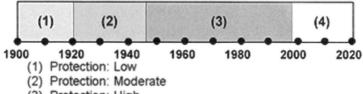

(1) Protection: Low
(2) Protection: Moderate
(3) Protection: High
(4) Protection: Reduced to low levels

Figure 2.1: The Pattern of Development of the Car Industry in Australia

manufacturers; small quantities produced; protection measures very low or non-existent.

- Common Second Phase (2): Industry coalescing; small manufacturers merge; production runs increased; growth is dependent upon the entry of US firms (GM and Ford) or UK or European firms; protection measures brought in to ensure a degree of local content and control.

- Australian Third Phase (3): Industry becomes centred around a small number of foreign car makers (Ford, GM Holden, Chrysler and UK makers — then Ford, GM Holden, Toyota and Mitsubishi); high levels of protection and subsidies to ensure the local industry continues to develop.

- Australian Fourth Phase (4): Protection measures reduced; More exposure to global producers, although this is partially offset by increased exports; local car makers rationalized and Australia's car manufacturing industry starts to decline in terms of employment.

The Situation in 2007

By 2007, besides the four major car manufacturers established in Australia, there were around 200 smaller plants manufacturing auto components, and hundreds of other suppliers of goods and services dependent upon the industry. Australian Bureau of Statistics figures for 2003 reported that there were 13.2 million motor vehicles registered in Australia. The automotive industry in Australia accounted for 6 per cent of manufacturing activity in 2001 and employed 63,000 people in that year. Total new sales in 2006 were around 950,000 (as has already been noted), and forecast sales for 2007 were 970,000 vehicles.[20]

In the first quarter of 2007 Australian new car and truck sales reached record levels. Toyota topped the list, 50 per cent more than GM Holden and more than double Ford's sales.

Imports of vehicles and vehicle components were high, and growing at an average annual growth rate of 10 per cent a year.[21] They were mainly from Japan, the United States and Germany and reflected the increasing interdependence of world trade. The Australian industry as a whole had an average export record, exporting mainly to the Middle East and New Zealand, which does not have a domestic industry comparable to Australia's.

Judging by the industry statistics, the Australian car makers should have had a rosy future, but by 2007 the scenario facing them was similar to that faced by makers elsewhere — falling market share and high levels of costs in comparison to the sources of imports.

Mitsubishi cut its workforce by 1,000 in 2005. In 2006, GM Holden announced a loss of $145 million in the 2005/06 financial year and cited problems with increased world competition and a cost structure that was too high. The company also announced that it was cutting back production by 20 per cent, which meant cutting shifts and reducing total employees by 1,400 to around 4,300. Another 1,800 jobs were lost in component manufacturers making parts as diverse as windscreens and thermostats, and the cause was baldly stated — the large manufacturers were outsourcing the supply of components to lower cost producers in Asia.

GM Holden in Australia has also been affected by the problems overwhelming GM in the US. In February 2005, GM cancelled plans to develop the next model Commodore as the basis of large rear-drive cars for the company worldwide. The cancellation of the Zeta program meant GM had less capital available to develop the new Commodore. According to Graeme Maxton of the Economist Intelligence Unit (one of the analysts who admits to the possibility of the termination of leading car makers in Australia): 'The Zeta debacle is a symptom of problems in GM that could crush the Australian operations.'[22]

There were, however, causes for hope at GM. The company's facilities in South Australia were being prepared to manufacture Pontiac G8s for export to the United States by the end of 2007. The projected quantity was up to 50,000 vehicles per year, which quantity would far exceed GM Holden's total exports for 2006 (around 31,000 vehicles), but in view of the falling US demand for large cars, this model may not be entering the market at the ideal time.

Ford has experienced falling sales of the Falcon, down about 7,000 in 2006 compared to 2005. The most popular European brand in Australia in 2006 was the Volkswagen.

Of the four Australian car makers, Toyota was in the strongest position, with its parent achieving good operating profit margins, increasing sales and expanding to the point where it could contemplate challenging for the number one world spot. Although its situation in Australia was not as bright as it was elsewhere in the world, and sales of the Toyota Camry have been falling, they have not fallen as much as the sales levels of the Ford Falcon and the Holden Commodore.

Ford and GM must be considered to have a precarious future in Australia because of the difficulties facing their parent companies in the US. If the corporate lifeboats have to be launched in the incoming flood, it is doubtful whether there will be seats reserved for Aussies. The possibilities of GM and Ford going bankrupt or being forced into a restructuring or merger in the United States must also cast a pall over the future of their Australian subsidiaries. Mitsubishi in Australia is also fragile and it was the smallest of the four local manufacturers. In September 2006 its Australian management had to deny rumours that Mitsubishi would close its local manufacturing operations.

It could be noted once again that the car makers were in these doldrums even before the advent of large quantities of Chinese-made cars hitting the market. The car makers have problems even in buoyant economic times, and if this is what occurs in the green wood, what will happen when the wood is dry? In other words, if they are struggling in the existing competitive conditions, what will happen when the competition gets much, much harder?

Overall, affected by the rise in oil prices, sales of medium to large cars in Australia declined by about 10 per cent during 2006. At the same time, Australia's continued economic strength overall contributed to an increase in total sales, and small car sales rose by 20 per cent in the same period. Sales figures for January 2007 confirmed that sales of small cars were increasing, and such cars had a 26 per cent market share. If these trends continue, small cars made in China will be well-placed to meet market demand and will probably find ready acceptance by the Australian consumer.

By 2007, the future for Australia's car making was very clouded, with the threat to car component makers already becoming serious and presaging bigger problems ahead. An analyst has already used the word 'crush' to describe what might happen to at least one car maker in Australia in the near future. The limited tariffs associated with the Automotive Competitiveness and Investment Scheme are no longer sufficient to offset the unfair advantage enjoyed by overseas players in the marketplace or to counter the rapidly growing threat of cheap quality cars and components from China.

Some participants in the automotive industry have recognized the threat in general terms, even if a full understanding of the impact of Chinese-made cars and components has not flowed through to the wider community. Some of the players in the Australian industry have sought a review of the tariff levels, with a view to increasing support from a level of $2 billion to at least $3 billion in taxpayer dollars over the term of the five-year plan. Their lobbying has been criticized in a number of quarters as just a plea for pork-barrelling (an interesting term derived from an old American practice of giving away the left-over scraps after a pig was slaughtered).

There are certainly strong arguments against protection measures, on the basis of the distortions that industry protection causes in an economy, and these arguments are well made by leading economists and analysts. The Secretary of the Australian Treasury, Ken Henry, summed up his view of the situation when government assistance is funnelled to inefficient industries: 'If growing businesses are being subsidized, or if governments step in to prevent other businesses from shrinking, then GDP is lowered by their command of the nation's scarce labour.'[23]

Ian MacFarlane, the former Governor of the Reserve Bank, has commented that although there were assumptions that manufacturing had 'foundered', it still shared in a 12 per cent rise in business investment in 2006.[24] The Chief Economist of the ANZ Bank, Saul Eslake, stated that as economies develop, manufacturing naturally declines in importance and people's increased disposable income is spent on services instead. He adds, 'Concerns that manufacturing might become extinct is emotional rhetoric unfounded by fact.'[25] The director of Access Economics, Chris Richardson, believes that it is 'inevitable' that most of Australia's car manufacturing facilities will have to cease making cars in Australia in the near future, but he believes that this is 'creative destruction' that will be followed by resources flowing into other more productive sectors of the economy.[26]

On the other hand, the local manufacturers have three strong arguments. First, the Australian government has reduced tariffs and protection that favoured the local industry, but the measures have not been entirely reciprocated, as some other car making countries, such as South Korea, maintain high protective walls, while in other countries such as Japan their markets work to effectively shut out imports. The principles of the WTO are not always upheld in reality.

Second, other sectors of the economy benefit from protection measures, or subsidies in one form or another. For example, the pharmacy sector is a protected industry, and lawyers and accountants, even newsagents, benefit from effective barriers against outside competition. These professions have had the political muscle to demand and receive protection and keep their bailiwicks free of the competition of fully open markets. The agriculture industry enjoys protection in various ways, although Australia's support for its rural sectors is minuscule compared to the massive benefits enjoyed by farmers in Japan, in the EU and in the US. If so many sectors within an economy can enjoy protection, then

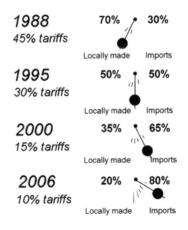

1988
45% tariffs
70% · 30%
Locally made   Imports

1995
30% tariffs
50% · 50%
Locally made   Imports

2000
15% tariffs
35% · 65%
Locally made   Imports

2006
10% tariffs
20% · 80%
Locally made   Imports

Figure 2.2: The Swinging Pendulum of Imports and Locally Made Vehicles

why should not manufacturing receive such a benefit?

Third, local manufacturers can point to the recent history of car making in Australia and demonstrate a link between reduced tariffs and rising imports — a link in timing, even if it cannot definitely be proved that there is a causal link. A further reduction in tariffs to just 5 per cent will probably be linked to a further decline in local operations.

As the pendulum swings between the relative market shares of imported cars and local cars, jobs are shed with each movement. Figure 2.2, drawn in broad strokes, illustrates the comparative market shares of imports and locally made vehicles at various periods when tariffs have gone from around 45 per cent to 10 per cent.

There are strong arguments on the other side of the free market versus protection debate, of course, as has been mentioned above. For example, it can be argued that these swings from locally made cars to exports reflect the fact that consumers are 'voting with their feet' in choosing smaller, more fuel-efficient cars in preference to the medium to large cars beloved of local car makers and churned out in quantity for what may once have been a captive market.

When Will the Chinese Tsunami Hit?

Later in this book, it will be argued that there are systemic problems with the Chinese car manufacturing industry which must be overcome before they can export quality cars to the world, and in the view of the author, the problem resolution process may take some years or more. However, some reports suggest that the veritable economic tsunami of cheap cars may hit even earlier than 2010. One writer suggests that the flood could flow in as early in 2008:

Chinese car makers could be flooding the Australian market with hatchbacks costing less than $10,000 within two years using Australia as a test bed before taking on the rest of the world.[27]

There are other analysts whose studies suggest there are already negative impacts for Australia from the growth of China's car industry and its foray into world trade. In South Australia, where there are Holden and Mitsubishi factories that account for around one half of the cars manufactured in Australia (as at 2004), the state government has concerns. Those concerns led it to commission a report into the impact of a free trade agreement with China. The report, authored by Andrew Stoler of the Institute for International Trade at the University of Adelaide, stated that the Australian car industry, particularly the car-parts sector, could not compete with low-cost Chinese car manufacturers.[28] Stoler noted that the value of Chinese component imports had nearly doubled in just four years, going from A$132 million in 1999 to A$246 million in 2003. South Australian industry is clearly vulnerable and its car plants could be among the first forced to close under the pressure of cheap Chinese cars and car components in the marketplace — whatever the assurances given by the current management (for these assurances are based upon current conditions).

Reacting to the Threat
In Australia there is, sadly, a high toll of wildlife killed on the roads. Kangaroos cannot outpace cars and trucks and are frequently hit by vehicles. There is one Australian species that has adapted a defence mechanism that was effective when the threat came from two or four-legged animals but that defence mechanism is invariably fatal when the threat is from a big, speeding four-tyred beast. That animal is the wombat. It is an extremely heavily built herbivore that burrows into creek banks and emerges to graze in late evenings and during the night. It is inoffensive and one cannot help feeling a twinge of affection for its small face, whiskers and slightly myopic gaze at the world. Because it is powerfully built, its response to danger that has been developed over ages is to sit still and hunker down. But if the danger first appears as the bright headlights of a car, then the wombat will tense and squat down

protectively, relying upon its bulk and build to repulse the enemy, as its species has done for eons. However, a speeding car is not easily repulsed by a marsupial reluctant to move. Not only that but the wombat, dark brown and dusty, is difficult to see against a dark surface. This inoffensive creature litters roadsides, and is amongst the saddest of all sad examples of road kill.

It sometimes seems as if the car manufacturers in Australia are like wombats, hunkered down but caught in the bright headlights of an approaching threat. Their response is to carry on doing things that they have done for generations, either not taking evasive action against the looming Chinese threat or even denying that it exists. That response simply makes them an easier target. Also, there is no protection in sheer size. Indeed, quite the opposite: Bulk can make it more difficult to run and evade attackers. For some manufacturers, slow to move and adjust to changes, there may not even be skid marks as they are rolled by faster and more focused competitors.

3 The Beijing Jeep and the Threat From China

The production of the Beijing Jeep has a chequered history and serves not just as an illustration of the development of joint-venture vehicle manufacturing in China but also of some of the problems that Western firms encountered on their first forays into the country and the Chinese puzzle of its regulations and business practices.

In February 1972 Richard Nixon became the first US President to visit the People's Republic of China, and his visit revolutionized social and international compacts, but the visit of President Ronald Reagan in April 1984 may have had the greater economic influence. At the time of Reagan's visit, it was felt that there would be an explosion of trade with the world's most populous nation, for its doors to the West appeared to be creaking open at last. A White House spokesman, commenting on the 1984 visit and its implications for the US economy, said that Western business would earn 'megabucks' in China.[29] He predicted that within five years, US investment in China's oil industry would be '10 billion to 15 billion', and that there would be 'perhaps hundreds of thousands of Americans and other Westerners in China.'[30] However, and not for not the first time, foreign predictions of China's possibilities would prove to be inaccurate.

Fast forward to June 1989, five years after President Reagan's visit. In Tien An Men Square, the very centre of Beijing, there were citizens calling for democratic reforms, and on the seventh of that month they were dispersed by troops and tanks with great loss of life — official estimates were that 223 soldiers and police were killed and around 200 civilians (probably an underestimation) died. Thousands were wounded and thousands more imprisoned.

Foreigners fled the country. At the time, there were not 'hundreds of thousands of Americans and other Westerners' in China. In fact Americans numbered only around 6,000.[31] Also, far from there being '10 billion to 15 billion' of investment in the oil industry, there was just over one billion US dollars' worth of investment.[32] The pattern of foreign involvement in China's development was proving to be rocky from the days of those first joint ventures. One company that rode a roller-coaster ride from optimism to pessimism was Beijing Jeep.

Chrysler Motor Company, through its subsidiary, American Motors, took note of the opening door to China presaged by the President's 1984 visit. There was a period of consultation with potential Chinese partners, large State-Owned Enterprises (SOIs) involved in motor vehicle manufacturing, and this introductory period was characterized by cultural misunderstandings on both sides. One such misunderstanding occurred when a group of Chinese executives were invited to American Motors' conference of dealers held in Las Vegas. The somewhat prudish Chinese were scandalized not just by the showy (and some partially dressed) people gambling away wads of money which represented fortunes to the Chinese, but also by the fact that American Motors spent over a million dollars just on the conference. This display represented profligacy to the Chinese (although some years down the track, they could more than match such displays).

In time these initial misunderstandings were overcome and there was an agreement between the American company and a Chinese joint-venture partner, a long-established state-owned corporation named Beijing Auto Works. In 1985, a new manufacturing facility was established in Beijing, designed and supervised by American expatriates. Some components were sourced locally but most were supplied through the shipment of parts kits from Chrysler in the United States. The vehicles produced were sold throughout China.

There were ongoing problems from the beginning of the operation. Parts kits were held up in customs for various bureaucratic reasons, causing production problems. The joint-venture partner was accused by American Motors of unfairly holding back payments due to the Americans, in some cases taking months to remit their share of the profits of the vehicles sold through their Chinese network.[33] The partnership was not as profitable as the Americans had hoped. The partners were not the first to be beguiled by the prospects of selling their products into a market of a billion-plus people, only to discover that high profits were illusory. Business analysts had a habit of making a superficial analysis of the Chinese market and producing sheaves of optimistic statistics. In most cases, those who sponsored such research and were tempted by optimistic business cases found that cracking the Chinese market was exceptionally difficult.

The crackdown in Tien An Men Square led to a crisis for Beijing Jeep. All the US personnel were directed to leave by the US head office, and by the end of June 1989, the production facility was entirely under the direction of Chinese management and staff. There was widespread pessimism, especially among American investors, not just at American Motors. A commentator wrote in 1989 that the conclusion to be reached from the short history of Beijing Jeep was that further joint ventures were unlikely and 'China is likely to remain a relatively poor country for a long time.'[34]

However, this was an unduly pessimistic assessment and there continued to be investment from Japan and Europe. Within two years, there was a renewed enthusiasm for the prospects of investing in the country. I witnessed some of this when I first went to Nanjing in 1992, and two years later when I went to the industrial city of Wuhan, where I worked at Wuhan Iron and Steel University (in one of the centres of reform of heavy industry in China) and later in the coastal city of Qingdao.

A Personal Encounter With the Beijing Jeep
John was a teacher in Qingdao, and over a Bitburger ale in a bar on the Fujian Road he told me how he was — and will always be — a proud citizen of the Old Dominion (the State of Virginia in the United States of America). John was also a big fan of Jeep, and he picked me

up to take me to the bar in one. At that time, he drove a five-speed Jeep Cherokee hard-top (manufactured in Beijing) — cost, new in China, 130,000 yuan (almost universally known as renminbi, 'people's money'). He could have bought a cheaper version — a soft-top, four-speed for just over 100,000 yuan. In the garage at his home in Virginia, he had a hard-top and a soft-top that he enjoyed taking out on expeditions throughout the natural wonders of the USA, Canada and even parts of Mexico. The two vehicles in his Virginian garage seemed to him to be near-identical models to those he could buy in Qingdao. If he bought his hard-top in the USA today, new, it would cost around US$30,000 — or the equivalent, at 2007 rates of exchange, of 240,000 yuan. This was nearly twice as much in absolute terms as the price John would pay for a near-equivalent vehicle in China.[35]

In other words, if the Beijing Jeep could be sprinkled with pixie dust and magically transported to the USA with all other factors being equal (disregarding taxes, etc.), then it would retail for well below the price of the US-made model, perhaps even one half the price. However, there were two big provisos with this scenario. First, GM would not import foreign-made models and wreck its own domestic market in the United States, and second, taxes and customs duties would affect the relative pricing. However, what if ....? What if there were wholly owned Chinese car manufacturers with up-to-date technology and excellent quality assurance who could produce vehicles with similar styling and quality to cars manufactured in the West? Would the Chinese have the motivation and desire to sell them in the West at prices that would ensure market dominance? Could it happen? What if John was back in his home state of Virginia and happened to be cruising through a new car market and found two jeeps, virtually identical — an American-made vehicle costing US$30,000, and a Chinese-made vehicle costing say US$20,000? Which one would he purchase?

Extend the analogy and put yourself in the picture. What if you were in a car yard in Australia and found two new Volkswagen Polos — one German-made for A$22,000 and one Chinese-made lookalike for A$14,000? What if you came across a manual 1.3 litre three-door Toyota Yaris, locally made and priced (September 2006) at A$14,999 and next to it was a Chinese-made identical car (maybe just with different badges) for A$9,999? Perhaps you do not want a small car, and a family-sized car is more to your preference. What would you do, then, if you walked to the next row and found an Australian-made Ford Falcon, new, for A$33,490 and lined up right next to it was a new Chinese-made Buick Regal that was the same size, same quality, with similar features, for A$23,000? Not even the most experienced and qualified car sales professional could find a better price.

It would be a bold person who would say that they would prefer to buy the locally made car, or the US-made car, or the European-made car, and pay a premium of 30 per cent, 50 per cent or even 100 per cent on the price. Provided the Chinese-made car had equal quality, or close to equal quality, with adequate sales and service back-up, then most people would buy the cheaper vehicle. That is simply human nature. Periodically there are 'Buy Australian' campaigns, but they usually founder when there are big price differentials between local and imported goods.

World Reaction to the Coming Storm

Do Western car manufacturers recognize the threat of increasing quantities of Chinese-built cars any more that Australian executives and managers? Do they have plans to meet the challenge when it arrives (other than lobbying for increases in tariffs and protection to impede the competition)? Are manufacturers making cars that suit the demands of consumers? Certainly some manufacturers recognize the challenge thrown down by the low-cost industries of China and India. Toyota is planning what it calls an 'ultra-low-cost car'. Its president, Katsuaki Watanabe, has stated that his company is focusing on 'low-cost technology' with radically changed design and manufacturing processes, and very low-cost materials, aiming to produce a car 'sub-Yaris sized' for a lower cost but the same quality.[36]

However, consider the latest models from American and Australian manufacturers — large, fuel-guzzling models, some bigger than their predecessors. These car makers may well be out of touch with the demands of consumers, who are asking for cars like those being made in China that are cheaper and offer better mileage. Such features are becoming crucial in consumers' deliberations as the price of oil surges — as is evidenced by 2006 figures in Australia and around the world which showed that sales of larger cars fell and there was a commensurate rise in sales of small to medium cars.[37] Consumers who were feeling the financial pinch were opting for smaller cars which were not only cheaper to buy, and were cheaper to run, but had a higher resale value than larger cars.[38]

Having said this, it must be added, in fairness to car producers, that perhaps it has been the consumers who have been out of touch with world trends towards sustainable development. Many consumers demanded cars that would enable them to lord it over the drivers of small cars, and do not value vehicle attributes such as emission levels. Many consumers still want a 'tank' to cruise the highways in what they perceive to be a superior and elevated position. Only a minority, and a very small minority at that, would confess to wanting a 'clean, green car'. Of the top-selling US-made brands in the US in 2006, big SUVs (sports utility vehicles) like the Ford F-150 and the Chevrolet Silverado 1500 came in at numbers one and two. The Ford Explorer came in at number six.[39]

A second point to make out of fairness to car designers is that many car makers do have innovative designs on the drawing boards. GM and Ford have a number of models at an advanced stage of design and testing to compete with the popular Toyota Prius. For example, Ford has two hybrids — the Ford Escape and the Mercury Mariner — already on the road.

China's wholly owned auto makers have joined others pushing the envelope of modern vehicle design, responding to current tastes and preferences. At the Beijing Motor Show of December 2005, First Auto Works unveiled a hybrid bus (named the Liberation bus — perhaps with levels of meaning in the name). The same auto maker launched a version of its trusty old Red Flag sedan that was a hybrid, utilizing Toyota technology under licence. The Motor Show of that year also saw the launch of a number of home-grown Chinese designs, including convertibles and sports cars. In contrast to some of the early indigenous designs, they were original, challenging, and owed few ideas or concepts to the West.

In relation to the question of keeping up with consumer tastes, manufacturers to some extent are in a no-win situation, because it takes a year or two to develop a new car model, and then more time to set up manufacturing lines, but consumer preferences appear to change much more quickly, sometimes as quickly as they notice the price of the tank of fuel that they have just put into their vehicle. So it would be unfair to overly criticize major car manufacturers for being slow to meet changing consumer demands; they are not slow, just tied into a harsh timing cycle that makes it hard to keep up with changes in motorists' whims. Having said this, it nevertheless seems a fact that some auto designers persist with designs that appeal to their peer groups — their own motoring circles — but fail to connect with the wants of the mass of consumers.

The manufacturers that have concentrated on larger cars are in difficulties. Ford, for example, is having to cut back on its production plans worldwide to levels not seen for more than 20 years. GM and Chrysler in the US are also cutting back production, as will be detailed later in this book. These cutbacks surely suggest that the auto industries in Western countries may not be well-prepared to meet a serious challenge, and even tougher competition.

Some executives downplay the threat of Chinese-made cars. Denny Mooney, general manager of Holden in Australia, was reported as saying, 'I'm not really concerned about cheap Chinese imports ... because they're having trouble supplying their own demand internally.'[40] On the face of it, this is a reasonable statement. If the demand within China continues to grow exponentially, then Chinese car manufacturers (both joint ventures and the expanding wholly owned companies) would find it hard to keep up with that demand. However, infrastructure issues, such as developing a service network and the legal and insurance framework, mean the demand for cars in China has very firm limits that are already being tested.

Putting this problem in simplistic terms, the average Chinese private car owner will soon need a local car service centre to service and/or repair his vehicle when necessary. That need is not yet critical for the simple reason that most cars are still new and not yet in need of chronic repairs.

There is also the problem with increased pollution that sets a practical limit on car ownership (or at least on the ownership of current types of car). In China, any visitor can see that there is near intolerable pollution in the big cities even now, and traffic problems with the existing levels of car ownership and use, so it is difficult to support the premise that the number of cars in China's cities can double let alone treble in the near future.

In the near future, the growth in manufacturing capacity in China will outstrip even the increasing domestic demand, so much so that China's own car makers (as much as the joint ventures) will look to exports to maintain their frenetic rates of growth. The challenge from China cannot be too easily dismissed, and nor should aspects of the growth of its car industry remain unresearched.

A Modest Program of Research
During my time in China, I worked in several cities during the 1990s. I returned again in the new millennium, and over four years, from 2002 to 2006, while employed at universities in Chengdu and Qingdao, I worked alongside a number of keen young Chinese postgraduate students on research projects. These projects were designed to ask (and if possible obtain indicative answers to) some crucial questions. Because of the implications of Chinese industrial development for the global manufacturing industry and for the Australian manufacturing sector in particular, I resolved to undertake research into the patterns of the development of the motor vehicle industry.

When (not if) the Chinese motor vehicle manufacturing industry becomes a major exporter to markets in North America, the European Union and Australasia then it must become a dominant force, because it has the legitimate economic advantage of large-scale production as well as the less legitimate advantage of an undervalued currency that leverages the efforts of its well-educated and largely docile labourforce. Admittedly, there is some movement in the exchange rate of the yuan to the US dollar under the constraints of a managed rate, but it is far too little. Also admittedly, there are (albeit small) movements in the real wages paid in China, especially now that the country is entering a turning point when the supply of labour may be less than the demand, at least in the coastal and urban east, and the massive flow of labour from rural areas to the cities is easing. However, disparities between China and the West are too great to be corrected quickly. These disparities give Chinese manufacturing industry substantial advantages compared to Western manufacturers, and it is certain that China will retain its highly advantageous position for years to come. In time, it may be challenged for dominance by its neighbour, India. The economies of both these countries have features in common — high rates of growth, low-cost structures and large, skilled, willing labourforces in urban centres. It is too soon yet to judge whether the 21st century will be the Chinese century or the Indian century, but it is not too soon to make the judgment that both India and China will seriously challenge the West's dominance of global trade in the very near future.

When China enters the world's motor vehicle markets on a large scale, and there is a tsunami-like wave of cheap, quality cars, will governments in the West accept the decline and probable near-extinction of their own motor vehicle manufacturing industries?

A similar phenomenon occurred in the 1970s, when motorcycle manufacturers in the West were swept away by a flood of cheap Japanese motorcycles. On that occasion, governments survived the flood because motorcycle manufacturing had come to fill a niche and was not crucial to domestic economies, and moreover motorcycle enthusiasts had gained themselves (probably unfairly) a reputation as 'grease heads' and rebels. As a consequence, motorcyclists who preferred old style big bikes were not in a position to lobby effectively for protection in a big way. Governments did not feel pressure to support the long-established and increasingly sclerotic motorcycle manufacturers in a meaningful way.

Car manufacturing in the 21st century has a different profile — resonating with national pride, as well as underpinning employment and providing a bastion for defence industries. When the full force of the tsunami is felt, and local manufacturers feel the suck of the surge taking the ground from beneath their feet, then there will be pressure to ramp up levels of protection. Will governments be able to resist that pressure? The answer to that question is unclear.

Will all parties have all the accurate information they need about the phenomenon about to hit? The answer to this question is much clearer — and that answer is clearly in the negative.

There has been research into some of the major factors relating to China's motor vehicle manufacturing industry, such as production statistics and the degree of automation, but many other factors that are crucial to an understanding of the industry are not well-researched. The factors considered in this book are based on those examined in a 1983 publication, *The Motor Vehicle Industry in Asia*, which discussed problems and opportunities facing the industry, especially when joint ventures were established and domestic car manufacturing industries developed.[41] That book described two problems facing primary manufacturing forms, notably the deterioration of quality over time, and increases in prices of product. It also discussed the poor performance of production control due to shortages of skilled labour, as well as problems with production equipment and quality of raw materials. These are the issues that formed the basis of the research into China's car industry that is discussed here.

'Convince us That it's Important'

But is research into aspects of China's car industry infrastructure really earth-shaking? What of the 'so what' factor? The 'so what' factor is expressed like this: 'You've done research on the car industry in China — so what? Convince us that it's important.'

Some may say that such research is not needed or is irrelevant because the export of Chinese cars to the West surely cannot constitute a threat. They assume that Chinese-produced cars will be small and tinny, low-cost but poorly made by world standards, probably rattletraps and not suitable for road and traffic conditions in the West.

There is a historical precedent of the countries in the West badly underestimating Asian peoples. That precedent was before the Second World War, when some writers, imbued with racism, insisted that the Japanese could not be a military threat for numerous reasons, including that their planes were flimsy and second-rate and that the Japanese themselves were not good soldiers, partly due to the 'fact' that they had poor eyesight due to their squinty eyes. The events of 1941 put those theories in the dustbin of history where they belonged, but many Western servicemen and women suffered through the poor equipment and strategies they were provided with to contest the issues with the Japanese.

There may be an argument that the Chinese cars that are exported in the first wave of exports will be small, possibly of substandard quality and with very basic features, much like the Daewoos and Hyundais of South Korean manufacturers when they were first made widely available in the West. There may also be an apparent argument that the Chinese will remain content with this niche at the bottom of the market — the niche for the cheap 'throwaway' car. However, the latter argument ignores history. For example, the first Japanese cars exported in quantity to the West in the 1960s — the Datsun and the Toyota Tiara — were indeed cheap and basic at first, and not really suited for the driving conditions encountered on America's freeways. However, the Japanese manufacturers were not content with winning a market niche, and a niche at the bottom of the market at that. Japanese manufacturers fought hard to improve their products and in a comparatively short time won a strategic position in the American market, against some of the toughest competition in the world, largely because the Japanese relied on a 'volume-oriented tradition and the use of aggressive pricing'.[42] Moreover, Japanese companies had an advantage over American companies because 'Japanese enterprises are growth-fixated to an even greater extent than US companies'.[43]

These comments about the Japanese perfectly reflect the instincts and attitudes of Chinese manufacturers also. They also are 'growth-fixated', and they have a 'volume-oriented tradition' (if anything, even more so than the Japanese). Moreover, one has only to observe what has happened in the textile and footwear industries now dominated globally by the Chinese to agree that inherent in their strategy is 'the use of aggressive pricing.' It is beyond doubt that when the Chinese have the capability to enter a new market, they will seek a major position in that market. They will offer products across the range of the market seeking to dominate mass markets. Some niche markets, perhaps the very top of the luxury-car range or parts of the SUV range, will be left to Western manufacturers, not the other way around.

Basically, Chinese executives and managers are lean and hungry in a way that executives and managers in the West are not, or at least not since the likes of Henry Ford and Alfred Sloane. When the Chinese export their products, they will seek a dominant position in the market and not be satisfied with a small proportion.

This thesis is supported by industry analysts:

> There's no question that the Chinese strategy is to sell the cheapest cars on the planet. It will seek to dominate market share at the low end then look to improve quality and price, just as the Japanese did before.[44]

> In the 1990s, you had people spending $13,990 on a new Hyundai instead of a second-hand Toyota. The next step is people spending maybe $10,000 on a new Chinese car instead of a second-hand Hyundai. The effect will be to pull the whole price structure down.[45]

So, is a study of car manufacturing important in the Grand Scheme of Things? The key to modern economic development has been industrialization. At the heart of industrialization in the nineteenth century was the expansion of railways and the telegraph, but at the heart of industrialization in the 20th century was the increasing private ownership and use of the car. Phenomena such as urbanization were dependent upon the convenience of personal transportation. Car ownership was crucial to economic development, and central to the formation of the type of lifestyle now lived in developed nations. Private car ownership did something more — it reflected the development of an individual's confidence and self-esteem, and spoke to something elemental deep within everyone. In economically advanced parts of the world, by the latter part of the 20th century when car ownership had become widespread, people identified themselves with their cars. Their 'four wheels' became more than just transportation. Their car often had a name. People chose a model of car which matched their personality — or what they hoped they could be. Some cars were big and stately and others were sporty and nimble. The car was personalized, and sometimes it carried stickers to proclaim the owner's beliefs. In an age when some workers spent as much time in their car commuting as they did in recreation in their home, the car became a supportive and comforting envelope to get themselves through the world.

The car has taken up a crucial place in the psyche of modern man and woman. It contributes to the feel-good factor that keeps people well-adjusted and able to keep their place in the world. Hence, a study of car manufacturing is very important in the Grand Scheme of Things, especially if there are big changes about to hit the local industry. The importance of the feel-good factor will be revisited later in this book.

The prospect of a looming economic storm is a critical one, and research into the nature and the effects of such a storm is urgently needed. The research that follows in Part Three indicates (although admittedly does not prove) that demand and supply factors in China will result in the mass production of the sort of vehicle demanded by Western consumers and a surge of exports, with a substantial force behind it, that sweeps over obstacles in its path.

Governments in the West may resort to a number of strategies to counter the impact, but all of the strategic choices they make will have implications for globalization. They can support globalization and free trade and import large numbers of Chinese cars at whatever cost to the local manufacturing industry; or they can erect tariff barriers, bring in other trade protection measures and subsidize local manufacturers to meet the Chinese competition; or else they can pressure/persuade the Chinese to freely float the yuan (the major distorting factor of the global level playing field if it is not allowed to reflect inflationary pressures inside and outside the Chinese economy).

To summarize this chapter, the Western automotive industry must be transformed or else global trade practices must be transformed. Over the past 30 years, China has been transforming itself from what has been called an iron rice bowl economy based on large State-Owned Enterprises (SOEs) to a 'gourmet table' economy of equally big private corporations, and the young and hungry Chinese giants need to feed their appetite for trade and markets. They are hungry and they are looking outside China to continue to satisfy appetites for growth.

4 Motorcycle Manufacturing in the West and in Japan

The thesis of this book — that high-quality Chinese-made vehicles and auto components will undercut, then dominate, domestic car markets in the West under the existing practices of globalization — may seem a far-fetched proposition, given the comparative strengths of the industry in the West and the industry in China. However, something similar has happened before, in very recent history.

Consider the situation in the world motorcycle manufacturing industry in 1960. In Britain and the United States, there were nearly 50 manufacturers, most with long histories going back 60 years, with their manufacturing capacity and the skills of their workforces developed during the First and Second World Wars with the benefits of large government contracts.

The three brands that had the greatest share of the market in the United States and Britain were Triumph, BSA and Norton. In the words of one writer, the British motorcycling industry had been 'the imperious leader since the 1920s'.[46]

The Triumph motorcycle company had manufactured bicycles since 1888 and started manufacturing motorcycles in 1902. Harley-Davidson commenced in the following year. These quickly became iconic companies, well-founded and apparently here to stay.

By the Second World War, other well-known companies included

Norton, Ariel, Indian, BSA, Matchless and many others. The manufacturers had a range of products that were tried and trusted, with an emphasis on some larger machines which have featured in the popular mind. There was a hard core of motorcycle supporters in motorcycle clubs.

In mainland Europe, the situation was different in some respects, for much of their industry was still recovering from the destruction of the war years, but they had substantial government support for their operations, and their products sold well in their home countries, as well as being exported to Britain and the US, where some had a solid reputation (e.g., the BMW touring motorbikes).

In Asia, four new manufacturers had been established in Japan, but in 1960 they were only around five to fourteen years old, with no history. One new manufacturer had previously produced pianos! Another was a loom manufacturer. They produced a restricted range of motorbikes, with an emphasis upon small and very small machines that provoked derision when seen in Britain or the US. (The author recalls a comment received while riding a Honda in 1971: 'Hey, mate — get a real bike, not a plastic one!') Japan was still suffering the effects of the extensive devastation of the war years, when many industrial plants were levelled, and many skilled workers killed by bombing or by the privations that followed immediately after the war. The Japanese economy had recovered with an influx of US investment during the Korean War, but it still had a way to go.

The four new manufacturers operated under names that sounded odd in the West, and they named their products with weak-sounding appellations (such as the Honda Dream) instead of resonant names like Dominator or Commando. Honda was the oldest of the companies, although it dated only from 1946 and its first product (a beast of just 98cc called the Dream, which was to be a recurring model name) only came out in 1947. Suzuki dated from 1952, Kawasaki from 1954 and Yamaha from 1955.

Yet within ten to fifteen years, the four Japanese manufacturers had taken the major share of the motorcycle market in the West, and their only effective competition was with each other. Within another ten years their dominance had advanced still further and they had bankrupted almost all of the British and American manufacturers. The Japanese Big Four had become elephants among mice.

Only one or two British and US brands survived, because they came to occupy small and specialized niches in the marketplace and attracted a cult following. Harley-Davidson, for example, once the largest motorcycle manufacturer in the world, managed to cling on the way denim jeans do — largely as a symbol of rebellion, although it is a rebellion of the comparatively wealthy who can afford the cost of the chromed 'soft-tail'. Its reputation as the first of the super bikes — a twin-cylinder machine of 55 cubic inches — won it iconic notoriety when Arnold Schwarzenegger rode one to outpace a Mack truck in *Terminator 2*.

In Europe, Ducati survived on the strength of its appeal to a sophisticated European clientele (yet was purchased in time by a US company), and BMW on the strength of its reputation for German engineering and the support of its diversified parent company. Smaller companies survived with a degree of a patriotic loyalty in their home countries. Yet some of these survivors still needed government funds and assistance as life preservers after the perfect storm of deceptively well-made and competitively priced Japanese motorcycles hit in slow-motion in the 1960s to the mid-1970s.

Western Motorcycle Manufacturers Before 1960
Who were the Western motorcycle manufacturers, and where did they come from? Gottlieb Daimler attached an internal combustion engine to a frame and thus produced the first motorcycle in 1885. The basic shape of that first motorcycle has not changed, despite all the refinements and remodelling over the years. Since Daimler, there have been numerous motorcycle manufacturers, although in 2006 only a few large-scale companies remain. The roll-call of names that have vanished is a long one. Consider some of the following motorcycle companies that were once so well-known and trusted in the marketplace.

The British manufacturer, Triumph, has been mentioned. The company was founded by a German, Siegfried Bettmann, as a manufacturer of bicycles based in Coventry. In 1902, Bettmann produced a bicycle with an imported Belgian motor attached. Three years later, he marketed a Triumph with an English-made engine. Bettmann hit upon an inspired marketing strategy when he decided to prepare his machines for motorcycle racing, and Triumphs were successful in early races, one of which was a circuit of the Isle of Man.

The company expanded during the First World War, producing more than 40,000 machines for use in transport and communication duties. Triumph built upon its sound position during the 1920s and 1930s, when a motorcycle was often the poor man's mode of transport. In 1925, Triumph manufactured 30,000 machines a year. It weathered the general downturn of the Depression and commenced making cars as well. During the Second World War also, it increased production to meet government orders. Coventry was heavily bombed and production suffered, but there was an upside, for the government assisted the company to diversify its operations into other provincial centres, and a town named Meriden, just out of Coventry.

After the war, Triumph continued to prosper in the late 1940s, but in 1951 it fell as a takeover target to BSA. The name 'Triumph' continued, however, and was applied to a new design launched in 1959 and (with an eye to the US market, perhaps) named the Bonneville, with its suggestion of attempts on world speed records on the salt flats at Lake Bonneville. By the end of the 1960s, it had a good market share, including selling nearly 30,000 motorcycles a year in the United States.

BSA, the major player in British motorcycle manufacturing after the Second World War, had started as the Birmingham Small Arms factory, initially manufacturing arms for the troops in the Crimean War. The company turned its skills with machining small units into building bicycles from 1880 and motorcycle manufacturing in 1903. They built their first fully BSA-designed and manufactured machine in 1910.

During the First World War, Triumph expanded its motorcycle production while BSA reverted to the making of weapons. When peace came again, they were well-placed to invest in new models and facilities. BSA prospered in the 1920s with its range of well-designed models from its sports machine, an overhead valve model of around 500cc, to its small two-stroke 175cc model. By the 1930s BSA was expanding aggressively and bought out a number of other motorcycle and motor vehicle manufacturers, including Sunbeam in 1936. From this extended base of resources and expertise, BSA produced its well-known Star M ranges. The Star range went from the single-cylinder Blue Star series (with engines in various sizes from 250 to 500cc) to the grandly named and famed Empire Star models. The M range was a more basic machine, and was the basis for its extended production during the Second World War.

By the late 1930s, BSA had more than a 25 per cent share of the UK market and claimed to be the largest motorcycle maker in the world. It had more than 60 factories throughout the United Kingdom. There could be no suggestion that these motorcycle manufacturers were amateur, or second-rate, or small-scale operations. They were major companies, with aggressive and go-ahead management.

During the Second World War, BSA suffered like Triumph from war damage to its facilities, but nevertheless they produced more than 120,000 machines for the Allied armies. In 1944, they took over Ariel Motorcycles. After the war, BSA continued its strategy of acquisitions and mergers.

Matchless Motorcycles was established as a manufacturer of pedigreed racing machines. Both the founders, brothers Charles and Harry Collier, were racing enthusiasts. Their first machine had a French engine married to a bicycle frame, and the first all-British motorcycle came out in 1902. The company expanded steadily, and in 1931 took over another firm that had a strong interest in racing bikes — AJS (named after the initials of its founder, Albert John Stevens). The Matchless Motorcycle Company continued to produce both Matchless and AJS machines, with engines of cubic capacities from 250 to 500cc, and styles from racers to roadsters. In 1938, it became Associated Motorcycles (AMC). Associated Motorcycles bought out Norton in 1951, and lost large sums attempting to expand into the American market. Norton as a separate entity had some success, but its parent company was in difficulties by 1960.

Royal Enfield was also one of the early English companies, starting in 1900. They developed motorbikes for the larger and prestige end of the market, and they also expanded manufacturing capacity to meet lucrative wartime contracts. In the 1950s, they were expanding into India, where they captured a large share of the market.

Ariel motorcycles also started production in the early 20th century, in 1903. They made motorbikes for the top end of the market. Their models were acclaimed as among the best designed machines in the world and, in the 1930s, among the fastest. An innovative four-cylinder machine (the Square Four) was one of the largest motorcycles in production, and much sought-after. As mentioned above, it was taken over by BSA during World War II. The name 'Ariel' continued and there were a number of models brought out in the 1950s, from a four-stroke 650cc model to a two-stroke 250cc machine that was a cross between a motor scooter and a motorbike.

Across the Atlantic, there were also prominent American manufacturers, although they did not come to have as much appeal to the American motoring public as did the UK manufacturers in Britain. This was perhaps because the American public found cars more affordable than did their English cousins, and the distances involved in the US made cars a more agreeable means of transport.

Harley-Davidson was a notable American motorcycle maker. It was set up in 1903 by three men — William Harley and Arthur and Walter Davidson — in Milwaukee. From the first single-cylinder model, the Harley-Davidson company produced a range of models that were renowned for their engine designs and, in time, for the distinctive timbre of the exhaust note which later competitors tried to imitate.

Indian is another name from the history of motorcycles. From its inception in 1901, it expanded into the market, and its Chief range, with a distinctive Indian-head logo, dating from 1922 became popular. However, its models were outmoded by the 1950s and it declined from that time.

In Europe, there were motorcycle manufacturers that had greater or lesser success over the years than some of the companies noted above. Ducati was formed in Bologna in 1926, originally to make radio components. It grew rapidly in the 1930s, but it did not begin manufacturing motorcycles until the Italian government nationalized it after the war and had it make motorized bicycles to address Italy's acute transportation problems. Ducati's first small motorcycles were just 60cc and 100cc, but they were used in racing and their successes on the track underpinned the growing fame of the company. In 1958, the Ducati 175 was exported to the United States and quickly built a following.

Moto Guzzi was another Italian manufacturer that did well from the 1920s and 1930s, and became renowned for its machines painted in the bright red of Italian racing. Moto Guzzi recovered after the war, producing large machines for the army and its popular Falcone tourer for the young and the restless.

The Bavarian Motor Works (Bayerische Motoren Werke; BMW) had its origins in an aero-engine manufacturing company of the First World War. The challenges of building lightweight engines developed engineering skills that were also appropriate for motorcycle makers, and in the 1920s the first BMW motorcycles, 150cc and 500cc models, were coming off an assembly line at their Munich factory. In 1929, a 750cc BMW set a world motorcycle speed record (134 mph/216 kph). After expansion and destruction during the war years, motorcycle production resumed in 1950, and by 1952, had reached a level of 30,000 per year. The company branched out into car production as well, and was successful in marketing a range of small cars, but made substantial losses by 1959 when it tried to compete in the luxury car market.

There were many other European motorcycle manufacturers, from Husqvarna in Sweden (established in a weapons factory in 1903) to the moped specialist Puch in Austria (which was notable in going from building motorcycles to building mopeds in the 1950s — a reversal of the history of most other manufacturers). Although most of these companies retained a following on their own turf, few of them could win and hold a hold a beachhead on the world motorcycle stage.

The bulk of the world's motorcycle market was held by machines that bore the names Triumph, BSA and Norton. It appeared as if their operations were sound and their shareholders and stakeholders could look forward to future prosperity. The truth was that their hold on the market was fragile, and that perhaps they had become complacent and over-confident. From their executive offices, top management could scan metaphorical horizons and wonder where any challenges could come from.

To use a metaphor, the Western motorcycle manufacturers saw their hold on the market as like an orange — full and round, and well able to be squeezed for juice. The real situation was that the market may have appeared robust and promising, but it was like an orange that had been hollowed out from within, and when the squeeze came, there was no flesh inside to resist.

In a country distant from the United States and Europe, there were small manufacturers dreaming big dreams. They were about to unleash a storm on world markets by taking, first Manhattan, then most other cities.

In the storm that was about to happen, there were very strong parallels with the situation confronting Western car manufacturers in the 21st century.

The Coming of the Japanese Motorcycles
Honda

The main force behind the perfect storm of Japanese motorcycles of the 1960s that hit the world industry, and especially the United States and Britain, was Honda. A recounting of its activities in some detail also serves as a description of the development and impact of the other manufacturers of Japan's Big Four — Yamaha, Suzuki and Kawasaki. Honda was the oldest of the Japanese motorcycle companies, although it dated only from 1946, when Soichiro Honda founded a machine tool and engineering business in October of that year. Honda set up his company in Hanamatsu, in the Shizuoka Prefecture, a small city about 100 kilometres south of Tokyo, not far from Mount Fuji. The new company prospered, and the manufacturing of engines became its main business, so in 1948 it was renamed the Honda Motor Co. Ltd. At that time, it was capitalized at one million yen, or around US$7,000 at the currency rates prevailing then.

In October of 1949, an event of great significance occurred for the company, although it was not recognized as such at the time. An engineer named Takeo Fujisawa joined the company, and he would prove to be one of the most talented managers of the 20th century. His skills drove

71

the expansion of Honda. In 1952, the company made its first exports — of the small F-type motorcycle to Taiwan.

Both Honda and Fujisawa knew that the key to expansion was to be found in overseas marketplaces. The field where exports promised greatest prizes was the United States. However, when a Honda team reviewed possible regions where they could sell their products, they recommended to their top management that the company should concentrate on Asia, and possibly parts of Europe. Their argument was that the United States market would be too tough to crack, and motorcycle sales were declining there anyway. Fujisawa responded to their recommendations with a blunt rejection. He told Honda that the US market was a pacesetter, and that the correct philosophy to follow was to take on the toughest challenges first.[47]

Fujisawa himself travelled to the US in 1958. Honda faced a major problem in determining the best way to handle its exports. Typically, for literally hundreds of years, Japanese exporters dealt through Japanese trading companies called Sogoshosha. These traders arranged transport and negotiated customs and the myriad problems involved in trading from one country to another. Honda's problem was that these traditional traders could not provide the follow-up services crucial to the motorcycle industry, such as ongoing services and maintenance and the supply of spare parts. If Honda wanted to be a major player in foreign markets, it would have to set up its own system of distribution apart from the traditional Sogoshosha model. This they decided to do, despite the difficulty and the expense involved.

Fujisawa held a meeting of some of the Americans dealers he had selected to be part of the Honda distribution network. He told them of his plans 'to sell 7,500 units.'[48] One of the Americans sucked his teeth and said that was a tough ask, because 'BSA and Triumph together only sold 6,000 units a year in the US'. Fujisawa responded, 'I was talking about 7,500 each month.'[49]

Fujisawa's goal was indeed a challenging one. For 1958, the total motorcycle registrations in the US were 450,000, and 60,000 of those were European imports such as BSA, Triumph and some German and Italian models. It was a peak year for Western manufacturers, and few managers or even industry analysts foresaw the risk to traditional markets from small competitors from a strange and distant country. By its own calculations, Honda was aiming at sales figures that constituted 20 per cent of the total existing market — and that was just for starters.

Fujisawa believed he had an ace — or more than one ace — up his sleeve, for he had identified weaknesses in the American market. There were just 3,000 motorcycle dealerships, and most of these were part-timers, open only for the weekend or a couple of days each week. Fewer than 1,000 were full-time motorcycle dealers. There were systemic problems, for inventories were low and dealers tended to buy on consignment. After-sales service was generally poor. These were classic signs of complacent players in a marketplace without strong competition from lean and hungry rivals.

Besides the systemic problems, there was an image problem. Motorcycles were sold to customers out of oily, dirty bike shops, by types described as grease monkeys.[50] Fujisawa wanted to change the very image of motorcycling and of motorcyclists. He had a strategy that involved finding new dealers, not cramped and cluttered bike shops, but sports stores, hobby shops, lawnmower dealers and hardware stores. The people who sold Honda motorcycles should be clean, preferably wearing ties, and work out of sparkling new premises that displayed shiny new bikes.

Fujisawa established American Honda Motor Co. Inc. in June 1959. He chose to set up its offices in Los Angeles, where the climate was conducive to riding motorcycles. Sales initially were well below expectations, barely 200 units in six months. Then a major problem arose. Many bikes were being returned with mechanical problems such as bad oil leaks. This was unexpected, and Honda's thorough research into the situation revealed that Americans drove their bikes differently from the Japanese. Due to America's distances and wide open roads, American riders drove faster and for longer periods than Japanese driving on the typically narrow streets and roads of their homeland. The images of Marlon Brando in *The Wild One* (incidentally riding a Triumph) cruising along wide highways inspired many to don their leathers and head off into distant vistas, winding up their machines to the max. Honda motorcycles had borne up to the conditions riders in Japan subjected them to, but had not been designed for the harsher treatment heaped upon them by American riders.

Honda was quick to remedy the problems. They undertook a rigorous testing program and improved the machines so that they could cope with American conditions, and with the proclivities of Americans. Only a few years later, Datsun and Toyota would prove to be equally quick learners in the car industry. An author made a comment that may be applicable to both car and motorcycle manufacturers: The early Japanese imports were 'weak, uninspired copies of outmoded English designs and while cheap, they did not sell well. As soon as they were upgraded to fill the needs of the American market, the Japanese … "miracle" began.'[51]

Despite Honda remedying the faults in their first imported models, sales increased only slowly. However, the company was building its distribution network all the time. By the end of 1961, there were 500 Honda dealers in the United States. At the beginning of 1963, a new advertising campaign struck a chord and sales took off. The campaign emphasized the new image of the motorcycle. No longer were they the machines of the 'grease monkeys' and the 'rev heads', but they were the cool transportation of the young and the carefree. The new slogan was inspired: 'You meet the nicest people on a Honda'. It appealed to young people, and especially to young women. It was comparatively uncommon for women to ride Harleys or Nortons, unless as pillion passengers. The new Japanese machines were aimed not just at male riders, but also at the class of riders who 'held up half of heaven'.

At the same time as their marketing strategy was yielding benefits, the company was reaping the benefits of another shrewd strategy — heavily investing in motorcycle racing (just as Siegfried Bettmann had done with his new Triumph motorcycles 50 years earlier). Every time a Honda motorcycle won a big race, it demolished another piece of the outmoded stereotype that small Japanese motorcycles had once endured. By the end of 1963, Honda's sales hit 100,000 units for a twelve-month period and took just over 50 per cent of the market — in other words, outselling all the domestic and foreign models on the US market put together. From then on, the only serious competition for Honda would be Japanese.

Honda entered the European market in May 1961, when it established European Honda in Hamburg. It also started manufacturing small cars, but the car industry in the United States was firmly in the grip of the domestic Big Three, and the early Honda cars made little headway until the Honda Civic appeared in the early 1970s, followed by the Honda Accord.

For a short period in the late 1960s, some of the larger American bikes such as Harley-Davidson, and British bikes such as the Triumph Bonneville and the Norton Commando, held their own in the niche of the market that was the preserve of big machines. Honda determined to take this niche as well and in April 1969 unveiled one of the classic motorcycles — the four-cylinder CB 750, called Dream just like so many of the other Honda breeds. Its very appearance was eye-catching at the time. There was a row of four chromed cylinders and carbies, and double exhausts on either side of the back wheel. Its tank was massive, and painted and badged in attractive semi-iridescent colours (whereas manufacturers like BSA and Matchless were content with 'any colour you like, as long as it's black'). The seat was long and made for two, where the seats of its British competitors barely allowed a pillion passenger to squeeze in. This was indeed a 'dream' motorbike.

The production of such a motorcycle was a statement that Honda, and by extension other Japanese manufacturers, would not settle for dominance in limited sectors of the motorcycle market, but sought a pre-eminent position across the board. The CB 750 rapidly gained a place in the market and its market share continued to increase, helped by the even larger Gold Wing 1000 brought out in 1975.

Yamaha

Yamaha had a history that shared many elements of the history of its larger rival, Honda. It grew out of a musical instrument manufacturing company founded by Torakusa Yamaha in 1897, and it is the only one of the Big Four Japanese manufacturers that only produced motorcycles long after the death (in 1916) of the man who gave the company his name. It was the company's chief executive, Gen-ichi Kawakami, who made the move into motorcycle production (so, if things had been slightly different, Yamaha motorcycles could have been called Kawakamis, a name which does not fall as easily from the tongue). The company made its first motorcycle in 1954, a single-cylinder 125cc two-stroke. The new bike proved a winner and Yamaha Motor Company was spawned in 1955, making small two-stroke machines. In 1960, Yamaha entered the United States market with some success, partly riding on the back of Honda's publicity. It made a name in its own right by entering its machines in road racing competitions from 1958, and won a championship in 1964. Yamaha was differentiated from Honda in that its products were generally two-cylinder two-strokes, of around 250cc, although it launched a 650cc model in 1970. By 1973, Yamaha was selling a million motorcycles a year, and seven years later topped 2 million a year.

Suzuki

Michio Suzuki set up a business making silk looms before the First World War. The business prospered but there was a limit to the demand for new looms and Suzuki's eye was taken by the automotive industry, which at that time depended upon imports. In the late 1930s, Suzuki developed a small car design, but the war intervened before it could be produced. After the war, he turned instead to motorized bicycles, first using small engines left over from war production, and then manufacturing his own engines of 30cc. His first home-built design appeared in 1951, and was followed by a 60cc model. By 1954, Suzuki was a major player in the home market that was being dominated by Honda, but remained wedded to the small bike sector of the market and for that reason was slow to follow Honda and Yamaha into the export trade. It was not until Suzuki could establish its credentials with a 500cc model in 1967 that it could seriously compete on the world stage. The T500 Cobra was a reliable machine that was well-priced. It out-performed comparable motorcycles, and it soon won a good market share. Suzuki increased its presence in the big bike area of the market in 1976 with the GS 750 , followed by the GS 1000 in 1978.

Kawasaki

The fourth of Japan's Big Four was the last to enter serious consideration. The Meguro company was the oldest motorcycle manufacturer in Japan and was taken over by Kawasaki, who in 1966 proceeded to manufacture and market a motorcycle of 650cc. It was not a marked success, and the company brought out two smaller models that had more appeal. The company made a decision to aim at the high-performance market and its Mach III model brought out in 1969 won a good following. Over the next decade, Kawasaki built on its reputation for high-performance machines by producing motorcycles across the range from big to small, as well as a series of off-road bikes.

By 1974, all the major Japanese motorcycle manufacturers were operating at full capacity, or close to it, at a time when manufacturers in the US and UK were faltering. The Japanese currency, the yen, was weak against the dollar, so this added to the advantages the Japanese enjoyed in the American market. Later in that decade, the Japanese set up subsidiary manufacturing operations in South-East Asia to expand their manufacturing capacity as well as to position themselves advantageously in important new markets. When the Chinese economy opened up, they were well situated to sell their product into China, as well as to invest in joint ventures.

Western Motorcycle Manufacturers Since 1960

Since 1960, the history of UK and American motorcycles has been one of decline and failure, with only a few sparks of success to ignite brief periods of optimism. When the markets for small to medium-sized bikes had been captured by the Japanese by the early 1970s, there was a brief respite when Triumph and Norton brought out large models that briefly held the line in the marketplace, but when the large Honda and Suzuki and Kawasaki bikes appeared, that respite proved to be short-lived.

In 1974, at a time when the Japanese were operating at the limits of their capacity, in Britain, BSA-owned Triumph was virtually finished as a viable and independent manufacturer. There were cost-cutting programs which led to strikes and redundancies, and then there were more strikes because of the redundancies. It was all a vicious circle which made economic decline more rapid. Triumph's flagship factory at Meriden was suddenly closed in February of that year and more than 3,000 workers were made jobless. Yet the market for motorcycles had not collapsed — at the same time Yamaha (not the largest of the Japanese manufacturers) was celebrating the completion of more than 20 million motorcycles.

In 1973, the Labour government which was in power in Britain at the time attempted to resuscitate the industry by supporting the formation of a new consortium, called the Norton Villiers Triumph group, and injected £10 million worth of capital. Even though this was an extreme measure, it was doomed to failure, because there were too many entrenched interests and the industry suffered badly from the 'us versus them' syndrome — or, in other words, the management-labour divide. In response to the closure of Triumph's Meriden plant the workers staged an occupation, a sit-in that went on for months but only postponed the inevitable demise.

The Norton Villiers Triumph consortium burned up the government cash and was on the point of sinking in 1975. Just to survive, the group required far more government capital than it was politically possible for the government to provide. NVT did not sink entirely for a period, but just managed to bounce along the bottom of the pond in the late 1970s, largely through increased sales in the US (sparked by an overall expansion of the market driven by the efforts of the Japanese exporters). There was also, ironically, a lucrative but short-lived contract making bikes with Yamaha engines. By 1983, it was clear that the efforts of the consortium were doomed, and the motorcycling operation at Meriden was closed for good. A property developer bought the site for housing, and had the name of 'Triumph' included as an adjunct to the purchase, as if the great motorcycle name was just a throwaway bonus.

The developer, John Bloor, licensed the name to a small manufacturer, and Triumph motorcycles had one more re-birth. This time, it was a very small-scale operation at first, but gradually built up to a more substantial production level in the 1990s. The new Triumph catered for a niche market — the aficionados of the marque, many of them baby-boomers with the money to spare to massage fond memories. In this guise, as a quasi-toy for the nostalgic retiree seeking some of the excitement of their youth, Triumph (and Harley-Davidson for that matter) have come up with an increasingly popular product.

The year 1973 also saw the demise of BSA, once the force to be reckoned with in the world's motorcycling industry. The company had made a number of disastrous decisions in the 1960s, misreading the marketplace when it produced a tricycle, and failing with its new small commuter bikes (where the Japanese succeeded). BSA, like the other British manufacturers, lost a true innovative edge and its designs were outmoded, and seen to be outmoded by most consumers. It incurred large financial losses and was taken over by Norton in 1971. Its subsidiary, Ariel, collapsed in 1967, after some ill-considered new models that were flops in the marketplace.

In the late 1960s, Norton had produced a large motorcycle that received a strong following — the 650cc Commando. In 1974, as part of Norton Villiers Triumph, it produced a larger 850cc engine for the Commando and the model continued for a few years more, but eventually it could no longer compete with large high-performance Japanese machines which continually proved their mettle on the racing track. The name of Norton disappeared from the mainstream marketplace in 1977. Ironically, the last model of motorcycle to bear the Norton name was an Italian-derived 50cc moped, so Norton went out not with a bang nor even with a whimper, but with a gentle putt-puttering.

Royal Enfield was another once well-known name in British motorcycles. It had grown, and had set up a well-regarded operation in India after World War II under the Enfield title. In 1970, however, the British business was closed, although the Indian manufacturer continued to operate profitably, providing a large number of machines to the Indian Army and police forces under supportive government contracts. They concentrated on a limited model range, mainly the Enfield Bullet, with a 350cc or 500cc engine. The Indian company prospered where British and American companies folded because they knew their market, did not overextend themselves and, crucially, had a high level of government support. In 1978 they even put in a bid to the liquidator of Triumph to buy the name, although the bid of just £55,000 was rejected. In 1997, the Indian company did have some success in winning a new name when it purchased the right to use 'Royal Enfield' on its machines, instead of just 'Enfield'. There is surely an irony in that an Indian manufacturer valued the appellation 'Royal' for its products at a time that the British sold that name so cheaply.

The firms founded to concentrate on racing motorcycles — Matchless and AJS — folded when Associated Motorcycles was taken over by Norton-Villiers in 1967, and the Matchless and AJS names were defunct by 1969. The once-popular motorcycle manufacturer, Indian, tried to remain in business on the strength of its well-known logo alone, licensing its Indian-head to badge Matchless and Enfield bikes, but the strategy was a failure and Indian was one more Western motorcycle manufacturer to disappear from the scene in the 1960s.

The iconic name in motorcycles, Harley-Davidson, felt the impact of the Japanese storm, and had a track record in the 1960s not much better than the UK firms. In 1965, it produced a big heavy bike called the Electra Glide which became popular among the aficionados, but it was a product that was at odds with the appeal of the smaller bikes Honda and Yamaha were importing for the young who needed basic transport. Under financial pressure, Harley-Davidson was taken over by American Machine and Foundry (AMF) in 1969, although it continued to produce Harleys. Twelve years later, Harley-Davidson was re-established as a stand-alone motorcycle manufacturer of top of the range machines that have a niche of their own, and prospered again in the new millennium.

Of the European manufacturers, Ducati's promising start in the United States just before the coming of the Japanese was snuffed out. It had been the second largest distributor of motorcycles in the United States, but could not match the rapid expansion of the Japanese dealer network, and just managed to survive at the bottom of the dealers' league table. In Italy, Ducati continued to operate as a government-owned company until it was privatized in 1985.

Moto Guzzi ran into financial problems at the end of the 1960s and tried to maintain its fortunes with the production of a range of big bikes, but it was sold to an Argentinean businessman in 1973.

BMW prospered from 1960 onwards because it had diversified into a wide range of industrial products, from cars to aeroplane engines. Its motorcycles had a loyal following in the United States and strong support in Europe, so production of new and innovative machines has continued. However, BMW was not a serious challenger to the Japanese dominance in America and the UK. The Swedish manufacturer Husqvarna is a diverse conglomerate that over its long history made a number of manufactured goods from sewing machines to chainsaws to motorbikes. Husqvarna, despite its reputation for making quality off-road machines, also hit financial problems and declined as a motorcycle manufacturer.

The list of failed motorcycle makers is a long one.

Reasons for the Collapse

Why did all these motorcycle manufacturers in Britain and the United States and elsewhere generally collapse so quickly, with so little effective resistance to the Japanese challenge?

Some popular theories held that Japanese motorcycles took hold of the market because they were cheap and low quality, but mass-produced in huge quantities. Such theories are badly wrong and totally misleading because they suggest conclusions that are at odds with the truth. Once Japanese motorcycle manufacturers resolved some teething problems associated with adjusting to American conditions, Japanese machines proved to be superior to Western products — as evidenced by their successes on racing tracks. Not only were the machines superior, but their management was superior. The companies behind the products were well-run and their executives focused on what they had to do and wanted to do.

Central to an understanding of why the Japanese assault decimated long-established Western companies is an appreciation of the quality of Japanese management. They planned their market strategies well, identified weaknesses, and provided an inspiring product. They were motivated by a hunger that was absent in their Western competitors who had grown complacent. This view is supported by informed commentators, who confirm that it was the 'work ethic and good management' of the Japanese that led to their success, not the price of their cycles.[52]

When the large motorcycle manufacturers, particularly in the United Kingdom, tried to meet the challenge of the Japanese, they cut costs and cut corners in production. The results were industrial unrest (that unrest increased costs and cut production — the exact opposite of what was needed) and a decline in production quality. At the time, some derided the Japanese products as 'cheap and plastic' as noted above, but in fact it was the Western products that suffered in terms of quality, and suffered from inefficient production practices. The British in particular were hampered by their nineteenth-century industrial practices, and the antagonism between management and labour. No large manufacturer in the West achieved the same working relationship and cooperation that prevailed on Japanese assembly lines. On the one hand, in the West there were workforces that were divided essentially into groups of individuals with fiercely opposed motivations, and on the other hand, in Japan there were workforces that cooperated as teams.

Management in most Western manufacturers also failed to rise to the strategic challenges. There were few executives who were as hungry as Takeo Fujisawa, and prepared to strike out with a totally new approach and distribution system, setting tough goals. Instead, British executives seemed to rely upon a succession of management and financial consultants, whose reports were swallowed up in committees and meetings.

One of the British responses to the Japanese motorcycle tsunami was a policy of mergers and acquisitions. Such a policy had been used by the market leaders in Europe in the 1920s, and had been successful then in building their businesses. However, if one amalgamates struggling manufacturers then the very weak can drain the strong, and that was what happened. Mergers result in a loss of company spirit and loyalty, as employees and professionals see themselves in a shrinking job market and react either by protecting their own position at the expense of someone else's, or by leaving the industry altogether for more promising fields of endeavour. Mergers also distract managers and drain their energies in resolving internecine disputes instead of devoting all their energy into engaging with the marketplace. Mergers also make political differences heat up, and political divisions, while they can be a source of creative tension in a dynamic environment, can also be the kiss of death to struggling organizations. It may have been better for the few manufacturers that retained some market share, like Triumph, to stand alone and take their chances rather than be merged into the Norton Villiers Triumph group with the result that all suffered. When Triumph was resurrected, it was an example of how a root and branch reorganization, and changes in industrial practices, could have made a difference 20 years earlier.

One other factor that contributed to the demise of British manufacturers was a small car that became a phenomenon. The Morris Mini was brought out in 1959, and was priced so cheaply that it no doubt took sales away from the motorcycle market, especially the market for larger bikes and motorcycle sidecars.

But if one central theme is needed to sum up all these factors that killed most Western motorcycle manufacturers, then it can be expressed in one word — vision (or rather, lack of it). Many Western motorcycle manufacturers looked backwards, not forwards. They wanted to bask in the successes of their glory days without accepting that times had changed and they had to move on. The industry had perhaps become introspective, with enthusiasts and experts and practitioners who saw themselves as part of a small and knowledgeable group of aficionados. Their inevitable downfall proved that there was no such thing as a privileged position for Western management.

The vision of the Japanese was that they were in an industry of mass transport, not one catering for the preferences of a biking elite. Also, their vision was aimed at the young and the newly emancipated generation of the 1960s and '70s, as epitomized by Honda's inspired and winning slogan.

The governments of the United States and the United Kingdom intervened to an extent, supporting the Norton Villiers Triumph consortium for instance, but they did not make the massive investment, or enact the protection measures that would have been required to stave off the Japanese. They did not take major measures in the 1970s because the motorcycle industry was relatively small, and the workforce not numerous, and indeed it would have required a major injection of capital to make the domestic manufacturers really competitive, as well as radical changes to work practices that were not possible in that political climate.

But, the question raised earlier can be repeated — could governments in the West stand by in the 2010s if their much larger car industries came under a more serious threat of collapse under pressure from Asian competition, and especially Chinese competition? There have already been major structural adjustments, and significant lay-offs in both the US and UK. What more could their corporation managements and governments do — or more to the point, what would they be allowed to do under WTO provisions? Some agricultural sectors in developing countries (e.g., the sugar industry in Cuba) have collapsed under the weight of global competition, with associated unemployment and hardship. What if the autoworkers of the United States and Britain faced a similar situation of collapse, to the point that the industry no longer existed?

Could a number of big Western car makers disappear entirely — or be merged out of existence? The questions hang in the air.

5 Car Manufacturing Outside China and Japan

The World Outlook

Before moving on to a comprehensive discussion of the automotive industry in China in Part Two, it is useful to include in this opening part a summary of the situation in world car manufacturing outside China. The situation of the Japanese car industry deserves, and receives, a separate chapter.

In terms of numbers, the US motor vehicle market is the largest in the world, with estimated sales of around 16.5 million cars and light trucks in 2006 — three-quarters being domestic production. The total European vehicle markets also account for around 15 million light passenger vehicles. In the estimate of the Scotiabank Group, about 49 million new cars and light trucks were sold around the world in 2006.

However, although these levels of sales seem to indicate a healthy industry, there is a major problem. The overall situation for the world auto manufacturing industry is in a critical condition in most countries due to over capacity, and current levels of production are unsustainable. In 2006, world production capacity was around 70 million vehicles (cars and light trucks), but actual sales represented just 70 per cent of production capacity, which means that considerable plant and potential are under-utilized — and China, and other developing countries, are ramping up their productive capacities despite the over-supply elsewhere.

The critical condition has come about because of a perfect storm of factors. These include the expansion of the industry into China, India and eastern Europe, and the increasing productivity in those countries at the same time as productive capacity in the US and Europe is aging, yet workers are still tied into relatively inflexible labour contracts, and consumer expectations are changing. The more efficient manufacturers — some of the Japanese firms (Toyota, Honda, etc.) and the German firm BMW — are weathering this storm better than some others, especially when they are a part of much larger and diversified conglomerates. Other world car manufacturers besides the Japanese are enduring worse problems of their own making because many are still tied to large models that may have a consumer following at the moment, but are not meeting changing mass preferences for smaller and more fuel-efficient cars.

Against this background, the Chinese industry is expanding rapidly and its cheap, quality components are already having an impact. That impact is not immediately obvious to most consumers because component parts are largely hidden, and anyway consumers — the end-users — do not go into the back rooms of their car servicing agent and therefore seldom get any chance to read the labelling on the box that names country of origin of car parts. The impact of Chinese cars will be more obvious to the population at large when wholly Chinese-made cars appear lined up for sale in main street car yards. And that day may not be far distant. The recent development of the Chinese auto industry has been so rapid that it must soon shoulder its way into a place in those main street car yards.

World Motor Vehicle Manufacturing Outside China — a Snapshot in 2007

The situation of the world motorcycle manufacturers in 1960 can be compared with that of the world motor vehicle manufacturers in 2007. Immediately, one crucial difference becomes obvious. In 1960, the motorcycle manufacturers were generally solvent and trading as they had done for years, even if they had become complacent and took their market for granted. In 2007, many of the major world motor vehicle manufacturers are in financial difficulties and grappling with problems, due mainly to the overcapacity issue noted in the beginning of this chapter. In the United States, considering the situation of the Big Three, it is no exaggeration to say that the largest (GM) is in crisis and Ford is not much better off. Chrysler (which of course has for eight years been part of the German group headed by Daimler) is also under immediate threat, and has had to make painful cutbacks and plan for more.

Currently, car makers, especially in the United States and western Europe, face not only financial pressure but also challenges from such factors as higher oil costs, and issues related to global economic competition. A growing emphasis on protecting the environment also provides a challenge. Many countries are determining new emission standards and encouraging manufacturers to develop alternative fuels. For example, there are new emission controls in the European Union, and after a staged introductory period, from 1 January 2006 newly manufactured cars must meet tough standards that determine maximum allowable emissions of the four main vehicle pollutants — carbon monoxide, nitrogen oxides from diesels, hydrocarbons and exhaust particles. These standards will of course hit all car makers — domestic and foreign — that want to sell their products in the EU countries.

The four largest car makers in the world in 2007, in terms of global unit sales of cars and light trucks, are General Motors (all the corporations that are part of the GM group, including Daewoo, sold over 14 million cars and light trucks in 2006), Toyota (sold 8.2 million cars and light trucks in 2006), Ford Motor Corp. (sold 6.1 million cars and light trucks in 2006) and DaimlerChrysler (sold 4.2 million cars and light trucks in 2006).[53]

Table 5.1 overleaf provides a snapshot of the comparative listing of the major world car makers in 2005, with revenue figures and ranking according to *Fortune 500*. Because the ranking is by revenue of the groups as a whole, the ranking does not correspond with the volume of vehicles each corporate group produces. Neither does the ranking mirror profitability of operations. If profitability was somehow factored into the ranking, then Fiat would suffer, for one.

The rankings are likely to change quite quickly as Toyota increases revenues and GM and Ford cut back production and regroup into 2007 and beyond. On GM's web site is the proud statement that the company has been 'the global industry sales leader for 75 years' but this statement no longer stands true. In the first quarter of 2007, Toyota passed GM in terms of worldwide sales, selling 2.35 million cars and trucks in these three months, compared to GM's sales of 2.26 million cars and trucks.[54] However, if GM chooses to include all the vehicles manufactured by associated entities within its group, it could still make a fair claim to be the world's largest vehicle manufacturing group.

The margins at the top of the world ranking list are all relatively narrow. Also note that the two largest Chinese car makers, FAW and Shanghai Auto, are understated in this ranking because total revenues are converted to US dollars, and the yuan is undervalued. If the ranking was in terms of units produced, then they would be higher on the list. As an additional point about comparative rankings, in the course of 2006, Shanghai Auto nudged aside FAW for the title of largest car maker in China.

Table 5.1: The World's Largest Auto Manufacturers in 2005 (by Revenue)

Corporation	Total annual revenues (in 2005 in US$ billions)	listing	Fortune 500
Top twelve			
GM	192		5
DaimlerChrysler	186		7
Toyota	186		8
Ford	177		9
Volkswagen	118		17
Honda	88		31
Nissan	83		41
Peugeot	70		60
BMW	58		78
Fiat	58		79
Hyundai	57		80
Renault	51		100
Others			
Mitsubishi (25th largest)	19		345
FAW (31st largest)	15		470
Shanghai Auto (32nd)	14		475

Source: *Fortune 500*, July 2006.

Car manufacturing in the United States and western Europe to the 1970s were the results of different paths of development. In the United States, the car market was intensely competitive and US consumers were very discerning, even fickle at times. The result over a hundred years or so was the development of three large privately owned car manufacturers that prospered in a wealthy and an open market and generally conducted their operations in an efficient manner, but with a clear understanding that their industry was an engine room of the world's largest economy (representing 5 per cent of the country's GDP and employing nearly 15 per cent of its workforce). Their work practices were among the world's best in the industry over the long term. In Europe, the car market in each of the major European nations was generally more protected, with strong government investment and involvement in the business strategies of national flagship car makers. Despite their different origins and patterns of growth, the situation from the late 1970s was that the automobile industries in both regions were under pressure from global competition, and the reactions of the car makers reflected their historical perspectives.

In the early 21st century, the situation was less clear-cut, due partly to the fact that there had been numerous mergers between the big manufacturers and their operations had largely become transnational in nature, although some of flagship firms remained strong in their national consciousness. For example, Renault remained quintessentially French in the eyes of the French, even though it was in alliance with Nissan, and depended in large measure upon its Japanese partner for its ongoing strength. Mercedes-Benz cars are notable for 'sound German engineering', even though they are a part of the transnational DaimlerChrysler group. Public perceptions are always very slow to follow corporate restructuring, and whereas the brands remain strong in national consciousness, global corporate ownership and partnerships associated with those brands are not so well known. The situation has been complicated by the rounds of mergers alluded to.

The mergers between car makers in the latter part of the 20th century were intended to strengthen the bigger players in the global industry, but not all the mergers were successful. Some, such as one of the first mergers of the 1970s — that of UK auto makers combining with British Leyland to form what was then the third largest car maker in the world — worked to the disadvantage of the strong players because their lifeblood was drained trying to maintain critically weak operations. Ford's mergers/takeovers of Jaguar and Volvo did not provide immediate benefits in cash flow or profit. GM's swallowing of brands such as Daewoo, Subaru, Suzuki and Saab did not deliver all the benefits or produce all the market advantages hoped for. It may be that Daimler-Benz's giant merger with Chrysler diverted management expertise and resources to try to make the new project work, at the cost of 'taking their eyes off the ball' and risking a beaning. In terms of stock market value, they have been beaned already, because the merged group has a market capitalization even less than that of Daimler-Benz before the merger.

Volkswagen has taken over a range of brands, from Bentley to Skoda, and SEAT to Lamborghini, and has generally maintained the whole lot on an even keel, but it faces the challenge of making the group sail faster in rising seas. Fiat — Italian to its very hubcaps — has accumulated other Italian brands such as Ferrari and Alfa-Romeo, but the merged group has not excited foreign suitors, largely because its legacy costs are as high and as threatening as those of GM and Ford.

One of the largest of the world's car makers — Toyota — generally spurned mergers (apart from the much smaller and compatible Daihatsu) and it became stronger, not weaker, in the marketplace.[55] Toyota chose a strategy of building upon the strength of its core brand to create new brands, such as the Lexus in the prestige car sector, and that strategy has been very successful. It is said that 'a cobbler should stick to his last', which means if you make shoes, you will be most successful carrying on making shoes and not being tempted to make other things. Many of the world's car makers were tempted to diversify into new brands and ranges that did not sit well with their core expertise and they paid the price for their failed strategies.

All these mergers and the takeover of numerous national brands by global conglomerates makes it difficult to summarize world car making, because the brew of brands and national industries gets stirred together in the global pot until it is difficult to identify a specific taste. However, the following discussion, at the risk of over-generalizing, makes an effort to present a snapshot of world car making in various countries and regions. It is an essential part of understanding the background to the growth of the Chinese car industry, and how that industry is likely to flood world markets at a time when those markets are weak and subject to a host of storms and squalls.

Car Making in the United States in 2007

In the United States, all the Big Three of the car industry — General Motors, Ford and DaimlerChrysler (US operations) — are based in Detroit. They face a strong challenge in matching the productivity of Japanese car manufacturers which are making inroads into the Big Three's traditional market shares.[56] In 2004, Toyota surpassed Ford as the second-largest car maker in the world and is increasing its production even as the largest manufacturer in the US — General Motors — is struggling to retain its market share and, as mentioned, in 2007 has ceded world leadership to Toyota. For the year ending March 2006, Toyota reported a profit of more than US$12 billion, making it the world's most profitable manufacturer. GM, on the other hand, lost US$10.6 billion in 2005. Consequently, GM and Ford are planning changes to restore their levels of profitability, but such plans include closing plants and cutting back jobs before 2010.

There are a number of excellent and up-to-date sources for analysis and current statistics on the US car market. Such sources include the US Bureau of Economic Analysis, Plunkett Research organization and the National Automobile Dealers Association. They can provide further reading for those who seek more detailed statistics relating to the following section, which is intended only as an outline snapshot to set the context for the later material on the car industry in China.

General Motors (GM)

GM, which once sold half the new cars manufactured in the world, still sells close to one-quarter of the new cars and passenger vehicles marketed in the United States, but its US market share of 25 per cent in 2005 fell to 24 per cent in 2006. It made almost US$200 billion in sales in 2005 and that represented sales of more than 9 million vehicles, but its losses amounted to around 5 per cent of its total revenue and its world market share declined from 14.4 per cent to 14.2 per cent. When the company announced annual losses, it said that the year 2005 had been 'one of the most difficult years' in its history.[57] The loss was, in the company's words, explained by 'fierce pressure from Asian car makers and soaring pension and healthcare liabilities'.[58] The company also bore the brunt of an increasing price of fuel, which has increased around 10 per cent a year and hit a psychological benchmark of US$3 per gallon in the United States in 2006.

It is not as if the workers in the auto plants in the United States do not put in the hours to remain competitive. At an average of 1,822 hours per year in 2003, they work longer hours then the French (who work the fewest hours of the industrialized countries at 1,431 hours per year) or the Italians (1,591 hours per year). However, these hours at work are eclipsed by Asian workers. For example, South Korean auto workers have the highest annual rate of all the industrialized countries, putting in an average working year of 2,390 hours. This means that if the Koreans have the common average working year that includes absences of around ten days for public holidays and ten days for annual holidays, also two days off on weekends, then they work a total of 238 days a year, and must work ten hours a day to accumulate these working hours. (If they have only one day off a week, then they must work on average of 8.2 hours a day each day for their six-day work week.) Add to this calculation a lower wage, fewer benefits and also comparable productivity through the same or even superior technology, and it is clear why Western car manufacturers cannot survive — all other things being equal.

GM's management has been taking evasive action as its Asian competitors close in on it, almost like smaller predators on a wounded giant. Like the moves of a wounded giant, however, they have been painful ones. The company remained reliant on vehicles that were proven sales performers in the extravagant years of the 1990s — large sports utility vehicles — but found that consumers were turning away from so-called gas-guzzlers. Its Lincoln model, launched and hyped as recently as 1999, has been discontinued. GM has had to close a number of plants to meet a twofold challenge — high ongoing wages costs and the overhang of retirees on generous pensions negotiated in the 1960s and 1970s when the company was a colossus on the world economic stage and at that stage well able to afford the imposts.

Since 2005, GM has been offering redundancy packages — planning to lay off 34,000 workers in the United States and 12,000 in its European operations by 2008 — and trying to negotiate reductions in additional benefits such as healthcare costs in order to meet a target of US$5 billion in cost cuts. GM's unfunded pension liability has been calculated as being US$85 billion in current terms, and this enormous figure far exceeds the market value of the entire company (which has anyway been devalued by the liability). GM management estimated that health care costs added around US$1,500 to the cost of each vehicle it makes in the United States (Chrysler says US$1,400 per vehicle and Ford estimates US$1,100). These figures represent a penalty that the companies have to carry while running around the market racing track against less burdened rivals.

However, just as a giant has difficulty moving fast enough when confronted with nimble attackers, and bleeds from numerous small wounds, so GM is having problems recovering its health and vitality. The costs of meeting the pension and healthcare liabilities mean that fewer funds are available for retooling and installing advanced technology. Some analysts predict that, despite its cost-cutting plans, it may go bankrupt, or at least seek protection by filing for bankruptcy,[59] as early as 2008. Bank of America, for one, assessed the odds on GM filing for bankruptcy in the next two years at 40 per cent.[60]

Ford

In 2007, the Ford Motor Company, the second icon of the American history pageant, with over 300,000 employees, was also under pressure. Ford and its associated brands (Aston Martin, Jaguar, Land-Rover, Lincoln, Mazda, Mercury and Volvo) have been losing market share in the United States since 2000 and sales figures continue to fall in the first quarter of 2007. Since the mid-1990s, Ford's share of the US market had declined by a quarter.

In 2005, Ford had 18 per cent of the US market, but like GM, this share fell by one per cent in 2006. In 2000, Ford had had enjoyed a 25 per cent share of the US market. In that market, the company has been overtaken by Toyota and in 2006 had slipped to be the third largest car maker in the world's largest market. Some of its associated brands were either up for sale (Aston Martin) or mooted to be for sale in the short term (Jaguar).

These falls in market share were matched by declining profitability. Ford lost US$1.6 billion in the US and Canada in 2005 and another US$797 million in the second quarter of 2006, largely due to falling sales of larger cars, trucks and SUVs. One of Ford's SUVs, the Explorer, came out in a new version just as petrol prices increased and its sales nose-dived. Losses worldwide in the first quarter of 2006 were US$1.2 billion. Its losses worldwide for the full year 2006, including restructuring costs of 9.9 billion, were US$12.7 billion — the highest loss in the history of the company.

As a result, Ford shares fell to US$7.88 as at 18 August 2006, compared with US$9.50 in August 2005. Early in the year, it announced that it was forced to lay-off around one-third of its labourforce — no less than 38,000 assembly-line workers agreed to voluntary retirement packages. It would also be closing at least fourteen factories by 2012. Later, the company announced that, in addition, 14,000 white-collar jobs would go, and another two factories. The last time Ford had had to undergo enforced layoffs was in the 1980s, after the impact of the Oil Shock of 1973 had eventually worked its way through American markets and car inventories and model design and forced painful changes. In western Europe, Ford has been forced to close five out of eleven plants and lay-off 20 per cent of its employees, and will consider further cut-backs. Ford's investments in luxury European marques, which included names such as Jaguar, Volvo and Aston Martin, had poor returns, and these added to the low profits in Ford's European operations — down to just US$36 million in 2005.

A leading credit agency, Fitch, cut its 2006 ratings of Ford investments to the level of 'junk' territory, with a negative outlook, indicating that further cuts are likely. Fitch's report said: 'Volume declines in Ford's pick-up segment, along with continued declines in mid-sized and large S.U.V.s, are likely to accelerate revenue declines and negative cash flows in 2006'.[61] William Clayton (Bill) Ford Jr, the great-grandson of founder Henry Ford, resigned as chief executive and left the company that bore his family name.

At the same time, however, Ford has been expanding in some areas of growth. Its facilities in St Petersburg, Russia, had a target of 100,000 new cars a year, and its Turkish operation was also expanding, but overall it appeared that the company was at risk of further decline. Its management admitted at much when they stated that Ford anticipated holding only 15 per cent of the US car market in 2009, effectively a 40 per cent fall in market share since 2000.[62]

In early 2007, Ford's future was put under a further cloud when a leaked memo from management indicated that a plan developed in December 2005 to restore the company to profitability to 2009, called 'The Way Forward', was not achieving its targets. Sales were down on projections and 55 per cent of employees believed that the plan was not working.[63] It seemed that instead of finding a way forward, the company was at best treading water.

DaimlerChrysler

Chrysler went through a painful period of cost-cutting in the 1980s under the charismatic Lee Iacocca, but it never recovered its former glories. Chrysler's former operations in the United States now constitute the US division of DaimlerChrysler AG. In 2007, it looks as if the eight-year-old merger of Daimler and Chrysler is about to come to an end. Since the 'merger of equals' that made the group the fifth-largest car maker in the world, there have been more than 40,000 jobs lost and sixteen plants closed as a result of cost-cutting strategies. All those measures may not have been enough. In 2005, Chrysler made a profit but lurched back into loss in 2006 after a 5 per cent fall in sales and cuts in production. As was the case for Ford, the production cuts were of vehicles that were once big sellers but faced falling consumer demand and increasing inventories — SUVs and light trucks. As 90 per cent of Chrysler's sales were in America, and those American markets were hit hardest by the dramatic fall in sales of SUVs and big passenger vehicles, Chrysler was especially vulnerable to the change in market demand.

Chrysler was still big, with 85,000 employees and selling 2.7 million vehicles, but it lost US$1.47 billion during 2006. In the third quarter alone, the American division lost more than US$1.5 billion, which was more than twice the amount forecast. The company's US market share in 2005 was 14 per cent, but in 2006, this fell to 12 per cent.

Overall, DaimlerChrysler made a profit in 2006, but only because of the profitability of Mercedes-Benz. In February 2007, DaimlerChrysler management announced a new plan to achieve profitability for Chrysler operations some time in 2008. This new plan, one more in a series of strategies aimed at staunching the company's bleeding wounds, involved a further 13,000 job cuts. At the same time, the company recognised that a de-merger was on the table and put out feelers for the sale of the Chrysler operations. In May 2007, management announced that DaimlerChrysler would sell 80% of its stakeholding in the Chrysler Group to private euity group Cerberus Capital Management of New York for US$7.4 billion. Cerberus Capital Management is a specialist in restructuring companies sailing troubled waters. Ironically, one of the lifelines held out for Chrysler's survival was an alliance with the Chinese car maker Chery, and the development of Chery's small car lines to take market share in the United States and Europe.

The Dodge Caliber, whose size met contemporary demands in the marketplace, was selling well in Asia and Europe. But the Caliber was the only new small car presented by the Big Three American firms at the Detroit Motor Show of January 2006.

Back in May 1998, the merger of Daimler and Chrysler was heralded as a strategic masterstroke which had as its aim becoming the world's number one car maker. Barely eight years later, the group's management looked to the Chinese for help in recovering their place in the global car market.

US Car Parts Suppliers

For US car-parts manufacturers, their situation in 2007 was also one of being under siege from lower-cost competitors, for example the car industries of Brazil and India. The prime example of a US car-parts manufacturer that was struggling was Delphi, one of the world's largest manufacturers of car components. In October 2005, it was forced to lodge a legal application to seek protection through filing under Chapter 11. This move was a controversial one, because some in the US auto union movement (the United Auto Workers) saw it as a means to forcibly reduce workers' entitlements, even employ labour on a much cheaper hourly basis under threat of complete dissolution of the company, at the same time as top executive salary packages remained lucrative.

Delphi's plans to return the company to profitable operation not only involved revising the benefits and wages of its workforce, but also putting off around 20,000 workers, 60 per cent of its total workforce of 34,000 who were on hourly rates. Some 14,000 of the company's 24,000 employees who were members of the UAW agreed to voluntary redundancy offers. In addition, Delphi planned to reduce its global executive workforce, that is, salaried employees, by another 8,500 positions.

The pressure on Delphi had come from overseas suppliers who produce similar products with labour that was paid a fraction of the wages and benefits American auto workers receive. Once again, it was a case of the playing field not being a level one, although some would say it was the natural operation of globalization. The pressure from foreign competition was also being felt by the companies supplying components to Ford and to Chrysler. The discrepancy between wage rates — not to mention the ongoing costs of benefits — between US workers and foreign workers was huge. The workers at Delphi were paid the same rates as assembly line workers at GM, namely US$27 an hour, with attached benefits such as health and pension benefits, adding up to an additional US$50 an hour cost to the employer. As part of its plan to revise operations and costs, Delphi sought to renegotiate wage rates. The lowest rate they offered was US$9.50 an hour, just about one third of the pre-bankruptcy wage level, but the union negotiated a minimum hourly wage rate of US$14. These rates stand in comparison with Chinese auto workers' wages of the equivalent of around US$2 to US$2.50 per hour.

Manufacturers in the United States, as in other countries in the

West, suffer a disadvantage when, over time, unions have negotiated common wage rates and benefits across an industry. Such a strategy may have been useful in the past, when companies within national boundaries faced their main competition from other enterprises inside the country. However, as global trade has opened up, the situation of different companies within one country operating in a 'one size fits all' milieu makes it difficult to respond to international competition such as that threatened by China.

The woes of Delphi have particular resonance, for it was once a fully fledged part of GM, but GM set it up as a separate business in 1999. It may be that GM saw this move as a strategic means of establishing a firewall between the main company and the components manufacturer. The firewall was needed because it seemed that there was a looming conflict with the United Auto Workers over pay and conditions throughout the GM empire. The firewall may not be an effective one, for GM remained exposed to the woes at Delphi, because Delphi was its main components supplier. Therefore, the risk of bankruptcy of Delphi carried with it a strong possibility that the move could bring down GM as well, despite its being one of the largest corporations in the world (and despite the fact that such a bankruptcy would be by far the largest in history, threatening the livelihoods of nearly 150,000 employees and hundreds of thousands of retirees who drew a GM-funded pension). The knock-on effects would be felt by all the workers of the US car makers — up to one million employees. The stigma of bankruptcy would tarnish the image of GM for years, and certainly put its sales into a downward spiral, for consumers would naturally be reluctant to make a major purchase from a company that may not be around to service the product, let alone provide a series of updated products when trade-in time comes around.

The spiral of bankruptcy can be compared to some of the early aircraft, and their performance. When those early planes went into a spin, through the efforts of a ham-fisted or a distracted pilot, it was very difficult to pull the plane out of the spin. The only way to do so was to haul the stick over and turn the plane into the spin, the opposite course of action to what a pilot naturally believed was right. By such a manoeuvre, the plane's flying surfaces could once again effectively bite the air and control could be recovered. The alternative was continuing downward progress and a messy impact with the unyielding surface of planet earth.

Car Making in the United Kingdom in 2007

The British manufacturing sector was under pressure generally by 2007. During August 2006, a total of just 72,959 cars were made in the UK, a respectable figure in world terms but this was a decline of 19.5 per cent on the total for August 2005.[64] It is still a large segment of the UK manufacturing industry, but it is small compared to what was once the powerhouse of the worlds' manufacturing industry. Around one million manufacturing jobs in the United Kingdom disappeared between 1996 and 2005, and it appeared likely that the services sector would replace the manufacturing sector to become the mainstay of the economy, which is an ironic situation in the country that brought about the Industrial Revolution in the late 1700s.

The United Kingdom has had a long-established motor vehicle manufacturing industry and it was one of the pioneers of the transport revolution. It saw the development of a number of car manufacturers from the early 20th century, peaking in the 1930s. After the Second World War, many of those manufacturers merged (while retaining their distinctive marques) and survived with government support. In the 1970s and '80s, most passed into the hands of global car manufacturers. At that time, under the reforms brought in by the government of Margaret Thatcher, the country's markets were generally liberalized and labour laws wound back more than on the European continent, so that British car makers came under more pressure than those of, say, France.

The situation of the British car industry in 2007 was as perilous as in some other Western countries. The phenomenon of moving manufacturing to regions with lower wages and taxes and less rigorous regulatory regimes is likely to prove fatal to the chances of the United Kingdom remaining a major player in the world car making industry. This phenomenon has been called 'footprint migration', and will have an effect on much of western Europe's auto industry.[65] One journalist quoted Bob Lutz, the vice-chairman of GM, as saying, 'Everybody's talking footprint migration from high-cost countries in western Europe and North America ... Everybody is talking to the unions and trying to shift at least part of the production to Eastern countries. You don't have a prayer of breaking even on a new car unless it's built in the East. ... We're also talking about Korea, Thailand, Mexico and, in five years ... China.'[66]

The fact that the old British car makers were taken over by larger, global car makers largely resulted in interconnected manufacturing between a number of plants, which in time incurred new problems. By 2000, there were new pressures, although some of those pressures were not entirely external ones. Some of them are part and parcel of global competition and can come about as productivity at one branch plant is compared with another. For example, one company, Vauxhall, was taken over by General Motors and by 2006 was one of a number of UK plants being downgraded as it could not maintain competitiveness with other GM manufacturing plants in Europe. For many years, Ford had built a number of icons of the car industry of the UK — such as the Ford Escort and Ford Capri — but it ended its UK production of Ford-badged cars in 2001 (although it continued to make vans and components). Tony Woodley, general secretary of the Transport and General Workers' Union, claimed that 100,000 manufacturing jobs were being lost each year due to the British government's failure, 'to support manufacturing "champions" as happened in other European countries, including France and Germany.'[67]

Peugeot's plant in the heart of British manufacturing, Coventry (once the UK's Detroit) was closed in 2006. It had operated for 60 years and was the fifth major car plant closed in what one commentator dubbed a 'market driven massacre'.[68] The probable reason for the closure was that the operation could be transferred to a country in eastern Europe where wages were lower. The same commentator pointed out that most of those made redundant were unlikely to work again, for few laid-off workers from the Rover plant closure more than a year earlier had been re-employed.

It certainly appeared that market-driven policies had left the United Kingdom in a vulnerable position compared to other jurisdictions, for it was easier to lay off redundant workers in the UK than in, for example, France or Germany. This had the inevitable result that in a situation where there were two plants in a marginal situation, in the UK and another country with strict laws and provisions that made it costly to have forced redundancies, the tendency would be for management to lay off their British workers, because it was easier and cheaper, and close the UK plant. This equation might apply even if the UK plant was slightly more efficient and profitable, but not so much as to offset the higher costs of laying off employees elsewhere.

One of the few bright spots in gloom surrounding UK car making belonged to the German car maker, BMW, which operates a large and up-to-date facility at Oxford to build Minis, and updated the plant with the latest technology in 2005. However, a number of other plants were under threat of closure, including some of the biggest names that have graced the history of British car manufacturing, for example, Vauxhall's Ellesmere Port plant in Cheshire. Those plants, which were once pacesetters, can no longer match the productivity of plants in Europe. For example, a GM factory in Eisenach, eastern Germany, takes 15 hours to assemble a small car — the Astra. Vauxhall has been put under notice to match such productivity or face closure, with closure the more likely outcome.

The luxury car maker, Jaguar, suffered a big fall in sales to less than 90,000 in 2005, a 25 per cent decline over 2004. Jaguar, in 2007 part of the Ford group, faced annual losses of more than £300 million.

In Birmingham the collapse of MG Rover at Longbridge meant financial hardship for thousands of long-term employees of the motor industry, as well as an uncertain future. In the 1960s, MG Rover and its associated production facilities accounted for around half of Britain's domestically produced cars. The company had grown out of a business manufacturing the Rover Safety bicycle in 1885. During the Second World War, the revolutionary jet engine was developed in workshops associated with Rover. The Land Rover and Range Rover symbolized British outdoor life. Rover was one of the UK's oldest car makers, and its logo — a Viking longship — was a symbol of boldness, wealth and success. All deserted the company at the end of the 20th century.

In a management buy-out, Rover was purchased for just £10 from its previous owner — BMW — which had operated the business for six years but could not turn it around. The group of managers gave their venture the singularly inappropriate name of Phoenix Group, implying they could rescue the company from the ashes. However, the Phoenix Group, who won control of the venerable name of Rover MG for just the price of a round of beers, were accused of milking what was left of the company for whatever they could get out of it. MG Rover was Britain's last independent volume car maker but after the buy-out, sales continued to fall, by as much as 23 per cent in 2003, when the company posted its third loss in three years. What was needed was investment in new plant, and the most advanced technology that was available, but funds flowed out of MG Rover instead of into it, and in the end 6,000 auto workers paid for poor management with their jobs.

The Longbridge facility was sold by its administrators to a Chinese car maker. Nanjing Automobile Corporation bought what remained of the company for just £50 million. The other main contender was Shanghai Automotive. Nanjing pushed through the sale, not least so that they could benefit from the technology of Rover engines which, although no longer at the cutting edge, they planned to transfer to their plants in China. The Chinese company intended to maintain a much-reduced manufacturing line in Birmingham, mainly assembling vehicles using components manufactured in China. There was a certain irony in that the demise of Rover came about because of its uncompetitive situation, but also because the British government stated that it would not intervene to rescue the company as it no longer held to the principles of state intervention in industry and 'trying to pick winners'.

The entity that took over the plant is a State-Owned Enterprise in all but name, and its investment is underpinned by government bodies in China which are well-prepared to put public money into developing such facilities. Although the provincial government in Nanjing (in Jiangsu Province) may not fully fund the car manufacturer, the fact that it had a stakeholding and had contributed public funds acted as an incentive for private investment. Where government has contributed funds, private investors may assume, with some validity, that the fact that a public entity is involved means that there is some guarantee of support in case the enterprise comes under risk of insolvency. Of course, with this assumption, there is also the assumption that the government will support efficient management and will not stand by if inefficient management puts its stake at risk.

Another part of the UK icon since the early 1900s, Land Rover, had been acquired by BMW in 2000, but the Germans agreed in August 2006 to sell the Rover trademark to the Chinese company Shanghai Automotive Industry Corporation. The Chinese company had already bought the rights to Rover models from the MG Rover group in 2005 (and was outbid for the husk of the company, its equipment and plant, by Nanjing Automobile as noted above). In February 2007, Shanghai Automotive launched a re-born Rover which carried the traditional Rover radiator grille — and the new car was named the Rongwei 750 (which can be translated as 'Glorious VIP'). The advertisements emphasized its British heritage — 'British classic car' with 'leisurely gentility' and 'eager chivalrous spirit'.[69] It was priced from £15,000 (A$37,500) — much less than what the last of the Rovers sold for in Western markets. It was worthy of note that this reborn Rover aiming at the luxury (but competitively priced) market was not produced by a joint venture but was the product of an indigenous Chinese auto maker.

As one stakeholder of the UK motor vehicle manufacturing industry commented about the environment of the industry in 2006, 'Certainly we must move away from the idea of the state as a passive spectator of a series of industrial disasters. That is not, incidentally, the policy which is propelling China's spectacular industrial and economic growth.'[70] What he says is correct. The Chinese governments, at various levels, are very actively involved in funding and encouraging the development of Chinese industry, even as Western governments are hectored that they must stand back.

Car Making in Europe in 2007
In other European countries, there were pressures similar to those experienced in the United States and United Kingdom. The governments were in some cases more likely to intervene to maintain the national car

maker's level of employment. On Continental Europe, the sales of new cars in more developed countries such as France and Italy were relatively stable, but the markets were expanding further east, in the Czech Republic, Russia, Poland and the Ukraine.

The French manufacturers, Renault and Peugeot-Citroen, were not under quite the same threat as UK car makers like Rover MG, but they did face considerable financial pressure.

Renault in particular experienced a fall of nearly 40 per cent in its group operating profit in 2005, and its plants were operating at well under full capacity. In response, Renault was developing a strategy of aiming for 'green' customers, in part responding to calls from President Chirac to limit France's dependence upon oil in favour of bio-fuels and hybrid cars.

Renault received a new CEO in 2005, Carlos Ghosn, who had made his name controlling costs at Nissan, part-owned by Renault. Ghosn unveiled the new strategy of aiming for more environmentally friendly cars and affirmed that Renault would also seek to increase its sales in markets outside France from 27 per cent of its total sales to 37 per cent by 2009, when total unit sales were targeted at 3.33 million vehicles. Part of the sales growth was intended to come from the upper end of the market and from a range of SUVs, which strategy seemed to cut across consumer trends becoming evident in the US.

Peugeot-Citroen was also striving to keep its head above the surface of deep financial water. Their profit margins in the second half of 2005 and the first half of 2006 were under the 3 per cent mark. Their total earnings had fallen as well, by 20 per cent between 2004 and 2005.

Fiat in Italy was under financial pressure too, but had assistance from Italian banks and other business sectors who saw themselves as acting out of patriotic interests to keep the company afloat.

In 2007 Germany had the largest car industry in Europe, employing nearly 2 million people directly and many more indirectly. In Germany, BMW continued to be competitive in the global marketplace, selling 1.4 million cars worldwide in 2006 after achieving sales of 1.33 million in 2005. One of its most successful models was, ironically, a resurrected British icon of years past— the Mini. Germany was the only country in western Europe to see the opening of a new car manufacturing plant, that of BMW in Leipzig, in eastern Germany.

Aside from BMW, the other large companies in Germany were feeling the weight of global trends of falling sales in old markets and new manufacturers in new markets. Volkswagen — which included Audi and the British icon Bentley, and was one of the big investors in China (where it was losing money)[71] — was reducing its workforce by 20,000 workers and possibly as many as 30,000. It was also closing a number of plants where management admitted that some processes were no longer of world standard and the overall productivity of workers was comparatively low.

The admission on productivity was especially telling, because on average German auto workers were paid some 50 times more than their Chinese counterparts, and Volkswagen was the highest paying car maker in Germany, with wages around 20 per cent above the average for German manufacturing workers. Volkswagen's options were limited because it was constrained by an agreement with unions in 2004 that there would be no compulsory lay-offs, only voluntary redundancies — which meant in effect that Volkswagen would have to buy out its workers to reduce numbers. The company management had cut costs by nearly €4 billion in 2005, but had plans for a further extensive program of cost-cuts totalling no less than €2 billion to meet the financial challenges. In 2005, its profit margin of 2.6 per cent was worse than that of Peugeot-Citroen.

The other big German name, Mercedes-Benz, also had to undertake cost-cutting measures and planned to reduce its workforce by 16,000. Some in Germany predicted that European car making would have to gravitate eastwards and that eastern European plants would eventually account for 60 per cent of European production. The Chinese and the Indians would also bring more competition to the European marketplace in the short to medium term.[72]

Besides the cost pressures on European producers, there was also market pressure. Asian car manufacturers were active in Europe and Toyota, for one, had plans to pass a benchmark sales target of one million units sold on the continent in 2006. Toyota also planned to open new facilities in Russia and Slovakia, and expand facilities in countries like Turkey, to manufacture mainly small (and fuel-sipping) cars. Hyundai was developing a Czech plant to make 300,000 cars a year. Another Korean company, Kia, was the fastest growing brand in Europe in 2005. These companies were positioning themselves in the countries of eastern Europe where demand continued to expand.

Car Making in Other Nations
South Korea
South Korea presents a different pattern of development of its car industry for a number of reasons. First, the country was under Japanese control until 1945, and then suffered further conflict until 1953. There was no initial phase of developing an industry from small-scale home-grown innovators. Second, the domestic auto market in Korea was relatively small, so to survive the industry had to be export-oriented from the start. There was a strong similarity with the Japanese business structures called *zaibatsu* (later *keiretsu*) in that Korean businesses were organized into a number of industrial conglomerates called *chaebol*.

The South Korean car making industry began in the 1960s with plants assembling Japanese and American imported components, but developed quickly and built up export markets behind high protective walls. In 1962, the Korean government completely banned the import of finished cars. As the expertise of its car makers was built up, there were further laws reducing the amount of imported components allowed in domestically produced cars. In 1972, the government passed further protective legislation to control the auto market by decreeing that, for a period, there would be just two auto makers in Korea — Hyundai (which was associated with Mitsubishi) and Daewoo (which was linked with GM). There had originally been seven auto makers, but in the view of the government (under pressure from elements within the *chaebol*), the market was too small to accommodate them all.

Hyundai, now the flagship of Korean auto making, entered the industry as late as 1967, and the first vehicle it turned out was the Ford Cortina (with assistance from Ford of the UK). In 1972, Hyundai turned to another European vehicle manufacturer and entered into an agreement with Mercedes-Benz to manufacture buses. Hyundai was a true child of the global industry, because not only did it benefit from British and then German vehicle design and manufacturing technology, but it had strong links with the Japanese industry through a 15 per cent shareholding owned by Mitsubishi. In 1976, within ten years of its entry into the industry, Hyundai produced a design of its own — a cheap and basic car called the Pony, which over time became the Excel. Excels were exported in quantity from 1982. Daewoo was set up by GM, and utilized Nissan's small car manufacturing expertise and technology. A third large Korean car maker which dated from 1977, Kia, was a Ford/Mazda joint venture, but it remained in the shadow of the two larger Korean operations.

With the benefits of strong protective measures, and a low-wage labourforce, Hyundai and Daewoo and their associates established new plants and produced small, cheap cars for Western markets. Over time, the industry improved the initially poor quality and reliability of its products, and its factories passed the benchmark of one million vehicles a year in 1988, although production levels dipped shortly after that. The industry has not been without problems — it saw some industrial troubles and was heavily hit by the Asian financial crisis. However, the big car makers continued to be heavily supported by Korea's banks and government. In 2006 Korean-made cars made up 20 per cent of the total world production and most cars made were exported. Hyundai alone made 3.2 million vehicles in 2005.

Among the well-known Korean names besides Hyundai (now the world's 11th largest auto maker), are Hyundai's associate company Kia, Daewoo, Samsung (majority owned by Renault) and SsangYong (in which a Chinese car maker — Shanghai Auto Industry Corporation — now has a 49 per cent stake). It is significant that the Korean auto industry is also heavily involved in the production and export of car components. As noted earlier in this chapter, Korea's auto workers work the longest hours of any in the world.

As a by-the-way, there is also a motor vehicle manufacturing industry in North Korea, but it is very small. It was structured and operates along the lines of the long-gone industries of the Stalinist era in the former

USSR or China. There are a number of state factories dedicated to the manufacture of a particular class of commercial vehicle, for example, the Sungri General Auto Works makes heavy trucks comparable to the old-style Chinese Jie Fangs, the Chongjin Bus Works and Pyongyang Trolleybus Works are eponymous with their product, and the closest the North Koreans come to a facility that makes cars is the Pyongyang Auto Works which makes a small number of sturdy vehicles for military and official use.

India

Like Korea, India started with low-quality cars by world standards. Its domestic economy was heavily protected and the first cars built in India were to a well-tried and venerable British design that came from Coventry. Some knew the shape of the cars as the Morris Oxford, or Morris Cambridge. In India, they were called the Ambassador and the streets of Mumbai and Delhi and a thousand towns stirred by the dust of the home-grown yellow and black taxis. In the 1970s, the Maruti appeared — a small sedan similar to a Suzuki because it was a product of a Suzuki joint venture. The Maruti and the Ambassador became numerous, and Mumbai became the hub of the domestic Indian car making industry. Maruti was the largest car maker in India and the truck maker, Tata, also made cars and became the second largest manufacturer on the subcontinent.

The situation changed as India's leaders came to understand, as did the Chinese, that the path to increased prosperity lay in links to world markets. India offered international auto companies the benefits of an educated workforce, and wage costs, even for highly skilled workers, barely one-tenth those of developed countries. Market reforms and the opening of the Indian economy did not come about until the mid-1990s. At first, foreign companies set up operations in India to manufacture components. These components were as basic as nuts and bolts at first, but gradually became more complex as technology and local skills were built up.

The companies that came to India before 2000 were mainly American (GM and Ford) and Japanese (Honda, Toyota and Mitsubishi). The models that were assembled and sold into the Indian market were generally small sedans (like the Alto) or basic commercial vehicles. By 2005, Indian car makers were supplying exports to countries in the Middle East and South-East Asia. The number of units exported was not large by world standards (around 130,000 units in 2004) but has been growing rapidly.

It is worth noting that India's vehicle manufacturers plan to expand their exports, although they will not be as competitive on world markets as China's manufacturers in the short term, because in the author's opinion, increased demand in India can absorb increased production, unlike the situation in China. In India, there are well-established networks to service private vehicles, based on the motorcycle service networks. Indian-designed cars, as of 2007, tend to be more basic in style and features and hence are not as likely to appeal to markets in the US and Europe.[73] Although India's car industry is growing rapidly, it is starting from a lower base than the car industry in China and is unlikely to overtake its Asian rival within ten years. Indian consumers do not have as much disposable income as the Chinese consumer, nor have there been equivalent rates of domestic capital formation (including the rate of savings of individuals and families). As a final point, there is an inflow of capital into India, but it has been much less than the inflow of capital into China, especially from the Chinese diaspora in the West, also Singapore and Taiwan.

Nevertheless, there will be Indian cars entering global markets. Tata has plans to sell its Marina and Indigo small car models in the West in 2008. Mahindra, a manufacturer of light commercials formerly associated with Ford, markets light trucks and utilities in the West in relatively small numbers.

Statistics for the motor vehicle manufacturing industry in India are not easy to compare with other countries, because of the very large number of motorcycles that are produced. Each year, India produces around a million passenger vehicles and light trucks but more than 7 million motorcycles, so if motorcycles are included in some official statistics for 'motor vehicles', then the output of India looks very substantial indeed. In this book, motorcycles are not included in the general discussions concerning 'auto' manufacturing.

Russia

Russia, like China, made do with basic cars manufactured to obsolete designs during the years of Communist rule, but its industry has been modernized to a large extent in the past 20 years. It produces around one million cars a year and employs a workforce of 140,000. Domestic sales were growing by about 10 per cent a year in the early 2000s, and the domestic market was protected by tariffs.

The modern Russian auto industry has been developed through joint ventures, from BMWs made in Kaliningrad (once part of Prussia) to Fords produced in a plant near St Petersburg. The Volga, once a venerable vehicle for the commissars, has been upgraded by domestic Russian manufacturers — the Gaz Auto company at Nizhny Novgorod — and remains an affordable car for many Russians whereas the Fords and BMWs are out of their reach. In 2007, the disadvantage that Russian domestic producers faced was the lack of a modern high-tech engine designed for good fuel economy and able to meet modern standards for exhaust emissions.

Brazil

The car industry in Brazil, the world's fifth most populous country, is the tenth largest in the world. It is also one of the main pillars of the economy and a source of national pride. There has been substantial foreign interest in the Brazilian industry because it has a very large domestic market and is central to events across the entire South American continent. The President of Brazil, Luis Inacio 'Lula' da Silva, is a former auto worker. VW, GM, Ford and Mercedes-Benz are the first, third, sixth and eighth biggest corporations in the country (note that Toyota, while present in Brazil, does not have operations as large as these other companies).

The Brazilian industry started in a pattern common to many other countries, with small beginnings as local inventors came up with conventional and not-so-conventional designs. Then, in the 1920s, big foreign firms such as GM and Ford established assembly plants to put together imported component kits. The modern Brazilian car industry did not hit its straps until the 1950s, when the government of the day (with echoes of China's Great Leap Forward) decreed the Fifty Years in Five program to rapidly industrialize the country. The program was based upon policies to encourage import-substitution, that is, to have products made locally rather than being imported, and such policies included controlling foreign exchange and giving tax credits and subsidies, as well as severely limiting imports. Generally, the program was an overreach that failed, but there were pockets of success, among them the establishment of Sao Paulo as an auto manufacturing centre. In 1953, Volkswagen set up a manufacturing line for the venerable VW Beetle, and the German 'people's car' lived on in Brazil until 1985, long after it had been superseded on production lines in its native country. By 1961, nearly 90 per cent of the vehicles of Brazil had been made or assembled by Brazilian industry. By the end of the decade, Volkswagen accounted for 80 per cent of the cars motoring on Brazilian roads, and even in 1979 still accounted for 40 per cent of the 6 million cars tooling around the country.

The 1970s saw an explosion of growth in the industry in Brazil, an explosion confined and encouraged by strong protective barriers. GM, Ford and Fiat were among the local manufacturers who accounted for Brazilian production of 27 different brands, most small to medium-sized cars to meet domestic demand. In around ten years from 1965 to 1974, production went from 170,000 vehicles to 700,000. These were peak years, but the Oil Shock had a strong impact and was followed by industrial unrest centred in the auto industry. Brazil was forced to find increased foreign earnings to pay for imported oil, and the auto industry was reoriented from a focus on domestic production to a focus on exports. This was not difficult on the face of it, because the cars made in Brazil could be called 'world cars', being VW Beetles, Ford Escorts and Fiat Unos. These exports went first to other South American countries, and then to Europe and North America.

Brazilian cars did not fare well when they were exported out of their strongly protected local market. Brazil's auto workers were not highly productive (even in the 1980s they were about one quarter as productive as Japanese auto workers) and the finished quality of their cars was below par. The 1980s, seen generally as a period of expansion, saw instead stagnation of the industry even as Brazil's economy suffered from hard times and military dictatorship. There was falling investment, then inflation. The government responded in 1984 with pricing controls which further crippled investment. Overall, much of the 1980s has come to be seen as a period of lost opportunities for Brazil and for much of South America.

When democracy returned in 1985 the economy was ailing and needed a strong remedy. The potion for the ill patient was to be a dose of trade liberalization. In the early 1990s, protective policies were largely abandoned and foreign investment was encouraged by a new freer trading environment. Established foreign vehicle manufacturers such as VW and Mercedes, Honda and Toyota, announced that they would build new plants and update others. There was also an influx of new auto makers, mainly Asian ones, such as Hyundai and Kia. In 1996, when national production passed 1.5 million, the plan was to lift Brazil's auto production to 2.5 million vehicles by 2000. However, this goal was not achieved until 2005. The second leg of the plan was to increase the proportion of production that was exported, and by 2005 nearly 40 per cent of Brazil's auto production went into exports. By 2007, the Brazilian industry has taken an important niche in world markets — concentrating on the manufacture of car components as much as on complete cars.

There are, of course, developing auto industries in other countries, such as Canada, Spain, and Malaysia. These countries will not be described in detail, for to consider every country with an industry would make this chapter too long. Suffice it to note that most of the larger countries of the world do see auto manufacturing as an important segment of industry, and indeed auto manufacturing is even related to national status — a country comes to see itself as developed once it has a functioning car making sector.

Conclusion

In 2007, it is indisputable that a number of very large car makers are under intense pressure. The question has been asked whether the great American car makers GM and Ford could go bankrupt, or be merged with other corporations and lose their unique identity. Bankruptcy of these American icons is not impossible. At the end of the 20th century the airline industry in the US, the world's largest, saw many notable bankruptcies — among them Pan American Airlines. Pan Am was a true icon of the American aviation industry and its collapse was almost unthinkable. Yet collapse it did.

Enron and WorldCom were also very large corporations and perhaps analysts would once have scoffed at suggestions that they could collapse suddenly and create financial disaster for hundreds of thousands of employees, pensioners and shareholders.

There is no reason why automotive icons should not encounter the same fate as aeronautical icons.

In summary, the car making industry in the West, the most mature sector of the industry, is at greatest risk. It appears highly likely that even household names could disappear if current global trends continue. It is no response to say such things just could not happen. In 1912, it was said that the *Titanic* was unsinkable — yet the unthinkable happened.

In the motorcycle industry of the 1960s, Western manufacturers talked only to the 'grease monkeys' and the 'rev-heads' and seemed oblivious to the fact that there was a growing market of ordinary people — with clean, not oily, hands — who would welcome cheap reliable basic transportation that had good fuel economy and did not pollute the environment excessively. The size of the motor, the number of gadgets, and expensive features were not the prime attributes that the market in general wanted. Yet the motorcycling aficionados of the West reacted with contempt to the Japanese — hence sneering references to 'plastic Japanese bikes — not real ones'. It may be that executives in the motor vehicle industry have always talked mainly to industry insiders, and so have been slow to sense changes in the wind. If you love cars, then you talk to others who love cars and you build cars that you like and that they like.

Today, the price of oil is increasing, and it must increase even more. The burgeoning demands of the hugely growing economies in China and India must ensure that the price of oil will never again decline to the levels of the late 1990s. Fuel efficiency must be a crucial factor in the

6 The Development of Japanese Car Makers

marketplace, and yet US and other car manufacturers in the West have been slow to react and have continued to design new models which use even more fuel than previous models.

As this book examines how the rapidly emerging Chinese car industry will emerge to likely choke the Australian (and other) car industries to death, it is useful to look also at how the Japanese car industry developed, for there are strong parallels with its larger Asian neighbour, and lessons can be drawn from its pattern of development.

The early history of the Japanese car industry was not unlike the early years of auto manufacturing in China, except that the Japanese historical pattern ran its course around 20 to 30 years earlier than the Chinese.

The Japanese Auto Industry to 1947
The 'black ships' of American Commodore Matthew Perry prised open the doors to Japan and its markets in 1853. To that date, Japan had been closed to travellers and isolated from international trade. After 1853, foreigners brought in industrial and manufactured goods and the transformation of Japan began. As the foreign importers often colluded, their trading was subjected to heavy regulation, and from 1870 foreign investment was squeezed out, although the import of foreign technology was encouraged. Domestic businesses were established in areas such as light manufacturing, where locals were not subject to foreign competitors. Throughout the nineteenth century, although the country remained

largely an agricultural economy, the Japanese industrial sector grew rapidly as powerful trading cartels (the *zaibatsu*) used an abundance of cheap labour and local finance to develop diverse operations. By the early 20th century, Japan's imperial and militaristic ambitions led to an emphasis upon more widespread industrialization, although much of the technology and heavy machinery still had to be imported.

Japan's automotive industry began around the beginning of the 20th century, with a typical first phase of inventors pottering in their workshops to produce odd vehicles that invoked shock and awe in witnesses. The first car designed and built in Japan was a ten-seater steam-powered vehicle that one Torao Yamaba built in 1904 to get his large family around. The first petrol-engined vehicle dated from 1907, when the Automobile Trading Company, financed by one of the Japanese Royal Family, built a dozen Takuri cars using European technology. Only a handful of cars had been made in Japan until 1914, when an American-trained engineer named Masujiro Hashimoto produced a sedan with a wooden body and a 1.5 litre petrol engine. He worked for a newly established car company which formed its acronym from the names of the company's partners — Kenjiro Den, Rokuro Aoyama, and Meitaro Takeuchi — hence the new car was named the DAT. It was the first Datsun (the word 'Datsun' was applied to a 1931 model referred to as the 'Son of DAT' — but the word 'son' means in Japanese 'loss', so the logical name 'Datson' was jettisoned in favour of 'Datsun').

At around the same time, one of the *zaibatsu* which had been involved in trade and shipping brought out a car based on a contemporary Fiat design. The *zaibatsu* was Mitsubishi, based in Osaka and named not after a Mr Mitsubishi but from the Japanese words for the three diamonds which made up its trademark. Another competitor was the Tokyo Gas and Electric Industrial Company, which entered into an arrangement with Wolseley of the United Kingdom to make their cars in Japan.

All of these companies were small manufacturers at first, producing limited numbers of cars, and even by 1923 there were fewer than 13,000 vehicles in the country, of which less than 10 per cent were of local manufacture. There had been a boost to production in 1918 when the government subsidized the manufacture of vehicles suitable for military use. This created a relationship between vehicle manufacturers, government and the military which lasted until 1945.

The car did not become popular in Japan until a catastrophe hit. The Great Tokyo Earthquake struck in 1923 and demolished huge swathes of Tokyo and its port of Yokohama in the initial shocks and the fires which followed. Tramlines and railways were destroyed. Until they could be rebuilt (and there was a massive amount of rebuilding to do) the authorities and ordinary citizens needed to get around by motor vehicle. In the short term, thousands of vehicles were imported, rising from 1,900 vehicles in 1923 to more than 4,000 in 1924. They came mainly from the United States — from Ford and GM. These two companies set up manufacturing plants in Japan in the years following, Ford in 1925 and GM in 1927. By 1929, the number of vehicles in Japan had increased threefold in just six years, and this phase of rapid expansion, underpinned by foreign imports of vehicles and expertise, represents the typical second phase of automotive industry development.

However, the military link became more important in the 1930s, as Japan's imperial aspirations in China grew. The government chose to restrict imports and freeze out Ford and GM. Government funding and support saw new car manufacturing enterprises established. The most notable of these was a former textile firm named Toyota, founded as an auto manufacturer in 1933 by a notable inventor named Sakichi Toyoda (who changed the 'd' in his name to a 't' when naming the company to reduce the evidence of its family background). Nissan (first known as Nihon Sangyo — shortened to Ni-San) was created out of a merger of DAT and Jitsuyo the following year. A number of smaller companies merged to form Isuzu. A new truck maker called Mazda had started turning out vehicles in 1931. An engineer named Hatsudoki Seizo had come up with a design for the ordinary commuter — a tiny three-wheeled sort of bug that became very popular. His company became Daihatsu. In 1936, the government acted to exclude all foreign car companies by law and Ford and GM were forced to close. So most of the Japanese vehicle manufacturers that are huge in the 21st century were established in the early 1930s, mainly in response to the demand created by the Tokyo Earthquake, funded or authorized by the government, and with foreign competitors forcibly excluded. These motoring giants may not even have survived infancy without strict and uncompromising protection.

During the war years (which for Japan stretched from 1937 to 1945) vehicle production was geared towards the war effort. Nissan and Toyota concentrated on making aero engines, and the efforts of Mitsubishi were applied to manufacturing an aircraft that was initially much underrated in the West — the Zero-sen fighter.

By the time of Japan's surrender, its vehicle manufacturing industry was in ruins. It was to be re-established by the occupation force, which was directed by the Supreme Commander for the Allied Powers, General Douglas MacArthur, who believed that a key to the successful reconstruction of Japan was the resuscitation of the auto industry. One month after the surrender, the occupation authorities gave the go-ahead to the construction of trucks, although the production of small cars for civilian use was not authorized until 1947.

Thus the irony of the early history of the Japanese motor vehicle industry is that at crucial stages it was wholly dependent upon US car makers, notably Ford and GM, for its very survival. Japan's economy was opened by the US in 1853; the first car produced in quantity, the DAT, was by an engineer trained in the US; the US car makers provided the vehicles desperately needed after the Tokyo Earthquake in 1923, and American authorities planned its resurrection in 1945. This was a significant date for the industry, and indeed for Japan as a whole, as it represented a re-entry to world trade and a pivotal point in automotive industry development.

It can truly be said that the early Japanese auto industry had both a father and a mother — their father being the US car industry and their deeply protective mother being the Japanese establishment. However, The Japanese motoring *zaibatsu* may become like Oedipus, who when he came to maturity, killed his father.

The Japanese Auto Industry, 1947 to 1968

The Japanese auto industry took time to recover from its long period of isolation from world trade, and the distorting effects of militarism. Many people were impoverished by the war and rebuilding homes and services took precedence over buying a car. Also, local car makers faced outside competition because US servicemen were allowed to import their own cars while serving in the occupation forces, and they sold those cars locally when their terms were up. In 1953, when domestic manufacturers produced fewer than 9,000 cars, around 13,000 cars imported from the US were sold on the local markets. In time, these imported vehicles lost their popularity, mainly due to the difficulties of obtaining spares and servicing. Also, the reconstituted Ministry for Industry and International Trade brought in protective measures to cosset the recovering industry, such as bringing in tight regulations for the resale of second-hand vehicles (many of which remain today, although born out of measures to counter the import of cars by US military personnel).

The government provided financing for reconstruction, and they also provided another hugely valuable contribution. MacArthur and the occupying administration had sought to spread democratic principles throughout Japan, and part of that program was the establishment of strong labour unions. Previously, the big car makers had organized their labourforces as if they were military establishments. In the early 1950s, most workers joined the new unions and when Toyota and Nissan sought to lay off staff, they were hit by strikes. Toyota suffered its one and only strike in 1950 and Nissan was brought to the edge of bankruptcy in 1953/54. The government assisted the big zaibatsu by establishing labour laws that reduced the power of the unions, although the zaibatsu had to agree to a trade-off by agreeing to virtually life-long employment contracts and advancement by seniority.[74] The result was that a confrontational industrial management style — an us-against-them attitude — was averted. In the revived car makers, there would be a cooperative management/labour arrangement that stood the companies well for decades.

With financing, legislative and labour policies in place, the industry looked to expand. The problem was to design up-to-date models and implements new technologies. The three-wheelers produced by Daihatsu and others (with engines of around 500cc) had limited appeal. The key to development was to import technology from the West — yet another occasion when the Japanese industry had to look to foreigners to revive its fortunes.

From 1952, several joint ventures took root. The US manufacturer of Jeep (Kaiser Motor Company, later American Motors) entered into a joint venture with Mitsubishi to assemble Jeeps in Japan from kits of component parts referred to as CKD (completely-knocked-down) — exactly the same arrangements as those negotiated 30 years later for the assembly of Jeeps in Beijing.

Nissan negotiated with Austin of England to produce the technologically advanced and popular Devon A40 and A50, and based later designs upon the UK models. Hino entered into a joint venture with Renault to import component kits. Isuzu completed an agreement to manufacture the Austin A40's direct competitor, the Hillman Minx. It was notable that the Japanese went to European makers (with the exception of the Jeep) because European models — smaller and more basic than contemporary US models — suited their needs.

These ventures were all successful, but the Japanese partners probably benefited more than their foreign partner, because within a relatively short period of time, the Japanese adopted the technology and were producing their own Japanese-designed models which within a few years would take market share from their erstwhile partners. By 1960, the country's car production topped 300,000, and all the cars being manufactured in Japan were entirely sourced in Japan. It is likely that such a pattern of development — that the country's car production is entirely sourced within the country — will eventually be followed in China.

Throughout the 1960s, private car ownership expanded as wealth returned to Japan after the reconstruction era of the '50s. National income per head rose more than threefold in the decade 1955 to 1965. Industrialization and urbanization grew. The emphasis in car making was on the manufacture of small cars of less than 1.5 litres, aided by a system of road taxes and sales taxes which penalized larger vehicles. The price of such small cars halved from 1955 to 1965, making them much more affordable to the ordinary wage earner. The structure of the industry was different from the West in that the structure was like a very flat pyramid — around 20 big manufacturers sourced many of their components from a range of thousands of smaller companies,[75] which led to greater efficiencies and competition within the domestic economy (and the emergence of new players such as Honda). Foreign imports were largely excluded by quotas and high tariffs — for example, 40 per cent on small cars. Foreign investment was entirely excluded, which shielded the Japanese companies from takeover bids from the likes of GM and Ford and Chrysler.

Japanese car makers began to export in quantity from the late 1950s. Toyota entered the US marketplace with the Toyota Crown in 1957, but it did not make an impact. Its styling looked outmoded and old-fashioned. Other Japanese offerings such as the Tiara and Datsun looked cheap and clunky. Their design reflected a difference in global tastes — Asians have a different appreciation of beauty and style than Europeans, and US aficionados are different again (which is a basic truth that will make design of the so-called global car a nightmare of reconciling tastes). Japanese cars also suffered from the same design flaw (if flaw it can be called) as its motorcycles: They were designed to travel short distances on narrow roads at moderate speeds. At first, when US drivers hammered them at speed on California highways, they wheezed and folded. In time, Japanese designers rectified these shortcomings.

By 1968, as Japan sought to lift the level of its exports, it also sought to set up more assembly plants around the world, from South-East Asia to Brazil to South Africa to the US. Mitsubishi, Toyota and Isuzu trucks set up operations in Australia in the 1960s. Due to this expansion, Japan came under foreign pressure to grant a quid pro quo — open its markets to foreign competitors if it expected to get access to foreign markets itself. Accordingly, it relaxed some tariffs and allowed some foreign investment, although not without some conflict. It was only when the Americans put special import taxes on Japanese cars that the Japanese responded by lowering tariffs to a reciprocal level.

The late 1960s was also a time for mergers and takeovers among the Japanese vehicle makers. For example, Toyota took over Hino in 1966 and Daihatsu in 1967. Isuzu had not one but three tentative takeovers, the first with Fuji Industries, then Mitsubishi and then Nissan.

The Japanese Auto Industry, 1969–2005

From 1969, even as the Japanese government relaxed some it protective measures, exports of Japanese designed and made cars soared, reaching 22 per cent of its total production (which was still less than, say, the UK's or Germany's proportion of cars made for exports at that time — 42 per cent and 55 per cent, respectively). In 1971, more than a million cars left Japan for foreign markets, but greater things were yet to come. The Oil Shock (a big increase in oil prices due to conflict in the Middle East) hit in 1973, and most people suddenly wanted to buy smaller cars … and Japanese cars were just the right size. The next five years saw a skyrocketing increase in exports, to 2.5 million cars (out of a total Japanese car production of 5 million units). Japan had become the world's second-biggest car-producing country, and world's largest exporter.

Japan's success caused some tensions. Although protection of its domestic market had been reduced, it was still a hard market to crack, for the Japanese consumer had become enamoured of local vehicles and the typical US car — big, luxurious, and fuel-thirsty — did not appeal. The only foreign cars that sold well in Japan were the top of the range luxury cars from Europe, such as Mercedes-Benz, and they only sold in small numbers (around 45,000 in 1984 out of a market of more than 3 million — just 1.5 per cent). Some complaints about the global car market began to be heard, and the most vociferous complaints arose about the most successful competitor in export markets — Japan. US lobbyists pointed out to their government that Japan had two factors that tilted the world car markets playing field in their favour: They had a docile labourforce in their factories who were remunerated much less than their counterparts in the US and Europe, and their currency, the yen, was seriously undervalued, which gave them a strong and unfair price advantage.

The Japanese not only had these unfair advantages, but their own market was virtually a closed shop. Some European countries brought in quotas to limit the number of Japanese cars imported, and the US instituted a 10 per cent tariff. International pressure on the Bank of Japan contributed to a revaluation of the yen and foreign agitation subsided a little.

The big Japanese car makers used the respite they were granted to undertake a grand strategy to get around the lobbying and foreign governments' protective measures — the wholesale establishment of manufacturing facilities within foreign countries. Firms such as Toyota and Mitsubishi had long established assembly plants around the world, partly because they were taking advantage of even cheaper wages elsewhere to expand capacity which was reaching its limits in Japan, but now they built even bigger plants. These plants, for example in the US, had to pay wages at overall US levels, but they were not burdened by the same legacy costs — such as pension payments — as their home-grown competitors. Moreover, they set up new plants, which meant using the latest technology, in 'green fields' regions such as Kentucky where there had not been large manufacturing plants in the past, and this meant that they could train new entrants to the industry in Japanese procedures and work practices, which were by then in the front rank in global terms.

The history of the Japanese industry during the 1970s was not one of unrelieved success. Some companies either hit the rocks or came within a hair's-breadth of disaster. One such was Mazda. Mazda had invested in a number of new and innovative models, including cars with the revolutionary Wankel rotary engine, and the drain of these investments at the same time as the impact of the Oil Shock hit sales levels of its medium-sized cars and rapidly set the company on a course to hit large-sized rocks. Mazda was saved from bankruptcy by massive financial support from Japan's banks, the prime among them being the Sumitomo Bank. Once the crisis was passed, Mazda was able to set a course to safer financial waters.[76]

One of the accusations of unfair comparative advantage — Japan's lower wages structure — was offset in the late '60s by the fact that Japanese workers were less productive than their US counterparts, in fact, achieving no more than 20 per cent of the productivity of a US car worker in 1967.[77] However, due to aggressive efficiency drives, and introducing concepts such as Total Quality Management and Just-in-Time inventory management, the productivity of average Japanese auto workers crept up and by 1980 they were just as productive as their American counterparts, although they were still paid comparatively less. The principles of *kaizen* (continuous improvement) management of Japanese firms became the subject of study for management students everywhere.

The profits of the years of the 1970s Oil Shock provided profits and funds to re-invest in new technology, and during the 1980s Japan's car makers ploughed ahead with the installation of automated manufacturing lines, which gave them additional advantages in cost-savings as well as improved quality and reliability of product. They continued to establish auto manufacture and assembly operations in countries as diverse as Kenya and Trinidad.

In the 1980s, Japanese designers came to the forefront of global car design and took the lead in designing for new trends such as fuel efficiency and reduction of vehicle emissions.[78] They addressed these issues because their home country, small and crowded, found them particularly acute. Their government had brought in laws to govern the amount of pollutants that vehicles could emit, defining permissible levels of hydrocarbons and carbon monoxide. In addressing these issues, the Japanese were five to ten years ahead of governments in the West. Japanese designers also led the way in planning for safer cars and developing auto electronics, as well as making innovations such as front-wheel drive widespread.

The Japanese industry came under stress in the mid-1980s, when, at a summit of the major industrialized nations in New York in September 1985, there was major pressure put on Japan to revalue its heavily undervalued currency. In response to this pressure, the yen was revalued by 30 per cent and Japanese manufacturers felt a twofold squeeze as their pricing advantage in foreign markets was reduced and their wage/cost advantages were whittled away. The squeeze resulted in a renewed push for efficiency and cost savings, and these, coupled with the diversification of its operations across so many countries, enabled the industry to maintain its overall momentum towards growth and profits.

This efficiency drive was needed, for in the late 1990s and early 2000s the Japanese economy entered a period of sluggish growth caused by the aftermath of the Asian financial crisis and an overhang of debt in the financial system.

The pattern of development of Japan's car industry can be illustrated using the bar graph used in chapter 2 to describe the pattern of Australia's car industry development. Note that the industries in both Japan and Australia had similar beginnings to around 1940 (as indeed China's infant industry also made similar first steps).

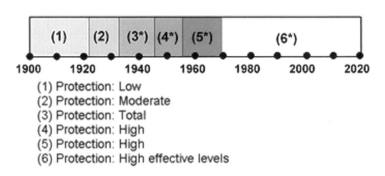

(1) Protection: Low
(2) Protection: Moderate
(3) Protection: Total
(4) Protection: High
(5) Protection: High
(6) Protection: High effective levels

Figure 6.1: The Pattern of Development of the Car Industry in Japan

- Common First Phase (1): Industry in infancy; many local manufacturers; small quantities produced; protection measures very low or non-existent.
- Common Second Phase (2): Industry coalescing; small manufacturers merge; production runs increased; growth is dependent upon the entry of US firms (GM and Ford) or UK or European firms; protection measures brought in to ensure a degree of local content and control.
- Japanese Third Phase (3*): Abrupt termination of international contacts; local industry concentrates on military/industrial needs; number of cars manufactured limited. Protection measures total — which means that foreign manufacturers were totally excluded from the mid-1930s.
- Japanese Fourth Phase (4*): Strict controls relaxed; local industry has small and obsolescent designs; joint ventures encouraged to bring in marketing and management expertise, also new technology and designs; some local designs are virtual copies of popular Western models. High levels of government investment and support and high levels of protection.

- Japanese Fifth Phase (5*): Mergers of local car makers into a smaller number of conglomerates; indigenous small car designs very similar to Western models; expansion continues and exports grow in importance due to undervalued currency and lower wage/cost structures. Relatively high levels of protection continue.

- Japanese Sixth Phase (6*): Local markets reach virtual limits and exports make up a major proportion of production; innovative designs achieve world-wide acceptance; plants are established in other countries using indigenous expertise and practices. Advantages of undervalued currency and low wages remain; protection levels are reduced, but social and cultural factors remain strong barriers to foreign competition.

Car Making by the Big Japanese Companies, 2005–2007

Japanese car makers have operated in an uncertain economic environment in Japan itself, given that country's recent sluggish economic growth, but in 2005 prospects seemed better, with a recovery under way. With that impetus, Japan's car makers maintained their growth and profitability, in contrast with the prospects facing many car makers in the US and UK.

In 2005, Toyota increased its sales in its automobile segment by 2 per cent and sales for the group overall increased to US$11.5 billion (up 6.6 per cent on 2004).[79] This was one more in a pattern of steady increases over previous years. The company held out optimistic prospects for the future, but nominated higher oil prices and changes in exchange rates as threats in the future.

Mitsubishi as a group (of which its car making operations are only a component part) increased its group sales by around 13 per cent from 2004 to 2005 to reach the US$16 billion mark, and its profits increased by 14 per cent. The group saw good prospects for growth in the massive market that is China, and recognized the huge and increasing impact China's growth had on supply/demand factors in the world's resource markets.

The subsidiaries of Japanese car makers in the US also continued their growth. To an extent, they had advantages over their American counterparts, especially in regard to pension and healthcare costs — for both of these are funded or part-funded by the Japanese government.

The advantages are not inconsequential and certainly tilt the field in favour of the Japanese.

Some Japanese companies do face the same challenges as the American Big Three, and ironically, these are the Japanese companies like Toyota, Honda and Nissan that chose to establish manufacturing operations in the US. Their challenge of coping with a retiring workforce does not have the same degree of difficulty as that faced by GM, Ford and Chrysler, because the employees of the Japanese plants in the US were hired under less advantageous contracts in regard to pensions and healthcare and the workforce in the Japanese operations is not, as a whole, as old because they were established much later than the Big Three of Detroit. The latter companies negotiated their generous plans in the 1960s when the US economy was buoyant (and lower life expectancies did not promise too much of a burden in funding retirees). Toyota, in its Annual Report of 2005, did not include details of obligations to employees in regard to pensions and healthcare, for they were considered to be too small to be material.

The earlier chapter that outlined the world car industry has described how Japanese car makers are now the world leaders. In many aspects of its development the Chinese car industry runs parallel with, but some decades behind, that of the Japanese car industry. In 2006, the Chinese industry, which in 1920 was larger than the Japanese, reached the level the Japanese reached in 1960. They have imported contemporary technology through joint ventures and built up their domestic market in isolation from the rest of the world. They have learned contemporary world's best management practices.

There is a parallel even in the presence today in China of the small and 'cute' three-wheeled car that was popular in Japan in the 1950s, but was phased out in the 1960s.

Most importantly, China has the advantages of both an undervalued currency and the much lower wage/cost structures that Japan used so well in the late 1960s and 1970s to parlay a place for itself in the front rank of auto manufacturing countries.

There is no reason to assume that the Chinese industry, having followed Japan's path although somewhat behind its neighbour, will not go on to emulate Japan's example of improving upon Western designs and using market savvy to ease out the older and less-efficient producers.

In the next part of this book, which looks at details of China's development and the growth of its auto manufacturing industry, the parallels will become clearer.

Part Two
The Chinese Automotive Industry and its Environment
7 'Cars for All'

In Nanjing City — Aspects of a 'New' China

Nanjing, a former capital situated on the Yangtze River and one of the largest cities of China, was a study in contradictions and curiosities. Mr Shu epitomized those contradictions. Mr Shu was an accountant at a modern fibre optic plant, a joint venture between the Netherlands and China. When I interviewed him in 1993 he proudly said that he was 73 years old yet still enjoyed working. Ever cheerful, he smiled as he told me how he was imprisoned during the years of the Cultural Revolution between 1966 and 1969 solely because he was an accountant who had once worked for a Western enterprise, for at that time all accountants were considered to be 'reactionary' and 'counter-revolutionary'. However, by 1993 his skills were in great demand, because as China's economy opened up to Western investment, joint-venture partners required accurate financial statements, not least for the purposes of reporting to stock markets and regulatory authorities in the United States and Europe. That was also the year the government promised its people cars for all within fifteen years.

Mr Shu took me to Nanjing's stock market, which was just one of many branches of the Shanghai stock market. It was situated in a large building that was formerly a French convent school. It had survived the Cultural Revolution because it was used as a warehouse by an iron foundry. In the backyard of the building there remained a stack of steel rods, and underneath a lean-to was a small group of men who were busy fabricating metal fencing. One was welding with only a pair of cheap sunglasses held to protect his eyes.

In the central hall of the main building, it was crowded and very noisy. I could look up through the wispy smoke curling around the ceiling to make out the remains of French baroque decoration — repainted at least, though chipped and spalling under the paint. At one end of the high ceiling, over what was once the podium of the hall, now lined with boxes of busy tellers conducting transactions, there was a decorated plaster feature. At its centre were the letters, 'A.M.D.G.' I wondered what French-trained Chinese craftsman had laboured to fashion the initials for the Jesuit motto *Ad Maiorem Dei Gloriam* (For the Greater Glory of God) in the days when Christian missionaries laboured there. Now the smoke of many cigarettes and the noise of excited Chinese investors ran and rattled around the pious old decorations.

Suspended from the ceiling by iron rods were electronic boards with continually updated messages on share prices. Most of the suited crowd were keenly following the messages and waging loud conversations with those nearest to them, who could have been companions or strangers. Dodging in and out of the crowd were young men and women in white shirts who were selling newsletters and newspapers. Mr Shu bought a paper and read me the front page, huddled close to my ear so that I could hear amid the hubbub.

'This says ...' he pointed to one column, 'that the people must labour to ensure control over the stock markets. This other exhorts us to invest in ventures that will advance the good of the people.' He smiled at me widely and dropped his voice (though that was hardly necessary, for no-one could possibly eavesdrop amid that noise). 'But people do not buy the papers to read that. They want to read these.' He turned to the back page and indicated rows of figures, the closing prices in the Shanghai and Shenzen markets. I noted one stock that appeared to be spiralling upwards. It was in the newly established Shanghai Taxi Company. The company had recently been floated and the investment money that poured in had been used to purchase 2,000 new Citroen taxis, made in China of course.

The two main stock markets in Shanghai and Shenzen were linked to many centres throughout China where branches operated, in Nanjing for instance, and the newsletters and newspapers provided up-to-date information on movements in stock values. Yet there was a curious ambivalence about the markets. The government at the time encouraged their operation, and welcomed foreign investors, even though foreigners faced some restrictions on their investments. Despite the official enthusiasm, however, the Premier then in office, Li Peng, noted that shareholders should not see themselves as being owners of the companies in which they bought shares. It was a statement that directly contradicted Western concepts of share ownership.

It almost seemed as if the investors were deemed to be, and indeed saw themselves to be, speculators and even gamblers, seeking increases in share prices rather than long-term returns on their investments through dividends. A taxi driver regaled me with his story of making a 200 per cent return from his investment in the local taxi company, and he was now looking for another 'good bet'.

The operation of the Nanjing stock market branch was one of the many contradictions in modern China with its centrally controlled economy still including Communist elements, like a very old wall hanging that was starting to fray and deteriorate with gaps and rotting strips dangling down. Investment was sought from foreign and local 'capitalists', but at that time much of it seemed to be applied to short-term profit and projects, rather than long-term investment. In 1994, I journeyed to the southern island of Hainan, to an iron ore mine, to give a presentation on modern management methods. Afterwards, the management commented that they had received a cheap loan to 'update plant' from a Scandinavian country, and had used the money to purchase 50 new Lincoln Continentals and 100 Jeep Cherokees. In the meantime, the operating equipment remained the outdated and inefficient product of Stalinist-era design.

In the 1990s, the aging heavy industry of China still needed much refurbishment. Mr Shu took me to visit the Ma'ashan steel plant just outside Nanjing where he had worked before being recruited for the fibre optic factory. During the Great Leap Forward it was claimed that such plants achieved prodigies of improved production, but years of isolation from the rest of the world took a toll. At that time, the equipment at the steel mill was antiquated and overused. A second-hand cold-rolling mill had been purchased from Japan, but the installation had run past its deadline and past its budget. The labourforce at the plant (around 18,000) had voluntarily deferred the receipt of one-third of their wages to help the plant over its financial problems (according to the management).

The plant's efficiency needed improvement. A manager told me that over the Spring Festival that had just passed, nearly 11,000 of the mill's employees were given a fortnight off to be with their families in the surrounding countryside, or in nearby cities such as Wuxi or Shanghai. Over that fortnight, production did not decrease — but increased markedly! The plant clearly suffered from over manning, for efficiency in industry had taken a back seat to expanding employment. Yet the picture of industry in contemporary China at that time was not a bleak one. On the contrary, industry was organizing and expanding in such a way that Chinese manufacturing, protected by currency controls, even then looked as if one day it would be able to overwhelm the manufacturing industries of states outside China.

In the 1960s there had been notable industrial achievements. Every citizen of Nanjing I met asked me if I had been across the bridge that spanned the Yangtze River. The bridge was commenced with Russian aid, until the Russian technicians were withdrawn at the time of the Sino-Soviet split, and the Soviets claimed that the Chinese did not have the skilled labour to finish the giant undertaking. Yet finish it they did — one case where the expertise and ability of the Chinese should not have been underestimated. The bridge stands as a symbol of determination and hard work, even if it is now overshadowed by even grander bridges such as those over the Wangpu River at Shanghai, and bigger bridges over the Yangtze at the great inland industrial powerhouse at Chongqing. On the approaches to the bridge at Nanjing, there are bronze figures in heroic pose commemorating the builders. However, there are also living 'statues' — guards with machine-guns in police boxes on either end of the bridge. At the time of the Democracy Movement that culminated in the Tien An Men Square incident, there were demonstrations in Nanjing also, and the bridge was occupied by students. I was told that the bridge was cleared by soldiers and that there were 'some casualties', although how many is still not publicly known.

On another visit to Nanjing, when I went for a stroll near the bridge I noticed posters. I thought they were for a sports event, but a more skilled translator than I (he was an Indian-Australian who hailed from Melbourne) told me that they announced a public execution. Forty-five criminals (one woman and the rest men) were to be shot in one of Nanjing's large sports stadiums. Most had been found guilty of murder, although a few had committed robbery with violence, and several had plundered a train. Forty-five had been chosen by the provincial governor's office to be publicly executed to mark the 45th anniversary of the Communist Revolution. I discussed the proposal with my Chinese friends, and almost all expressed some admiration for the grim parallel of 45 to be put to death to mark 45 years of rule, and the originality of the concept had a certain appeal to them. Of all the people I talked to about the public execution, Mr Shu was the most reticent about discussing it, for he sensed my own unease at using such an event as part of anniversary celebrations, but I found no one who dismissed the event and the gruesome accounting involved. Perhaps it was unreasonable to expect anyone to express criticism in such a controlled society. Despite the reforms and the opening to the West and the acceptance of foreigners, there remains a cultural gulf between East and West in China. Although it is no longer a case of 'ne'er the twain do meet', there are differences nevertheless, and often misunderstandings about values and customs. Outside the central court buildings, posters appeared that bore a picture of each of the condemned persons, with a summary of their crimes and their sentences. After the executions, a court official appeared with a tin of red paint, and on each poster he brushed on a large red tick — an emphatic statement that told everyone who passed that the sentence had been carried out!

A Young Man With a Dream

In Mr Shu's office, I met a personable young man who had been a university student at the time of the 'disturbances' of 1989. He was studying oceanography and graduated that year. Although he said that he had not been directly involved in any demonstrations, he commented that all the students of his year had been sent to other regional centres to work in menial tasks. He himself had been lucky in being sent to a distribution company where he had been in charge of the cashbooks, hence he was recruited to the fibre optic company when it opened in 1993, and was a part of the accounting team. He appreciated the opportunity to work in a European–Chinese joint venture. His aims were limited, and his greatest dream was to own a car. That seemed to be a common aim, and resonated across all classes of citizen. In 1993, the government made that promise to the people that within fifteen years, every Chinese citizen would own a car. It became, and remains, a potent promise.

At the time, I could not conceive where all those cars could be parked, let alone driven around the choked and choking streets of cities like Nanjing and Shanghai. If a hostile power ever wanted to damage China, they need not threaten the use of nuclear weapons. I believed then that if they simply made a free gift of 20 million cars to be shared among the populace, that would suffice to bring the entire economy to a halt as millions of drivers became ensnarled in the world's biggest traffic gridlock! On a serious note, I wondered whether the promise could be met. Could the domestic Chinese auto industry produce cars of sufficient number and quality to meet the incipient demand and fulfil the government's pledge by 2008? Could the domestic manufacturing sector produce modern high-performance products? By 2006, it was becoming clear that Chinese cities were being transformed by the car and the motorway, but the answers to these questions were still not obvious.

Yet the ingenuity, hard work and propensity to sacrifice of the Chinese people should never be underestimated. My friend Mr Shu was the oldest employee at the fibre optic company and looked forward to continuing as long as he was able to. He had had a mild heart attack, and took it as a sign that he did not have much time left and so he should work harder! Anyone in the West who was diagnosed with a heart ailment might take it as a sign to work less, not work more — but Mr Shu saw it differently.

The rest of the labourforce of around 300 men and women at the fibre optic joint venture appeared to be young and enthusiastic. They were, after all, the pick of the crop, for they had been selected from more than 80 people who applied for each and every vacancy when the joint venture had started. Most had university qualifications, and many of the technical staff had spent one or two years in Europe learning the latest in fibre optic technology. The product of the plant was of high quality, it had met world accreditation standards and received ISO certification. Transport costs to Europe and America were high, but the product was still well-priced in comparison to its overseas competitors.

This was the rub and the deep and terrible trap for globalization, especially for Australia's ability to compete in world markets. Those skilled and qualified workers were paid around A$100 for a 40-hour week, which included shift and weekend work without penalty payments. Holidays consisted of two weeks per year. Sick leave totalled three days. Public holidays numbered about ten per year. There were extra benefits such as free hot meals in the company canteen each day, subsidized housing and in some cases a monthly rice ration for each employee. Low labour costs were the answer to the question of why the product of the fibre optic plant could be competitively priced in Europe and elsewhere.

I have read (and drowsed over) many economics textbooks, and can recite classical economic theory about the comparative advantage that low-wage countries possess, but I recall that every one of those texts assumed that the low-wage workers had low skills and low productivity, and also assumed that as skills and productivity rose, so would their wage levels until their wages reached equilibrium with the developed world and the comparative advantage had gone. Not one textbook seemed to conceive of a situation where a country would have a very low comparative wage rate and yet many of its workers had skills and education comparable to workers in the developed world, and moreover they had comparable productivity. The situation is rapidly developing where the low-paid Chinese workers may be more productive, not less.

Around 2 per cent of the Chinese labourforce is employed in high-tech joint ventures. One might think that 2 per cent of anything would hardly make up a decent football team, but two per cent of the estimated Chinese urban industrial labourforce of 200,000,000 equals 4,000,000. That is a large number in anyone's terms, and it may indeed be large enough to be the spark in the transformation of China's economy despite the dead weight of old and antiquated heavy engineering plants in the State-Owned Enterprises.

Therefore, there is a whole generation in China who are well-qualified and hard-working, and who have the same aspirations as so many others in the developed countries of the world — to live well and to own their own comfortable home and to drive their own car.

The Contradictions

There were so many contradictions in the city of Nanjing at that time. I was conscious of one more when Mr Shu invited me to a farewell lunch at his factory. He took me to the large and well-appointed factory canteen. One table had been especially set up for the foreign guest (me) and the group from the accounts section. We used the best chopsticks and fine traditional china. Despite years in China, I was still comparatively clumsy with chopsticks. Then I noticed the clatter of cutlery elsewhere in the canteen. All the other employees had heaped platefuls of potato and meat that they were eating with knives and forks. The foreign guest was honoured with chopsticks and traditional fare (and struggled with the traditional implements), yet the locals were comfortable with Western food and Western cutlery and clearly used them every working day. Just one more contradiction in modern China.

The promise of 'Cars for all' is itself a contradiction. There is no way in the world that every Chinese citizen could have a car. In the time of Mao Zedong, there was a similar aspiration — that every Chinese citizen could own a bicycle. In its day, this also was a valued ideal that should not be underestimated in today's more sophisticated world, because it represented an increase in the overall welfare of the citizenry. Ownership of a bicycle brought about an increase in mobility and flexibility of employment. It was feasible and desirable that every Chinese should own one.

In the 21st century, the promise of cars for all is beguiling but unattainable. In 2006, fewer than two Chinese in a thousand own a car. The worldwide average is 90 per 1,000 — although this statistic is inflated by the high level of car ownership in the United States. If, out of a total population of 1,308 million (a 2004 figure), we assume that around one half are adults who are potential car owners, this equates to a figure of 650 million cars, and there is not enough raw material in the world to make this many. Moreover, this calculation ignores the growing demand for car ownership in India. The research into China's motor vehicle infrastructure that comprises Part Two of this book indicates that, even now, the limits of motor vehicle ownership are being challenged. China's big cities are becoming so polluted by vehicle emissions among other pollutants that the limits of habitability are not far away. The cities are becoming so crowded that space is at even more of a premium than it was in the past, when Chinese families were satisfied with cramped living accommodation.

So what will happen? The certainty is that the number of cars will increase substantially, because the promise of cars for all is such a powerful one. The promise also incorporates a strong feel-good impetus, for it contains within it implications that the Chinese people have prospered and come into their rightful position in the forefront of developed nations. However, there are limits to growth — and that is where the thesis of this book comes in. The output of cars and other vehicles will continue as a sign to the Chinese people that all efforts to meet their dreams are being made, but the physical restraints upon the fulfilling of the promise mean that that excess motor vehicle production must be exported elsewhere.

The next chapter looks at China's overall economic development as a background to discussion of its motor vehicle industry.

8 Economic Expansion and World Trade

An Historical Thumbnail Sketch of China and Global Trade

China has long been a world economic power, and its global trade began many centuries ago. The Greek writer Herodotus was aware of China in the seventh and sixth centuries BC.[80] In the fourth century BC, the Scythian people traded with Chinese in western China, exchanging metalwork and rugs for gold.[81] Silks and porcelain from China were used by the Greeks in the third century BC, although it was unlikely that there were direct contacts on a large scale. Trading goods passed along the so-called Silk Road between China and the West, although there was also a Silk Road of the Sea that started from the south of China and ended in the trading ports of Arabia, Africa and Egypt. Goods from the West such as perfume, dyes and jewellery were exchanged for tea, porcelain and silk. In the seventh century AD, the city of Guangzhou was established in the area of the ancient trading ports, and later, a Chinese admiral of the Ming Dynasty named Zheng He explored routes in South-East Asia, India and Africa.

Some say that there is nothing entirely new in history and that the tides of events are cyclical. The current situation of liberalizing world trade and opening China up to foreign influence has not been a new phenomenon. It has parallels with events in the distant past, events not well-studied in schools in the West because they coincided with a period of economic and social decline in Europe, and young students are often not aware that although Europe may have been in a state of stagnation in the mid to late first millennium, there was a period of expansion and growth of wealth in Asia. China and India were the giants of the world economy, and would remain so until the eighteenth century, when the Industrial Revolution enabled the smaller countries of Europe to use their new technology to take hold of a greater share of the world's wealth.

Nearly 1,400 years ago, a new regime came to power in China and opened the nation to an influx of foreign ideas, religion and trade. The Tang Dynasty that commenced in 618 marked the reunification of China and a widespread prosperity, as well as a blossoming of intellectual and spiritual life. For nearly four centuries to 581, China had been a collection of warring states, with a major division between north and south. The Tang Dynasty, which would last for nearly 300 years, imposed the structures of a reasonably efficient, economical and centralized state and brought stability to China. This stability made possible extensive economic development and the period of Tang imperial rule was a time of good government and booming wealth. It was also a window of opportunity, a time when the governing powers of China were confident and ready to develop new ways and new practices. There was remarkable tolerance in the new China of the seventh century, and in some trading cities there were communities of Jews, Moslems, Nestorian Christians, Armenian Christians, Manicheans and Hindus, all coexisting more or less peaceably under Chinese officialdom in their own quarters.[82]

During these 300 years, there was a golden age for world trade and economic development. It was not free trade as such, for there were numerous taxes and customs duties that merchants on the land and sea routes had to pay. There were also systems of licensing and trade secrets. For example, the Chinese kept close the secret of how silk was made. Eventually, perhaps through the agency of Nestorian Christians who brought the secret back to Baghdad, the world could confirm the previously disputed and seemingly far-fetched rumour that silk was made by worms! During this period, there was also a growth in scholarship and technology in the regions around China — even during the times referred to by European historians as the Dark Ages. Those same historians also wrote in detail about Christendom in Europe, without recognizing that at the end of the period, there were more Christians east of Damascus in greater Asia than west of Damascus in Europe.

This golden age of trade came to an end when growing nationalism in China resulted in the expulsion of foreigners. Trade recovered somewhat in later centuries, but was hit again by the coming of the Mongols. The broad Mongolian empire was itself a conduit for expanded trade between East and West, but their empire was not long-lived. The Mongol rulers of China were bloodily expelled in the fourteenth century and Kublai Khan's Xanadu became a ruin. In the seventeenth century, weak Chinese rulers asked for help from Manchurian warlords to protect the northern region of the empire and the Manchurians stayed to establish their own dynasty — the Qings.

European traders came to what they knew as 'Far Cathay' in increasing numbers from the eighteenth century. They gradually increased their commercial privileges, not least through the two so-called Opium Wars. From the mid-nineteenth century, imperial rule became weaker and the colonial powers drained political and economic power from the Celestial Empire. Not until the 20th century would the Chinese recover their full independence and once again open their domain to world trade and the exchange of ideas.

The Economy in China Under Communist Rule

The People's Republic of China was established in 1949. Under the initial application of Communist ideology, the government sought to control all aspects of social and economic activity. That meant that the manufacturing sector, including the small and nascent motor vehicle manufacturing industry, was run entirely by the state. Until reform in 1979, the economy was a 'poorly functioning command economy' that had a number of serious problems, including 'poor allocation of resources, a lack of incentives, irrational and arbitrary pricing, much waste of resources and a rigid and stultifying bureaucracy'.[83] Any one of these problems would have hampered the development of an efficient auto industry in China, but the package of problems acted to stifle the growth of China's auto industry, as will be noted in a later chapter.

In the command economy that was developed according to the dictates of Marxism-Leninism, very large industrial units were developed, and these were referred to as State-Owned Enterprises (SOEs), employing tens of thousands of employees, not always efficiently. Employees were not well-paid, but at least they had guaranteed lifetime employment, in employer-provided accommodation, usually with a rice ration as well. The State-Owned Enterprises have been the mainstay of the Chinese economy since the establishment of the current regime. Furthermore, they have been the main job providers in China. In 1995, for example, SOEs employed 45 per cent of total industrial workers and 70 per cent of the urban workforce.[84] In its early years, the rigidity of the Chinese Communist system, coupled with the guarantee of life's basic essentials, led to the system being termed the iron rice bowl system, implying that there were strict controls but at least everyone was provided with food and the necessities of life.

The SOEs served as production organs, whose production, resources and product distribution were all controlled by government departments, even down to details of day-to-day operations. For example, the central government gave orders to car factories. But how many cars they were to produce, to what design and for what purpose? Profit was a foreign concept, in more ways than one, and under this socialist system, private ownership of a car was out of the question. Those few limousines that were produced during the 1950s and 1960s were for the use of senior officials and party functionaries, as economic efforts were directed into other pursuits. One car did become symbolic of the era — the Red Flag limousine, first built in 1958. It was apparently based upon the design of the Mercedes-Benz 220,[85] and was built to convey a sense of solidity and pride. Like Henry Ford's early creation, it appears to have come only in black. Its hood emblem was a rippling red flag of chrome and coloured glass.

The government of the post-war period, under the leadership of Mao Zedong, Chairman of the Party, decided to direct activities into the development of heavy industry. This led to policy disasters that impeded the country's economic development. One such was Great Leap Forward of 1958, which was intended to create a modern industrialized economy virtually overnight but led instead to recession, and then a disastrous famine in 1959–61 which killed between 30 and 43 million people.[86]

Just a few years later, the Cultural Revolution hit the economy. The leadership called for a complete cultural transformation, which meant destroying everything old, including many cultural and social historical treasures. In a spasm of collective irresponsibility, mobs destroyed much of the physical and human fabric China needed to develop.

After the end of the Cultural Revolution, recognizing the disasters wrought on the Chinese economy, the country's economic managers made efforts to transform the centrally planned economy into a market economy conducted by efficient and profitable enterprises (while still retaining firm political control). The giant SOEs in their 1970s garb were not compatible with a free-enterprise economic system, so the government decided that economic reform had to entail reform of the SOEs, among other things. In 1978 (just two years after the pivotal event of 1976 — the death of Mao Zedong) the process of reform got under way, and in December of that year new leader Deng Xiaoping won widespread support for his reform plans at a gathering of the leadership referred to as the Third Plenum of the Chinese Communist Party's Eleventh Central Committee. This gathering proved to be a watershed for China's development.

Deng was able to carry the day despite extensive debates about ideology and orthodoxy because it was evident to those in power that China's economy had become stagnant and was under-performing, and that a comparative decline in economic power would be paralleled by a decline in China's influence in the worldwide political sphere. They recognized that access to world markets and a freeing up of domestic trade were necessary factors for development. In a masterly summing up that also saved face, they determined that 70 per cent of Mao Zedong's direction of China had been correct, but 30 per cent was wrong, and needed correction through a reform process. Deng and his comrades were able to bring about this radical change of direction because the country had become ordered and stable under their control, and the people were ready for reform and a market economy, provided it brought the consumer benefits that they had done without for so long. Deng could make the comment, 'It does not matter what the colour of the cat is, as long as it catches mice,' and survive. During the Cultural

Revolution, such a comment could well have been fatal. He also referred to the process of reform as 'groping for stones to cross the river', and it was indeed a slow process at first, with the leaders groping for their next steady foothold.

The reform process included access for foreign investment which had hitherto been banned. In 1979, there was a new law promulgated called The Law of the People's Republic of China on Chinese-Foreign Equity Joint Ventures, and it was enacted to enable foreigners to 'establish equity joint ventures together with Chinese companies ... on the principle of equity and mutual benefit'. However, the changes required that the Chinese partner have the controlling interest and at least a 51 per cent shareholding in the joint venture.

Despite the strict rules, foreign direct investment flooded into the country, but many of those first joint-venture partners got their fingers burnt. Although they were attracted by low labour costs and access to a huge market, there were systematic obstacles and in the 1980s at least labour productivity remained low. One study indicated that the productivity of employees in mainland China was as low as 60 per cent of the productivity of employees in Hong Kong.[87]

The Process of Economic Reform in China
The reform process in China occurred in three broad stages.[88]

1978–1984: Initial Reforms and Decentralization
During the late 1970s and early '80s, trade in East Asia and South-East Asia was expanding rapidly, through the development of labour-intensive manufacturing in the newly industrialized economies, and especially in the so-called Tiger economies of the region (Hong Kong, Taiwan, Korea and Singapore). China was able to take advantage of this opportunity. Three of these four Tiger economies were part-peopled by the Chinese Diaspora. That diaspora included many merchants and traders who had fled China on the accession of the Communists. When their homeland was reopened to foreign trade, they were prepared to take advantage of relationships and opportunities to reinvest their accumulated trading profits on the Chinese mainland. What was required was a confidence-

boosting policy that would encourage foreign direct investment and the injection of modern expertise and technology along with foreign capital. The beginnings of the reform policy provided such confidence, because the Communist government promised that China was re-orientating its economy to world trade and would deliver on its promises.

The Chinese economy expanded rapidly during this period, even more than was expected. For example, the Sixth Five-Year Plan (1981–85) set a target of a 4 per cent annual growth in gross industrial output, but the actual growth achieved was 12.6 per cent.[89]

As a central plank of the policies of this first stage of reform, decentralization of management was brought in. There was also wide-ranging decentralization in the agricultural sector (which, for example, allowed peasant farmers to grow and sell their own produce). The reform program that was set in motion was not just a top-down directive that came from on high. There was a stunning bottom-up aspect to the reforms. The 26,000 rural collectives that had been established by the Communists in the years just after 1949 were broken up by their peasant members and 'decollectivized' in barely three years. This meant that in place of the agricultural collectives, there was a proliferation of village-based and household-based enterprises that operated under private ownership. These new enterprises depended upon the operation of local markets for their survival, and the strictures of orthodox Marxist theory had to be substantially modified to allow for the growth of such markets.

In the manufacturing sector, still dominated by the SOEs, the initial change wrought by the decentralization policy was to increase the operational autonomy of senior levels of enterprise management. They were allowed to decide the allocation of their profits and had limited powers to determine production levels. Overall administrative control of most SOEs was decentralized to the technocrats in local government authorities. However, product prices were still set by central government, so in the manufacturing sector there was not yet a free market economy during this period.[90] The next step in the reform process would take this devolution of responsibility one step further.

1984–1992: Reforms of Management in Industry

The initial reforms set in place from 1978 were experimental to a degree. The government was not following a hard and fast plan, but was feeling its way in what was a new economic environment for the country. In the late 1980s, the reform process entered a second stage when there were continual amendments to the reform plans. At the Communist Party Congress of 1987, General Secretary Zhao Ziyang tried to reconcile the freeing up of the economy while maintaining a Communist government by stating that China was a developing country in the 'primary stage of socialism'. The government ensured that it kept a tight control by spelling out what state enterprises were expected to do, could do and could not do. Basically, management in the industrial sector was made responsible for the performance of their enterprises in a way that they had never been during the years of strict Marxist rule. The changes brought in were packaged in a system called the Contract Management Responsibility System (CMRS). The motivation for these changes was a drive for greater efficiency.[91]

Under the CMRS system, all SOEs signed up to individually negotiated contracts with the state organizations that exercised primary supervision over the enterprise. The contract specified the exact amount of revenue that should be turned over to the state. In effect this was a taxation regime based on gross revenue, not net profit. This new institutional arrangement brought in aspects of governance that would be recognized in the West, and to some extent separated the owners from the managers, but in reality, local governments still interfered in the operational decisions of the SOEs that came under their purview. There was a lot of jockeying for power and influence, and the dictates of a strong central government did not always carry the day. One commentator wrote, with a reference to an American auto manufacturer which has now become ironic: 'Powerful provincial leaders ... insist that the state-subsidized firms in their regions not be abandoned as bankrupt but instead be turned into winners, as the United States supposedly did with Chrysler Motors.'[92]

The reforms over these years showed initial promise, and industries such as clothing and textiles expanded into Western markets, despite protectionist measures such as tariffs and quotas. The growing trade between China and the rest of the world, particularly through its flooding of Western markets with goods that were cheap but of acceptable quality, was already provoking tension in the overseas markets when internal Chinese politics intervened. The opening of markets was taken by some to mean that there would also be an opening of political debate and the government decided to crack down on any outbreak of social dissent, for fear that the debates could get out of control and threaten the Communist Party's absolute hold on power. This crackdown occurred not only in the Tien An Men Square in Beijing, but in other centres around the country during a few chaotic weeks in 1989. There could have been serious consequences for China's economic development, as some Western investors withdrew, but in the period immediately after the Tien An Men Square clampdown, other countries in East and South-East Asia were experiencing fair economic winds and sought to expand their trade with China. There were new bilateral agreements with Korea and Taiwan.

In 1992, Deng Xiaoping, by then very elderly and revered by ordinary Chinese who had seen their lives and futures improved by the reforms he had initiated, toured the country, calling for new efforts directed to economic development.

I stood near the back of a huge and enthusiastic crowd in Wuhan, when Deng made a break on that whistle-stop tour and spoke briefly to the people gathered to hear him. I could not help comparing the excitement and the response of the crowd to that of the audience at a Beatles concert I had attended in 1964.

1993 – Present: Modern Enterprises System
In 1993, riding a wave of popular support partly inspired by Deng's tour, the Third Plenum of the Fourteenth Communist Party Congress endorsed the creation of a modern enterprises system, with provision for public shareholding and accountability to stock markets. With this continued freeing up of the economic system, foreign investment increased and China's growth expanded even more rapidly.

China has economic advantages in that it has large domestic markets, a large supply of labour well-suited for labour-intensive industries, and good natural resources. In the early years of Communist rule at least, it lacked a flow of investment capital (even though it has a high level of domestic capital formation through people's savings, the low wages mandated from the 1950s meant that these savings were comparatively low in absolute values when listed in world rankings).[93] Through the isolation brought about by the politics of the Cold War, and up to the 1980s, the country also lacked access to modern technology. It is the thesis of this book that when the inflow of capital and technology addresses the shortfalls in the car industry, then the other economic advantages of China's labourforce and markets will ensure its dominance in a range of global markets — all other things being equal and presuming there is no new round of impediments to global trade.

Under the Modern Enterprises System various forms of ownership and a detailed framework of corporate governance were introduced to SOEs. With the introduction of market competition to the state sector, however, Chinese SOEs declined in performance and productivity. The contribution of SOEs to total gross industrial output value between 1978 and 1995 fell from 78 per cent to 33 per cent.[94] By 1996, half of Chinese SOEs reported deficits, although perhaps a further third of them actually made losses even though they reported profits.

Despite the fall in official performance of SOEs, at the Fifteenth Communist Party Congress in 1997, then President Jiang Zemin reaffirmed the leading role of SOEs as one of the pillars of China's national economy and called for ensuring and promoting the reform of SOEs by law, although he recognized the economic problems posed by inefficiencies in their management and the fact that reforming so many very big enterprises would be very difficult. Consequently, the Party Congress extended the tenets of the reform process to medium and large SOEs, as well as transforming a number of SOEs into limited liability companies under Chinese Company Law. This new system was soon put under trial when a financial crisis struck Asia in 1997/98, but the impact of the crisis on the Chinese economy was limited. As China's currency, the yuan, was strictly controlled and not freely traded on world financial markets, it formed a buffer between China and the financial stresses affecting other states of East and South-East Asia. However, it was clear that there were storms on the other side of the wall, and since 1998 the Chinese government has encouraged large corporations to take actions that lead to greater efficiencies and tend to weed out the poorer performers.

Summarizing the Reform Process — the Ongoing Problem of the SOEs

The introduction of Deng's reforms and their continuation under later leaders brought about a transformation in the economy and growth took off. Over the period 1978 to 2005, China's gross domestic product has generally grown at a phenomenally high rate of around 8.0 per cent a year, achieving double-digit growth for sustained periods. This is a very high rate of growth in historical and world terms, and should be considered against the rate of population growth. Nevertheless, recalculating GDP on a per capita basis, this still works out as an average growth rate of 6.6 per cent per capita income.

During this period of intense and far-reaching change, the performance of reforming State-Owned Enterprises did not keep pace with the efficiencies wrought in the private sector of the economy, as had been hoped. The early SOE reforms from the 1980s to the early 1990s delivered generally unsatisfactory results. The impetus of reform was mainly focused on government-enterprise relations and enterprise management, rather than responding to open market conditions. There were a number of problems encountered by the reform process of SOEs during this period. The problems were those which commonly affect publicly run organizations and included excessive government intervention, lack of incentive and motivation mechanisms, excessive government investment in the wrong areas for political motives, and heavy employment redundancy.

One result of the reforms of laws and policies related to SOEs meant that they could be bankrupted — a practice hitherto not even imagined in China. The first SOE to go bankrupt was the Shenyang Explosion-Proof Equipment factory, which was bankrupted then its employees laid off and the remaining assets sold at auction to a Shanghai company in 1986. It was the first SOE to be bankrupted in China since 1949.[95]

The *China Statistical Yearbooks* of 1995 and 1998 revealed the extent of the financial losses and profits incurred by SOEs between 1978 and 1998. In 1978, the profits earned by SOEs totalled 50.88 billion yuan. These increased to 89.19 billion yuan in 1988, but then took a sharp fall to 38.81 billion yuan in 1990 as they were exposed to more competitive trading conditions. Another significant statistic concerned the total number of loss-making SOEs. Such enterprises incurring financial losses increased from 1988 to 1997, peaking in 1995, when a total of 29,668 SOEs made financial losses.[96] The overall production of the SOEs measured by output value increased into the new millennium. For example, from 2001 to 2002, the increase was around 12 per cent.[97] On the other hand, the SOEs were voracious consumers of industrial input, and various input measures, such as investment in fixed assets, showed disproportionate consumption. For example, investment in fixed assets in 2001 was more than 3,000 billion yuan and rose by 17 per cent in 2002.

One analyst has stated that the continuing dominance of SOEs in the Chinese economy is a serious hindrance on development. They soak up more than their share of investment capital, including foreign direct investment (FDI), and they do not permit the most efficient use of entrepreneurial talent. Also, just as there is not a level playing field in the global economy, so there is not one even within China itself, for the SOEs remain favoured players.[98] Despite their history of inefficiencies, which cannot be remedied overnight — and just as huge ocean liners cannot change course like a sports car — SOEs will continue to play a dominant role in some heavy industries and service sectors in the short to medium term.

In the late 1990s, the Chinese government undertook a number of strategies to drive the economy forward and encourage FDI, for example through the creation of Special Economic Zones, where foreign investors were given tax and other advantages to establish new businesses there. New economic zones were developed during the reform process. There were five Special Economic Zones (Shenzen, Zhuhai, Shantou, Xiamen and Hainan) and fourteen other cities where there was increased freedom of markets, as well as increased government investment in the central and western areas of China.

There was also an increase in mergers and restructuring. According to an enterprise survey carried out in nineteen of China's provinces, 75 per cent of small and medium SOEs had been subject to ownership changes by the end of 1999. Another survey, which covered 520 large SOEs, indicated that 70 per cent of SOEs had been transformed to corporations with a multi-owner system by the end of 1999.[99] By 2007, the majority of SOEs had become publicly listed companies or joint ventures with share registers made up of state and private shareholdings (although usually the controlling share was still held by the state). These enterprises which have undergone structural reform are generally termed Restructured SOEs. The performance of these restructured SOEs as well as the performance of privately owned small to medium enterprises (SMEs) forms the backdrop to the development of the domestic car industry and China's overall economic performance.

The experience of SMEs under the reform processes has been different from that of the SOEs. Since China's opening-up drive in the early 1980s, the private sector of the economy was formally encouraged to develop and was no longer just a complement to the state-owned economy, but in the revised Marxist ideology was considered to be an important constituent of the socialist market economy. However, the Chinese business milieu was constructed by the Chinese Communist Party on the building blocks of the centrally planned economy of the 1950s and there were lingering impediments and attitudes that remained from the pre-reform era. Private enterprises were discriminated against by government and state-monopolized banks in entering certain fields and obtaining finance. Also, many private enterprises were disadvantaged by being subject to double taxation and over-charged for fees and licences by local governments.[100] Private enterprises were also prohibited from entering certain sectors of the economy.

Despite some continuing disadvantage, the number of SMEs has grown and they have assumed an important role in the Chinese economy. In 2002, there were more than 2.7 million private enterprises in China (the great majority of them SMEs), and they accounted for 60 per cent of the country's total gross domestic production. They played a very important role in China's economic transformation, not only because they absorbed more than half of the laid-off workers from the large State-Owned Enterprises, but also because they improved the overall efficiency of the economy and stimulated a broad change in the attitude toward competition, even though hard-liners opposed this in some quarters.

The growth rate of private enterprises has exceeded State-Owned Enterprises in many aspects, such as employment, registered capital, tax revenue, gross value of industrial output and retail sales.[101] Entry to the WTO affected the development of the emerging domestic private economy in China largely due to the WTO requirement of setting up-market-compatible institutions.[102] By 2006, however, China's private enterprises, including SMEs, faced pronounced challenges and problems due to growing pains (i.e., a growing shortage of skilled workers and a 'brain drain') and domestic discrimination. The problems included relatively poor management practices, management constraints on SMEs, and labourforce issues such as the training and retaining of skilled employees (which is linked with motivation and job satisfaction strategies). Also, the unhealthy presence of *guanxi* and the credit crisis of 2002/03 have contributed to an unfavourable operational environment and problems that still have to be completely overcome. (The concept of *guanxi* will be discussed in later sections. The word is not easy to translate, but refers to networking and relationship-building.) This situation will act as a brake on the expansion of smaller enterprises associated with the motor vehicle industry and will be considered in a later chapter considering the impediments to the development of China's auto industry.

China's accession to the World Trade Organization in 2001 was a fillip to the economy, although it brought requirements for further reform in the regulatory and financial environment. Foreign direct investment in China, already substantial, experienced another boom in the years 2003 and 2004, and SOEs benefited, as did manufacturers,[103] although in 2004 the government stepped in to restrict the level of investment in SOEs involved in heavy industry. There remains a need for development in the banking, insurance and legal infrastructure to take advantage of all the opportunities offered by WTO membership (chapter 6 considers some of these infrastructure issues as they relate to the car industry). In 2007, it is likely that the full benefits of WTO membership have still not accrued to China, and nor has world trade felt the full impact of increased access to its markets, because transitional arrangements are still in place, though tailing off.

There are those who see no threat from the burgeoning Chinese economic growth. One of these is US Commerce Secretary Carlos Gutierrez, who has been reported as saying: 'China has built its economy on the basis of manufacturing of commodity-type products. ... What we have seen in the US is that our new jobs that are being created are in the area of higher value manufacturing, differentiation of products, higher technology, and in many cases new services.'[104] The Commerce Secretary felt that China would take a big share of the world's low-tech manufacturing while the United States and other Western countries would concentrate on high value-added products with higher technology. However, it may be that Mr Gutierrez was too optimistic about the abilities of United States workers to retrain and maintain a competitive edge — and that he was underestimating the abilities of the increasingly well-trained and technologically savvy workforce in China.

The economic reforms discussed above form the background to the development of China's motor vehicle manufacturing industry in the modern era. Through these reforms, China's economic managers have significantly improved the performance of the national economy and increased the living conditions of most Chinese, especially in the major urban centres and along the eastern seaboard.[105] Between 1980 and 2000, the total volume of China's international trade has multiplied more than ten-fold, with exports rising from US$20 billion to US$250 billion.[106] The volume of goods and services produced in the country has increased by a multiple of six. China has had an aggressive impact upon world manufacturing markets (and indeed continues to have). There is no historical evidence that China's economic managers will not continue to seek dominant, even controlling, positions in world markets.

Pride in a nation's achievements is closely linked to the feel-good factor that encourages business people to take risks and seek new opportunities in the belief that fate (or maybe luck) is on their side. One author encapsulates the feelings of optimism and pride that are abroad in China:

> A virtually natural arrogance arises from China's great economic achievement in the post-Mao era, the fastest economic growth over two decades, ever, anywhere on the planet. ... China's extraordinary achievement fosters a feeling that nothing can or should keep the twenty-first century from being China's century. The popular feeling is that it is about time that China again rise to the top of the heap.[107]

The same writer then notes that there was a similar feeling in Japan in the early 1990s, and beliefs that Japan would be the leader in the 21st century. Those beliefs were undermined by the extended financial crisis that hit Japan for much of the mid to late 1990s.

Another economist has summed up the profound nature of the changes to China's economy over this time:

> The Chinese reform era is not only a transition from socialist central planning, as reform may seem to be in Russia or Poland. The change is deeper than that. The last quarter century is a time when China has linked itself productively and comfortably to the modern, global economy and society that began to force revolutionary change in all aspects of life in the North Atlantic two centuries ago.[108]

Private car ownership in China has also been transformed in the last ten years or so. In the early stages of reform, as joint ventures with US and European manufacturers (such as the Beijing Jeep) were expanded, most of the production was sold to government authorities, SOEs or corporations. However, from 1992, as economic reforms took hold, and individuals and small enterprises grew richer, private ownership of cars increased, albeit from a very low base of just over a million cars at that time. Over the years 1996 to 2000, private car ownership grew by around 25 per cent each year. By 2002, as per capita income increased, the number of cars owned privately passed the 10 million mark and continued to grow at an even faster rate — increasing by nearly 70 per cent in 2003, for example. However, in the author's view, the question of how many cars can be absorbed by the Chinese domestic market is still unresolved. Of course, car ownership is certainly seen as highly desirable.

In China in 2007, car ownership has become a status symbol. The sign of a successful person, once measured by possession of such consumer goods as a mobile phone, is now more likely to be the ownership of a car. This is despite the high capital cost and high ongoing expenses such as taxes and parking fees. Indeed, some taxes are being imposed to try and limit the fast spread of private car ownership in cities whose bounds are groaning under the strain of high growth rates. In many cities, buyers of new apartments may pay almost as much for private parking spaces in the apartment complex. The price of petrol, while appearing cheap to Western observers, is comparatively high in terms of Chinese incomes. In addition, the tolls for intercity and intracity expressways are a significant cost of travel.

There appears to be an unusual market situation, linked to a population demographic, that may only last another ten or fifteen years. The idea of car ownership appeals across the generations, but whereas those aged 40 or more who are buying cars have the financial means to do so, those in their thirties or younger are less likely to be able to afford even 60,000 yuan for one of the smaller cars — for the cost of such a car would be more than a year's wage, or even two years' wages, for those on what is a good wage by Chinese standards. The people aged 28 and under, and therefore born after 1978, were brought up in the era of the One-Child Policy. During the years when Mao Zedong was Chairman, a high rate of population growth was encouraged so that the country could build up its human resources and even 'out-breed' its Cold War adversaries even if it could not oppose them militarily. One of Mao's sayings was, 'The more people we are, the stronger we are.'

Control of the population growth was one of the policy changes initiated by Deng Xiaoping. The government took steps to limit the population lest it outstrip resources, one consequence of which has been that the only child of adoring parents has been given whatever he or she wants — hence the description of a generation as the 'Little Emperors' and the 'Little Empresses'. By 2000, the oldest of that generation were of car-owning age, and naturally turned to their parents for assistance in buying one. The parents, who had been brought up in more frugal times, and had saved a considerable amount of their income (often because there were limited consumption goods to spend it on), were in a position to lend or give their offspring money to buy a car. The offspring tend to have a higher income than their parents and can afford the running costs, but do not have the capital cost saved.

This demographic situation may last until the parents hit 60 or so and look to retire and use their funds for a retirement apartment. Hence, this unusual demographic window that encourages the growth of the domestic car market in China, whereby younger people who cannot afford to buy a car find easy funds from family sources, will last until around 2010 to 2015.

This population characteristic may be one of the factors that act to reduce the current high rate of growth of car sales within China. Such a reduction in demand (due to many other factors or course, besides this demographic curiosity) will be significant for world markets, because if China's car manufacturers want to maintain a high rate of revenue growth, they will have to turn to increased exports to meet a shortfall in domestic demand. The consequences of the One-Child Policy are also flowing through the economy in other aspects. The policy has proven to be a major influence on the supply of labour also.

Around nine out of every ten of the cars sold in China are the products of joint ventures, reflecting the fact that the car is a status symbol and that foreign-designed cars have more appeal than a domestic design. The growth of the joint ventures may result in a situation where the foreign partner of the joint venture sells more cars in China than elsewhere and hence the Chinese market becomes the most crucial part of their operation, not unlike a case of the tail wagging the dog — but over time the tail gets smaller and the dog gets bigger! This is not an unlikely scenario. One of the bigger joint-venture partners, Volkswagen, sells more cars in China than in Germany, and has done so since 2003. The logical consequence is that more and more cars will be designed to suit Chinese tastes and needs and, due to the harsh taskmaster of scale, the rest of the world will have to accept these. The 'world car', or the 'global car' — perhaps something like the Ford Focus — will have to be acceptable in the long term to the Chinese consumer.

There is one more factor to be considered in this short summary and background to economic development and the Chinese car industry. Before it entered the World Trade Organization in December 2001,

China's car manufacturers were protected by tariffs. Larger cars (i.e., with an engine capacity over three litres) were protected from imports by a tariff of no less than 80 per cent, and smaller vehicles benefited from a tariff of 70 per cent. After WTO accession, these tariffs were not abolished, but only reduced to 50.7 per cent and 43.8 per cent respectively. By 2006, these tariffs were further reduced to 25 per cent and 10 per cent. So the domestic car industry in China has developed behind quite high tariff walls and continues to do so.

There is a further issue related to tariff protection of China's domestic car market. Imported car parts should, under Chinese law, attract a 10 per cent tariff, but cars with more than 60 per cent foreign-made components attract the 25 per cent duty. This actively discriminates against parts kits brought into the country for assembly in Chinese factories. The result is that there is an imbalance of trade in car components. The Chinese car component market increased 17 per cent in 2005, but US exports of car components to China went up only 6.5 per cent. In 2006, the United States, as well as the European Union, made a formal complaint to the World Trade Organization that China was taking measures to prevent the importation of foreign-made car components that competed directly with its own manufacturers. In February 2007, the United States made a further complaint that China was still subsidizing its own businesses, discriminating against imports and interpreting its basic tax laws in a way that was unfair to foreign competitors. In commenting on the matter, US Trade Representative Susan Schwab expressed the problem in its basic terms: 'We are seeking to level the playing field to allow US manufacturers to compete fairly with Chinese firms.'[109]

These complaints may take many months to adjudicate.

2006 — Issues in the Chinese Economy

In August 2006, a conference called China Update 2006 was held at the Australian National University. At the conference, keynote speakers expressed their opinions that China's economy was at a turning point, mainly because of changing supply/demand factors relating to the labourforce.[110] Several of the speakers foresaw rising real wages and living standards, continuing urbanization and a seismic shift to more capital-intensive production. Among the forces underpinning this turning point was a slowdown in the supply of labour as the One-Child Policy, in existence for a generation or more, affected population demographics, especially new entrants to the workforce. At this turning point of economic development, growth rates of around 10 per cent per year were still considered feasible provided there were increases of productivity linked to rising real wages.

Wages appeared likely to rise due to these supply/demand factors. In 1995, the average annual manufacturing wage in China was equivalent to somewhere between 2 per cent and 4 per cent of the average annual manufacturing wage in industrialized economies. By 2002, it had risen, but was still between 4 per cent to 8 per cent of the equivalent wage in industrialized economies. From 1995 to 2002, the average annual growth in manufacturing wages in China had risen 11.6 per cent a year, compared to an average annual growth of 3.1 per cent and 4.3 per cent in manufacturing wages in the United States and the United Kingdom. So China's real wages in the manufacturing sector have been rising, but the gap remains a yawning gulf. The productivity of manufacturing labour in China had also increased over the period. Interestingly, the equivalent manufacturing wage in India in 1995 was 70 per cent of the Chinese rate.[111]

However, at this turning point, from the point of view of the rest of the world, there were two problem areas — the need to address the continuing lop-sided valuation of the yuan against the United States dollar, and the need to increase domestic demand.

The value of the yuan had been fixed to that of the United States dollar for many years. China's Communist rulers adopted strict rules for foreign trade and currency exchange in the 1960s, for they were aware of the 'chaos in the management of foreign exchange' that had more than once threatened China's well-being.[112] From the very first phase of the reforms starting in 1978, they resolved that there would be an inflexible link to the United States dollar and that this somewhat simplistic but effective solution would avoid foreign exchange problems.

When, under pressure from its trading partners, the Chinese government agreed to allow the currency to float, they hedged their agreement. The exchange rate for the yuan against major Western currencies was not allowed to be freely floating, but could only move within a limited range. The result was not a float at all, but instead a 'managed rate' of exchange. The yuan moved within this limited range to be revalued at no more than 1.8 per cent against the US dollar over a twelve-month period, and the rate of exchange remained around 8 yuan to 1 US dollar in 2006. A rough and probably controversial rule of thumb can be used to calculate what the yuan should be valued at, if there was a level playing field in the world's markets.

The calculation works this way. Auto workers in China are paid around US$60–80 for a full-week's work at some of the modern facilities that are the equivalent of Western operations, for example at the Ford factories in Chongqing. Auto workers in the West who do virtually the same work may receive US$800 a week — ten times as much as their counterparts in China. On this basis, if the discrepancy is a factor of ten, the yuan should be revalued by a factor of ten (rather than the 1.8 per cent permitted by the Chinese government). Instead of the rate of 8 yuan to the dollar as at July 2006, a fair rate may be around 0.8 yuan to the dollar.[113] The difference can be highlighted, with the rate for the Australian dollar added:

Existing controlled rate of exchange:
    around 8 yuan to the US dollar
    around 6 yuan to the AUS dollar
A realistic rate based on comparative auto workers' pay:
    around 0.8 yuan to the US dollar
    around 1 yuan to the AUS dollar

Rough and ready as this calculation may be, it does indicate the scale of the problem and is one of the reasons why Western workers simply cannot compete against their Chinese counterparts.

There is an economic concept called Purchasing Power Parity (PPP), which essentially compares relative wealth of countries through the differences in purchasing power between those countries. For example, the different price of a Big Mac in McDonald's restaurants around the world is accounted for by differences in the currency exchange rates. The processes of arbitrage should ensure that the difference in the price of a Big Mac between countries should be about the same, in terms of the purchasing power of currencies. Any anomalies are put down to what is called friction. The cousin of PPP, Relative Purchasing Power Parity, suggests that differences in the exchange rate over time can be explained by differences in inflation rates between countries over time. Both theories float quite well and keep the water out — unless someone acts to spring a leak! When a currency is not freely floating to find its own level against other international currencies, then the concept of PPP cannot fairly be applied. The theory may still work, but the heavy hand of political interference in relation to the valuation of the domestic currency means that the practice gives a different result from the theory.

The issue of the relative valuation of the yuan raised passions during 2005 in the legislative chambers of the United States, particularly the Senate, where there were calls to impose a 27.5 per cent tariff on China's manufactured imports into the US unless the yuan was revalued to a greater extent than the limits allowed by government. There were strong feelings that the valuation of the yuan as determined by the government in Beijing contributed to the growing trade surplus China had with the West, due to the advantages its producers received from the under valuation.[114]

The issue of increasing domestic demand was more complex. Later in this book, it will be argued that there are significant short-term constraints on increasing domestic demand, particularly for the private use of motor vehicles, because there are numerous elements of infrastructure that cannot be conjured up overnight. Put simply, demand cannot increase as much as supply. This means that the excess production will be available for export, and although there will be some increases in real wages, and some further movement in the yuan, they will not be enough to offset the enormous comparative advantage China enjoys.

In relation to 2006 being a turning point, there were two events that might have appeared to be relatively minor in the context of the world's trade, but were very significant nevertheless. The first event concerned the first Chinese-made car to enter a Western market. In that year, one of the largest Chinese car manufacturers, First Automotive Works, launched the first Chinese-made car to be marketed in the United

States. The car was micro-sized, and is called the ZX40. It is electrically powered, and the design is based on the Daihatsu Move. It is the first Chinese-made car, but others are on their way, notably the Chery QQ, a small sedan that is comparable in styling and finish to Western cars (and in fact is the subject of legal action by GM, who claim that the design breaches their intellectual property; this action will be discussed later in this book). The Chinese joint-venture car makers who have been exporting their products (mainly components) to the West plan to expand further. For example, Honda has plans to export whole cars to Europe and DaimlerChrysler has plans to develop a Chinese-designed car for export as a Dodge.

The second event of 2006 that marked the year as a turning point for the auto industry in China was the fact that wholly Chinese-owned auto makers took the largest share of the new vehicle market in China. Wholly owned Chinese auto makers captured 28.7 per cent of the market in January of 2006, the first time since the entry of foreign investors and joint ventures that Chinese brands have taken a leading position in the market — ahead of brands from Japan (27.8 per cent), Europe (19 per cent), the United States (14 per cent) and South Korea (10.3 per cent).[115] These figures covered all automobiles, including cars, trucks and buses, etc. The statistics for cars alone revealed that in 2006, joint ventures made up the lion's share (over 90 per cent) of the new car market.

Overall, by 2007, the world's economies seem to have reached one more turning point, a turning point hinged upon geopolitical events and the pinch upon resources as new economies challenge the old. The world economic situation in late 2006 was graphically presented in a headline in a UK newspaper: 'Balance of power ebbs away from the US'.[116] The article went on to summarize how the world's marketplaces were in a state of transition: 'The world economy has put in its fastest growth spurt for decades over the past three years, and is still bowling along at a healthy clip this year, despite a tripling of oil prices since early 2004. China and India continue to grow at breakneck speed.'

What will the future hold for the world's economy? Clearly, from 2007, China's expansion will continue. The likelihood is that its economy will become the world's largest within a generation, having recently supplanted the position of the United Kingdom to take fourth place, and surely soon it will overtake Germany to be the third largest world economy after the United States and Japan. There have been projections that, by 2020, China's economy will be on a par with that of the United States, and it will have the second largest consumer market and the largest technology sector in the world.[117] By 2050, it is likely that China's economy will be by far the world's largest, probably with that of India in second place and the United States a more distant third.

On the streets of China — cycles...

... and more cycles

A modern highway in Wuhan in 1994
few cars (but heavy pollution nevertheless)

The Beijing Jeep
photographed at Number One Bathing Beach, Qingdao, 2006

Motorcycles from China in 2006
the Jianshe

An outmoded but contemporary Chinese-designed vehicle, unlikely to
appeal in the West — a three-wheeler from Jinan Industries

Empty four-lane highways -
the expressway between Nanjing and Yangzhou 1993

Semi-motorcycles and common workhorses
waiting for business, 2006

Hard working vehicles – the ubiquitous small tractor and trailer
and a Liberation truck in the background

Tractor in festive mood – Lhasa 2004

Luxury Cars in China - a Lincoln dressed for a wedding

The Chinese Buick (already gift-wrapped?)

No room for parking - Compound One

No room for parking - Compound Two

Good features and attractive as an economical small car made by Geely

What will we be driving in the West in 2015?
Must we accept other cultural preferences?

Unlikely to appeal in the West —a three-wheeled Chang Jiang light truck

Finding room to park —a three-wheeler four-door at the front door
(and it does not take up much more space than a bicycle)

The SAIC Volkswagen —the styling is becoming outdated, but still a good basic car

A symptom of the feel-good factor — everyone likes to have their own transport

A Chinese suburban street in the early 1990s
— very little traffic, other than pedestrians

Downtown Chengdu

Still horse-drawn vehicles – Kunming 2005

No room to park – Chengdu

9 Origins and Growth of the Chinese Motor Vehicle Industry

A Snapshot

In the United States, the auto industry has historically been dominated by three very large manufacturers, but in China no fewer than ten very large auto-making companies account for around 80 per cent of the country's automobile production. No one plant is so big that it dominates the market. The three largest are the First Automotive Works Corporation (FAW), Shanghai Automotive Industry Corporation and Dong Feng Motor Corporation. In 2003, the output of FAW Group and Shanghai Automotive was around 800,000 vehicles each and Dong Feng produced about 500,000. The output of each of the other seven companies ranged from 100,000 to 400,000 vehicles. All have high growth rates, and the fastest growing companies of the ten are Guangzhou Automobile Industry Group Co. Ltd, Beijing Automotive Industry Corporation and SAIC Chery Automobile. In 2006, Shanghai Automotive overtook China's oldest car maker, FAW Group Corporation, to become the country's largest motor vehicle manufacturer.

China may have an advantage in having a more diversified market with more players than the US, because it means that the market is more dynamic and faster to react to changes. The three major US car makers are behemoths, less nimble than the smaller Chinese manufacturers. In the past, some Chinese manufacturers have enjoyed higher profit margins than Western manufacturers, but that situation is changing, due partly to higher production capacity and domestic demand that is growing more slowly than capacity increase. There was a dip in sales in 2004 that squeezed margins throughout that year and into 2005, and led to losses for some makers, as will be detailed later in this chapter.

The country's top ten car factories in terms of sales were Shanghai Volkswagen, FAW Volkswagen, Guangzhou Honda, Shanghai GM, Beijing Hyundai, FAW Charade, Chang'an Suzuki, Zhejiang Geely, Dong Feng Peugeot Citroen and Anhui Chery. The three most popular brands in terms of sales were Jetta, Santana and Charade. Anhui Chery and Zhejiang Geely accounted for over 60 per cent of cars exported from China in 2005. Chery exported mainly to Iran, Malaysia and Egypt, and Geely to Middle Eastern countries and Africa.

Table 9.1: Motor Vehicle Production in China (Selected Years)

Year	Units produced (millions)	Percentage increase on 2002
2005	5.7	78.1
2004	5.0	56.2
2003	4.4	37.5
2002	3.2	
2001	3.0	
1996	1.5	
1991	0.7	

Note that in 2005, of the 5.7 million vehicles produced in that year there were sales of 5.8 million vehicles, roughly half of which were cars, which means that the shortfall between domestic production and sales must be met by imports (and of course if some domestic production is exported, then there must also be additional imports to offset this).

Using these statistics as a starting point, it is possible to forecast motor vehicle production, one of the important sources of supply. The forecast production of motor vehicles has two scenarios, one based on an average 17 per cent increase each year (based on the rate of growth in 2005/06) and the other a 14 per cent average increase each year (a conservative official estimate). If projected sales figures for the larger car makers for the second half of 2006 are met, then the year on year increase will in fact be 19 per cent.

Table 9.2: Motor Vehicle Production Forecasts — Two Scenarios

Scenario 1: Production increases by an average of 14 per cent per year

Year	Units produced	
2010	11.3 million	
2009	10.0 million	
2008	8.7 million	
2007	7.6 million	
2006	6.7 million	(17 per cent increase over 2005)

Scenario 2: Production increases by an average of 17 per cent per year

Year	Units produced	
2010	12.5 million	
2009	10.7 million	
2008	9.2 million	
2007	7.8 million	
2006	6.7 million	(17 per cent increase over 2005)

Hence the forecast figures for China's motor vehicle production in 2010 estimate a total production of somewhere between 11 million and 12 million vehicles. Note that this scenario does not take into account changes to the level of imports, the other major source of motor vehicle supply. Nor does it take into account movements in the levels of inventory from one year to the next, so admittedly, it is a very simple model — but the increases in production and supply of motor vehicles are so large that the broad conclusion is valid.

A Short History of China's Car Industry

China's car industry was started by the big American car makers — which looks ironic, given current developments and the global challenge that the Chinese are about to throw down to the Americans.

The genesis of the industry was at the very beginning of the 20th century. A turning point in China's history was what was called in the West the Boxer Uprising, and in China the incidents surrounding the Society of the Fists of Harmonious Righteousness. After the skirmishing ceased in 1901, there was a new influx of foreigners from Europe and the United States, some arriving as missionaries and others ready to do business and make their fortunes. Some of them brought motor vehicles, although these first cars suffered severely on China's roads. It was probable that there were early attempts to develop cars and trucks in China, and equally probable that few prototypes advanced to quantity production. Among the problems were the servicing of the vehicles and, more importantly, the lack of a reliable fuel supply network. Travellers had to organize their own fuel supplies in depots along their planned itinerary.

The revolution against imperial rule in 1912 and then the First World War disrupted orderly economic development, and prevented the growth of large manufacturing corporations. Germany lost its colonies in the north to Japan, which occupied much of the country. Of the other main colonial powers, the UK and France had their financial problems, and Russia was in the throes of a civil war. The United States was, however, flexing its economic muscle and preparing to take a larger share of world trade.

The US had never taken up formal possessions in China in the way the other colonialists had, but there were many American missionaries and business people spread over the country. The Americans may be credited with taking the first practical steps towards building the Chinese car industry, mainly through the efforts of Ford (then the biggest car maker in the world, making around one half of all the world's cars in 1926) and General Motors, its main rival. This pattern of development, of the industry being put on a firm footing in the 1910s and 1920s by the efforts of Ford and GM, is similar to the pattern of development in Australia and Japan, and of course many other countries.

Henry Ford had exported his robust and practical Model T to China soon after he commenced large-scale manufacture. The first Fords were trundling along China's cobbled roads in 1913. There were Ford cars, Ford trucks and also Ford tractors. Ford saw the potential of the Chinese market, and he also saw the possibilities of establishing China-based plants. In 1920, he brought a number of young Chinese men to work in and study at Ford's manufacturing plant in Detroit. By 1923, there were about 100 Chinese in Ford's workforce.

GM entered China slightly later, in 1925. Rather than seeking to develop a local industry, the strategy of GM's new head, Alfred P.

Sloane, was to import fully assembled vehicles to win a share of China's market. GM chose to sell Buicks, as being the car best suited for Chinese conditions, and was moderately successful at this, importing and selling around 100,000 cars in ten years by the time the international situation once again deteriorated and the war between China and Japan flared. The other substantial foreign player in the Chinese car market during this early period was German. In the late 1930s, German heavy industry was expanding, largely due to the demands of rearmament. Mercedes-Benz saw China as a large potential market for heavy vehicles, and set up an assembly plant in Shanghai.

Nearly twelve years of war followed — the longest period of conflict for any of the participants in the Second World War. Japan invaded from the north and along the coastline and made headway wherever its columns could be supported by warships, aircraft and armoured vehicles. That meant that it could force its way up the Yangtze River, occupying the industrial areas of the lower Yangtze from Shanghai to Nanjing to Wuhan. It could not, however, force its way through the great gorges of the Yangtze, and so Chinese industry was able to survive and grow with Western aid in the west and southwest in the cities of Chongqing, Chengdu and Kunming. The aid included the provision of trucks and heavy vehicles — GM and Ford made. It also included Jeeps (then made by Willys). The Japanese were still conducting aggressive campaigns in 1944, occupying vast new swathes of territory towards Changsha, until the atomic bombs in 1945 brought surrender. The conflict between the Nationalists and the Communists continued and it was not until 1949 that the Communists prevailed and established the People's Republic of China. During the war years, there was contact with, and trade with the Western democracies, even though such trade was maintained with great difficulty through 'crossing the hump' — that is, crossing over the natural barrier of the mountains in the southwest by air and by dirt road. Many of the trucks that made the crossing were left in China as part of the package of aid.

There were two superpowers in the period post-World War II — the USA and the USSR. The Americans (with the British at their side) were firmly on the side of the Nationalists by 1949. This meant that the

US would not assist the development of a Chinese car manufacturing industry after the Communist victory, and neither would it sanction the export of American cars to the country. The British followed the same policy. French and Italian industries had too many problems of their own in rebuilding their domestic industry, not to mention the Germans and Japanese. Therefore, when the new Chinese government faced the challenge of modernizing the country, and sought assistance to establish auto factories, they turned to the USSR. Effectively, their industry was cut off from technological developments in the West and foreign investment, just as the Japanese had been isolated in the 1930s and 1940s.

Nevertheless, the Chinese established an indigenous and extensive auto industry. In 1951, to huge fanfare, the first sod was turned to build the factory of the First Automotive Works (FAW) in the northern city of Changchun. It may have been significant that the city was not that far from the far eastern regions of the USSR, close enough to obtain ready assistance from Soviet manufacturing experts, but it may also have been that the government in Beijing was anxious to re-establish prosperity in a region that had been under Russian then Japanese control for a generation. The First Five Year Plan (1953–57) of the new government had as a central plank the transformation of the former Japanese colony of Manchuria into a base for industrialization, and that region received the lion's share of industrial investment. It had also seen growth during the period of the Korean War.

The Soviet experts who came were extremely proficient at their trade. They had to be, for they had had to learn it under the stresses of the war the Soviets called the Great Patriotic War. The first model of vehicle for the new manufacturing line was a Soviet medium-sized truck, and it started rolling off the new production lines in 1956. It was the precursor of the Jie Feng — Liberation — truck. In time, these were developed and became larger and larger. Eventually, Liberation trucks were monster vehicles, and the veritable kings of the road (if the word 'king' can be used in a Communist country). They mainly came in only two colours — sky blue or ocean green. It can be said that the country was built on the back of Jie Feng trucks.

The Chinese Communists had a falling-out with the Soviets during 1957, partly because there was a breakdown of trust over such issues as strategic policy and sharing of nuclear technology. From then on, the Soviet advisers were withdrawn and Chinese manufacturers were largely on their own. Mao Zedong announced that the Chinese people alone, under the Communist system, would be able to close the gap quickly between China and wealthy countries in the West, including developing a technologically advanced manufacturing industry. This was the basis of the Great Leap Forward of 1958 that has been described in an earlier chapter. The policy was a disaster overall, but the period did see the FAW company produce the Hong Qi (Red Flag or Red Banner) saloon, as well as three-wheeled vehicles and micro-cars known as Jiaxing, and a medium-sized car called the Xiali, which was used as a police car and transport for company managers. The Red Flags came in various models: a Da Hong Qi (Big Red Flag), which was used for limousines, and variants for hearses and ambulances; and a more basic model, the Xiao Hong Qi (Little Red Flag). The quantities produced were not large — around 8,000 vehicles in 1957, increasing to more than 40,000 in 1965.

Other large vehicle manufacturing enterprises followed the example of FAW. A second large auto manufacturer, called, logically enough, Second Automotive Works (SAW) was inaugurated soon after FAW. The SAW facility was established in the south, in the Cantonese-speaking area of China. Its products included heavy trucks and buses, and these were badged as Dong Feng or East Wind. The Beijing Auto Works was set up in 1952 to produce light passenger vehicles for military and semi-military use. They were based upon the Willys Jeep. BAW made cars from 1958, the same year as they established a branch operation in Tianjin. Other very large motor vehicle makers established in the late 1950s were Chengdu Trucks and Buses (in the west of China), Chang-an (makers of light commercial vehicles) and Beijing Commercial. By this time, there had also been a big growth in smaller operations which were manufacturing components and were publicly owned, generally funded by local and regional governments where it was not feasible to establish an auto manufacturing facility to turn out complete vehicles.

The prewar industrial centre of Shanghai had suffered during the years of Japanese occupation and was slow to recover, partly because the new Communist government in Beijing had a lingering suspicion about the socialist credentials of the Shanghainese. However, by 1960, the Shanghai Auto Works had been established and was turning out the Fenghuang sedan, also aptly named the Shanghai sedan.

Overall, in the early 1960s, prospects did not look rosy, for the economy was in a state of collapse and there was famine in some parts of the country after poor harvests and economic blunders the year before, so much so that that some referred to 1959 as the Year of Hungry Ghosts. However, from 1963 to 1965, the economy recovered, and the SOEs in various provinces put their efforts behind regional governments bent on rapidly establishing auto factories of their own as a centrepoint of development and a symbol of modernity and prosperity. At the mid-point of this decade, there were over 400 motor vehicle manufacturing and assembling plants throughout China, mainly making buses and trucks, as well as motorcycles modelled on pre-war American designs. Many of the larger plants came under the purview of FAW, which was among the largest manufacturing concerns in the country. Shanghai grew in importance as an industrialized centre. In Beijing in 1964, Beijing Auto Works, manufacturer of a cloned Willys Jeep, produced a locally designed equivalent of the Jeep that had no name but was designated the BJ 212.

Another bout of ideological madness struck China and its manufacturers in 1966, when Mao declared his war on old ways of thinking and doing things and the Great Proletarian Cultural Revolution spread all over the country, disrupting life in general as well as the new auto manufacturing enterprises. The excesses of the Cultural Revolution would not start to peter out until 1969.

Metaphorically, the earth moved in February 1972, when Richard Nixon became the first US President to visit China and a new era in international exchanges and economic relationships began. There was not yet international investment in the local auto industry, but the stable economic environment and the promise of expansionary times ahead fuelled industrial growth in China.

The country was immune from the Oil Crisis of 1973, because it was virtually self-sufficient in oil production and refining, having extensive oil-fields in the far west in Xinjiang and Qinghai provinces among other areas. By the end of the 1970s, there were nearly 500 auto makers, and many times that number of component manufacturers making parts for cars and trucks and buses and light commercial vehicles. However, not many of these were efficient producers for they were working under a command economy. The private car market was non-existent. Most Chinese rode public transport and most vehicles produced were buses and trucks. However, the domestic industry was about to feel a blowtorch to the belly — the coming of joint ventures which offered the benefits of new investment and new technology, as well as new work practices. The advent of the joint ventures was broadly similar to the coming of joint ventures to Japan in the late 1940s, another of several parallels that makes the pattern of development of the Chinese auto industry a broad reflection of that of the Japanese.

The entry of the joint ventures was only possible after Chairman Mao Zedong had passed from the scene. His death in 1976 marked the pivotal point when the Chinese motor vehicle manufacturing industry was opened to the world. At that time, Chinese motor vehicle production was around 150,000 vehicles per year.

Joint Ventures
When the Chinese reform process was under way and the country was opened up, to a degree, to foreign investment in 1984, there were many who saw the huge marketplace on offer and made simplistic calculations. These were along the lines of, 'If only ... one Chinese in a hundred buys our product, and there are one billion Chinese, then that means we can sell 10 million products in China!' The mantra sounded good, but took too little account of the complexities of the country and its economy. Over the next 20 years, many a foreign investor would lose money and withdraw, disappointed, after a foray into the Chinese marketplace.

From the mid-1980s, there were many investors queuing up to enter China, and car makers from the US, France, Germany and Japan were eager, and sometimes somewhat naive, partners in joint ventures. Each of the new foreign ventures seemed to choose a broad swathe of territory for their own in setting up shop, establishing facilities in the north, south, east and centre of the country.

The local car makers in their turn were keen to develop trading relationships with their Western and Japanese counterparts. The bigger enterprises, such as FAW and Shanghai Auto, cultivated more than one relationship and in time set up joint ventures with a number of international auto makers, sometimes shrewdly playing off one national corporation against another. Although it had been the American President, Nixon, who had made the move that eventually led to the re-establishment of relationships between China and the rest of the world, the world's two biggest car makers, both American, were not the very first to enter into joint ventures with Chinese partners. That honour was reserved for Chrysler, and a posse of European firms.

Not until 1984 did two big Western companies set up auto manufacturing joint-venture operations in China. One that has already been mentioned, the Beijing Jeep, was a venture of the Chrysler Motor Company subsidiary, American Motors,

Figure 9.3: Sites of the Main Car Making Joint Ventures up to 2000. Joint-venture operations included: Beijing — Chrysler; Shanghai — VW and GM; Wuhan — DFM-Citroen and Ford; Guangzhou — Honda.

and Beijing Automobile Works. The second venture was established in October 1984 in the industrial hub of Shanghai, when First Automotive Works and Volkswagen got together to form FAW-Volkswagen. Volkswagen also entered a second joint venture known as China Shanghai Volkswagen Corporation. Although Beijing Jeep had an uneven history, the Volkswagen joint ventures moved on to successful trading and rapidly built a major market share. The Jeep appealed to business customers seeking high-status vehicles, but the Volkswagen sedans like the Santana, the Passat, the Gol and the Pol had a far wider popular appeal. They were small cars, basic and relatively easy to maintain, with good fuel efficiency, and were suitable for use as taxis.

At Wuhan, near the geographic centre of China and with important train and ship transportation links, the French saw their opportunity. DFM Citroen set up a manufacturing facility in 1992, and had a range of models on their lines, including the Elysee, the Picasso, the Xsara and Citroen ZX (which also became popular for use as taxis).

With the coming of the joint ventures, total vehicle production in China increased rapidly. In 1983, the quarter-million vehicle mark was passed, and production increased by 30 per cent in 1984, then 40 per cent in 1985. In 1988, China's total vehicle production was a half-million units. In 1993, production of cars and small vehicles had doubled and passed one million units, although virtually all of these were sold to corporations for business and semi-business use.[118] Two years later, as the VW and Citroen factories hit their stride, nationwide sales passed 1.25 million.

The two biggest American manufacturers did not come onto the Chinese joint-venture scene until the mid-1990s. First Ford took a local stake in 1995 when it joined with Jiangling Motors Corporation. Two years later, GM entered into an agreement with Shanghai Automotive Industrial Corporation to set up a new plant and build a range of Buicks, including the Excelle, the Regal and the Sail. Details of Buick sales in China follow in the next chapter.

A Japanese manufacturer, long-involved in motorcycle production in China, went to Guangzhou in 1998. Honda invested in the southern city and started to produce its Fit sedan for the small car market, the Accord as an up-market model and its Odyssey for the people-mover segment of the market.

Amidst all the publicity that the large auto companies received when they establish operations in China, another aspect of the phenomenon sometimes gets overlooked. Besides the auto companies, auto component parts manufacturers were also setting up joint ventures to take advantage of the opportunities such a strategy offered for access to China's domestic manufacturing market, as well as the comparative advantages obtained for their operations in global markets. One such example was Delphi Corporation, the giant component manufacturer established in the US by GM (and whose financial woes are discussed later in this chapter). Delphi was one of the first component companies to set up in China in 1993, and it expanded rapidly, reaching a level of US$700 million in sales after ten years and forecasting increased sales in the years ahead.

The Three-Wheeler Phenomenon in the Development of Car Industries

There are several photos in this book of the three-wheeler cars and light commercial vehicles of China. They feature because such vehicles are common, although possibly becoming less popular with the consumer as more sophisticated vehicles become more affordable. There are large production facilities for three-wheeled vehicles in Chongqing and Shandong. The latter, Shandong Shifei Corporation, has a capacity of a million light trucks a year, in addition to passenger vehicles.[119] They were a major feature of the early years of the development of the auto industry in China (and also in other national industries).

Three-wheeled vehicles (sometimes called tri-cars or micro-cars) come in various forms. There are motorcycles with sidecars, and also sports motorcycles which are in tricycle form (the latter comparatively rare and eye-turning, possessed mainly by the cycling aficionados). Then there are the three-wheeled enclosed vehicles. The smallest are like motorcycles or motor scooters with a twin-wheeled rear axle, and these are ubiquitous as auto-rickshaws, taxis and light delivery vehicles throughout Asia. Every tourist to Indonesia or Thailand or India has been whizzed about crowded city streets, in and out of traffic, by cheerful tuk-tuk drivers whose patter invariably includes a joke about their 'air-conditioning'.

The largest three-wheeled vehicles are trucks of two tonnes or more, sometimes with a single-pot engine mounted over the big front wheel, carrying big loads with persistence rather than speed.

The mid-range enclosed three-wheeler is the small car or van, and this type of vehicle is the main subject of the phenomenon and a feature of the pattern of development of a national car industry. In the early stages of development of a national or regional car industry, local manufacturers will produce a small enclosed three-wheeled car that accommodates three adults or a small family. In France, after the Second World War, there was a parallel with the emergence of the Deux Chevaux — reputedly designed to accommodate a farmer, his wife, and a sack of produce in the smallest possible space (albeit with four wheels).

Why build a three-wheeled car? The answer is that it is small and technologically simple. There are no twin front wheels which require complex steering boxes — the single front wheel is direct and quickly installed. The drawback to the design is that there is limited space for a motor, and too big a motor would make the vehicle unstable over its front wheel anyway, so three-wheeled passenger vehicles generally remain small and low powered. Most contemporary Chinese three-wheeled passenger and light commercial vehicles have single-cylinder engines of around 200cc. Their low speed is an asset, for the vehicles generally are unsafe when braking too hard. The exception, the three-wheeled trucks, maintain their stability because they are very slow, and also because a low load over their back axle guarantees they will not easily tip. Although most three-wheelers are not speedy vehicles because of the inherent instability of the design, this is no drawback in crowded cities, on narrow streets and alleyways. The three-wheeler owner has to be a pragmatist, travelling to his or her destination with a minimum of speed and fuss.

The three-wheeled car is also highly manoeuvrable, which is an advantage when driving in cities that are hundreds of years old and whose streets were designed to be just wide enough for a manpowered cart or sedan chair.

Another attractive feature of the design is that its simplicity and small size equate to cheapness. The consumer who wants only to venture about his home town can obtain a vehicle that is cheap to buy and cheap to run.

An exception to the above general comments about three-wheeled passenger vehicles was the Morgan sports car of the UK. The Morgan had a wide appeal, and it was both stable and manoeuvrable, because it was of 'tadpole' design, with two wheels at the front and one at the back, instead of the single front wheel which characterizes contemporary Chinese (and Indian) designs.

The Japanese car industry also went through a phase when three-wheeled models — both cars and small trucks — were common. Mazda was building three-wheeled trucks in the 1930s and 1940s. A three-wheeled Hino truck was produced in quantity until the 1960s. Daihatsu's first car in 1930 was a three-wheeler and the company was built up specializing in such cars. In 1957, Daihatsu produced a 'tri-mobile' for export, and in 1958 gestated a three-wheeler called the Bee, probably so-named because it could buzz around here and there. The Bee tooled around the streets with a 540cc engine and a three-speed gearbox. Its engine was comparable to four-wheeled cars of the time — Suzuki's first car, the Suzulight, had a 360cc two-cylinder engine, and Subaru's first car, that also appeared in 1958, had a 356cc two-stroke (although Subaru offered a buyer the option of going for the power of a 422cc version). Mitsubishi's Minica of 1962 had a 359cc engine that could whip the car up to a maximum speed of 89 kph (55 mph). Cars were not built for speed in those days and in those places, seldom was it murmured, 'speed kills'.

In Germany and Italy, especially after 1945, small three-wheelers appeared. One model achieved cult status — the Messerschmitt, produced by the company that produced the most numerous fighter plane of the war. The Messerschmitt was not renowned for the grunt exerted by every one of its 175cc.

Even Australia had a three-wheeled vehicle, although the Edith, produced from 1953 to 1957, was not a runaway success.

In the United Kingdom, the three-wheeler was displaced by another small car — the smallest possible four-wheeled vehicle — called appropriately the Mini. The Mini in its initial form was very basic, with a boot big enough for a bag of groceries and no more. In Italy, the Fiat Bambino filled a similar niche in the marketplace, edging out the small outmoded three-wheeler.

The comedy film *Mr Bean* encapsulated a widespread feeling about three-wheeler cars and vans when Mr Bean's Mini was shown stealing the parking space of the Reliant Regal, a three-wheeled van. If the Mini was not nudging the Regal aside, it was edging it off the road, leaving it tipped over on the roadside. The scenes tapped a psychological vein. Perhaps the modern motorist has become contemptuous of the three-wheeler, much as teenagers become ashamed of the toys of their infancy, while still being a little fascinated that once they valued these things.

The three-wheeler is more than an oddity. Its presence and declining popularity generally marks a turning point in the development of national motor vehicle industries. People buy the three-wheeler initially because it is cheap and simple, but somehow the image does not unlock pheromones in the motorist's brain. The three-wheelers are not as speedy and the possession of such a car does not convey an image of wealth and sophistication. As four-wheeled vehicles become available in time, the conveyance with a wheel on each corner displaces the three-pointer. Four wheels invoke the feel-good factor.

In urban centres in China, although the three-wheeler is commonly seen, few aspiring motorists seem to hanker after such a beast. Instead the consumer demand is for cars like those on the streets of the modern cities of the West. Hence the Chinese consumer has passed a milestone on the way to the development of a sophisticated car industry that is on a par with global aspirations. There is an irony in the fact that just at a time when one of the largest consumer markets is turning away from the small and seemingly outmoded three-wheeler, new and fuel-efficient models, with up-to-the-minute styling, are being developed for commuter use in urban areas. However, these new models (which do not yet have wide acceptance) are being produced for the same reason the three-wheelers of an earlier age were produced — to provide cheap and economical transportation in congested city streets.

The Joint Ventures in 2007

In China, almost all the domestic car makers established before reforms started have entered into joint ventures, some of them with more than one foreign partner. In 1999, 650,000 cars were produced by the joint ventures. In 2005, cars made by the joint ventures accounted for around 90 per cent of total new car sales in China (and 80 per cent of all motor vehicle sales).

As at 2007, the number and spread of joint ventures makes too long a list to enumerate in detail here. Many of them were established during 2003, which saw an influx of new entrants to the market, including Korean and additional Japanese firms, and 2004 was a disappointing year for sales, in part as a result of oversupply.

The foreign joint ventures that operated in China in 2007 were many, and only the main ones are mentioned here. They included VW and Mazda in the northern city of Changchun, site of the first FAW operation, and GM and BMW, which were set up in Shenyang in 2003. Beijing remained the site of DaimlerChrysler operations and also the Korean car maker, Hyundai, which made small sedans and SUVs.

In the city to the south of the capital, Tianjin, the joint Sino-Japanese joint venture of FAW and Toyota, also established in 2003, made the Charade, the Terios, the Vitz and the Vios models. Nissan was established in Zhengzhou. Nanchang was the site of Isuzu and Ford joint ventures — Ford manufacturing the small Fiesta and the medium-sized Mondeo. Near the coast at Yancheng was another Korean joint venture — Kia (associated with Hyundai). Nanjing had the Fiat production line. The industrial hub of Shanghai hosted the long-established VW and the more-recent GM operation to produce Buicks. Haikou had a Mazda joint venture.

In Sichuan's capital, Chengdu, there was a joint venture with Toyota. In Chongqing on the Yangtze, long a manufacturing centre since World War II, there were Ford and Suzuki joint ventures.[120] In Wuhan, there continued to operate the French DFM-Citroen venture (now part of the Peugeot auto group) and in Liuzhou there was another GM plant. In Guangzhou, Honda made a range of vehicles from the small Fit to the Odyssey, and there was also a Nissan plant turning out Sunny and Bluebird sedans.

The expansion of the joint ventures in the 2000s was conducted with a fever that was not unlike that of the gold rushes of the nineteenth century. In the words of a leading analyst: "This acceleration in the adoption of privately owned cars has sparked a "gold-rush mentality" which manifests itself in tremendous investments on behalf of European and American car makers [also Japanese and Korean] in on-the-ground production

Figure 9.4: Sites of the Main Car Making Joint Ventures as at 2007
Operations included: Changchun — VW and Mazda; Shenyang — GM and BMW; Beijing — DaimlerChrysler and Hyundai; Tianjin — FAW Toyota; Zhengzhou — Nissan; Nanchang — Isuzu and Ford; Yancheng — Kia; Nanjing — Fiat; Shanghai — VW and GM; Haikou — Mazda; Chengdu — Toyota; Chongqing Ford and Suzuki; Wuhan — DFM-Citroen; Liuzhou — GM; Guangzhou — Honda and Nissan.

capacity through joint ventures with local manufacturers'.[121]

In relation to the experience of the joint ventures in 2006, the many new players in the marketplace diluted the shares of the early entrants. The performance of the one-time market leader, Volkswagen, fell off as new foreign models entered the marketplace and there was a greater diversity of choice for consumers. Although VW's models remained well-suited to Chinese conditions, consumers were tempted by a wider range of models with more contemporary styling and design. VW's percentage of sales in 2001 was 50 per cent, but decreased to 40 per cent in 2002, 30.8 per cent in 2003, and reached a low point of 16 per cent in 2005. The lesson from their experience is that Chinese consumers cannot be taken for granted but have become discriminating and well-informed. This point was borne out by the research projects undertaken and described later.

Besides Volkswagen, another German company that was described in the earlier chapter on motorcycles, BMW, had been in China since 1994, when it received a licence to import and market its products, mainly sedans for the prestige market. BMW entered into a joint venture with Huachen Corporation in March 2003 to make cars locally for Chinese consumption, mainly through the assembly of component kits for BMW Series 3 and Series 5 sedans in Huachen's existing facilities in the northern city of Shenyang. By October of 2003, the first Chinese-made BMW was on sale.[122] However, the initial sales levels were disappointing. Only 8,860 cars were sold in 2004, which waslittle more then than half the target of 17,000 units set by BMW.[123] The less-than-expected level of sales meant that some 60 per cent of the production capacity was under-utilized. The reasons were varied but 2004 was generally a disappointing year for car sales in China (belying the myth of a continually increasing demand that would soak up every available car manufactured). BMW also suffered from entering the top end of the market which was already well supplied by imports.

Wholly Chinese-Owned Companies
The structure of the Chinese auto industry appears to become more complex day by day. The big Chinese-owned companies have been involved in the joint ventures discussed in the preceding section, but sometimes they have completed joint-venture agreements with a number of foreign companies, some of whom are bitter rivals in Western markets. For example, Shanghai Automotive's protégé Chery has grown to be the nation's fifth biggest car maker and could rival SAIC itself. Chery has entered joint-venture agreements with DaimlerChrysler, although SAIC is a major Chinese partner of GM in the Chinese market. The number of joint-venture agreements continues to grow. The main Chinese companies that are partners to these agreements also continue to develop independent operations.

In addition to the bigger Chinese car making companies, the older SOEs still turning out outmoded small and commercial vehicles, and the increasingly bewildering network of joint ventures, there were new entrants to the industry. Some of the large manufacturers of household goods or agricultural machinery have turned their hands to manufacturing motor vehicles. Geely is a case in point — it started in 1986 as a maker of refrigerators. Other companies, such as Great Wall and Brilliance, developed from bicycle and motorcycle manufacturers. These new companies started small, but proved to be not just nimble in the marketplace, but fast-growing as well. Geely has achieved a production capacity of 200,000 vehicles a year just 20 years after starting from scratch as a manufacturer then a producer of motorcycles, and just six years after starting quantity car production and making 8,000 cars in its first year. It had a sales target of 200,000 vehicles in 2006, and like Chery was looking to exports to improve upon these sales levels. In the first half of 2006, 10,000 cars were exported and Geely will be among the first Chinese companies to export cars into Europe, starting from existing bridgeheads in the Balkans and the Ukraine. The company has utilized a short cut to economical production, designing its small car models, sedans and hatchbacks around components manufactured in China for Citroen and fitted to Geely-designed car bodies.

In 2005, FAW was only just hanging onto its status as China's leading motor vehicle manufacturer and it employed more than 137,000 employees (but when the sales figures for the full year 2006 are compiled it will probably surrender first place to Shanghai Automotive group.) FAW ranked 31st in the ranks of the world's car makers. Besides its headquarters in Changchun, FAW operated all over China, from the north as far as Sichuan, China's largest province in the west of the country. It had joint ventures in China with Toyota (making the hybrid Toyota Prius) and Audi, as well as joint ventures outside China, for example in Russia, where it made a Russian version of the Zhongxing Admiral. It made a modest move into the US market in 2006, testing the waters with an electric version of the Daihatsu Move called the ZX40. The wholly Chinese-owned subsidiaries of FAW also have ambitious plans. Tianjin FAW manufactures the Xiali, which is aimed at the first-time Chinese family car buyer.[124] Its 2006 sales target was 200,000 vehicles. The company is also developing an up-market model for the Chinese market, and has named it the Weizhi.

Shanghai Automotive, heir-apparent to the title of largest Chinese car maker, continued to expand aggressively in 2006, as did its subsidiaries. Chery Automobile, linked with Shanghai Automotive, was aiming at a sales target of 281,000 vehicles, which would represent a 50 per cent growth rate over sales in 2005. Chery's management aimed to be one of China's top three auto companies within three years and it was aggressively seeking to increase its exports to a level of around one-third of its total production in 2006.

Later chapters will provide more detailed research on the profiles of those who are purchasing cars in China, but generally they are divided into two groups — the very wealthy who purchase high-value luxury cars as much as a status symbol as anything else, and the mid- to high-income earners in the cities who are purchasing their first car for the utility of it. The overall percentage of the population who can afford to buy a new car for exclusively private use remains small, at perhaps 1.5 per cent to 2 per cent of the population, but in absolute terms this small percentage represents 20 to 25 million people (not counting their families/dependents). This constitutes a potential new car market far larger than that of the UK or Germany.

While the pattern of development of China's industry to 2007 has been very similar to that of Japan, and protection measures at each period of development were comparable, the speed of development has not been the same. China's industry, in the most recent phases, has developed faster. For example, indigenous Chinese car designs have emerged just five to ten years after the establishment of some operations, whereas in Japan it took nearly twice as long for competitive indigenous designs to emerge.

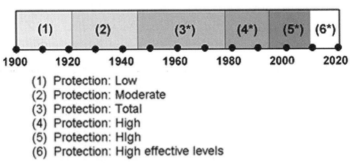

(1) Protection: Low
(2) Protection: Moderate
(3) Protection: Total
(4) Protection: High
(5) Protection: HIgh
(6) Protection: High effective levels

Figure 9.5: The Pattern of Development of the Car Industry in China

Allowing for the different speed of development at some stages, the development of China's car industry follows nearly an identical pattern to Japan's, namely the following phases:

- Common First Phase (1): Industry in infancy; many local manufacturers; small quantities produced; protection measures very low or non-existent.
- Common Second Phase (2): Industry coalescing; small manufacturers merge; production runs increased; growth is dependent upon the entry of US firms (GM and Ford) or UK or European firms; protection measures brought in to ensure a degree of local content and control.
- Japanese/Chinese Third Phase (3*): Abrupt termination of international contacts; local industry concentrates on military/industrial needs; number of cars manufactured limited. Protection measures total.
- Japanese/Chinese Fourth Phase (4*): Strict controls relaxed; local industry has small and obsolescent designs; joint ventures encouraged to bring in marketing and management expertise, also new technology and designs; some local designs are virtual copies of popular Western models. High levels of government investment and support and high levels of protection.
- Japanese/Chinese Fifth Phase (5*): Mergers of local car makers into a smaller number of conglomerates; indigenous small car designs very similar to Western models; expansion continues and exports grow in importance due to undervalued currency and lower wage/cost structures. Relatively high levels of protection continue.
- Japanese/Chinese Sixth Phase (6*): Local markets reach virtual limits and exports make up a major proportion of production; innovative designs achieve world-wide acceptance; plants are established in other countries using indigenous expertise and practices. Advantages of undervalued currency and low wages remain; protection levels are reduced, but social and cultural factors remain strong barriers to foreign competition.

In its very early years, in the first phases of its pattern of development, China's domestic automotive industry struggled because of its small and under-developed domestic market for private car sales. Even in the 1980s, those domestic sales were too small to finance the large investments needed for modern facilities and to develop new models.

Entering into joint ventures in the 1990s and early 2000s with the major auto companies of the US, Europe and Japan has helped kick start the modern auto industry in China, but it has also resulted in a comparatively sudden increase in the number of models and the number of cars available. Consequently, China's auto makers have become large enterprises — behemoths — even by world standards. For example, FAW has established 35 major plants around the country, with a capacity to manufacture nearly a million vehicles a year, and since its inception has turned out more than 5 million vehicles. The situation of such a large industry with many diverse players is not easy to summarize, but some broad brush strokes can be marked out on the world canvas in the following section.

The Situation of China's Car Industry in 2007

China's demand for motor vehicles reached a level of 5.8 million units in 2006, around one half of them cars.[125] This represented a rise of 17 per cent on the demand in 2005. A significant event occurred in 2005, when for the first time China became a net exporter of motor vehicles — that is, the level of exports first exceeded the level of imports. The amount of the excess was modest, less than 10,000 vehicles, but it was a milestone nevertheless.

The continued high growth in China's GDP (expected to continue to increase at a high rate, 8–8.9 per cent in 2006) was a factor in a change in the nature of car ownership, which was already seen to be shifting from institutional ownership to private ownership. However, there was a declining profitability in the industry and auto industry analysts were expecting greater price competitiveness. Xu Changming noted three factors driving the expected price cuts:

1.   China's vehicle production capacity in 2005 was around 1.8 times the domestic demand, and the production/demand gap was expected to grow (this supports the author's thesis, with implications for the probable flood of exports to the West).

2.   A number of new joint-venture manufacturing enterprises have expanded production capacity. These include Shanghai GM, Beijing Hyundai and Guangzhou Honda.

3. There is a very large 'overhang' of inventory — cars that were unsold in previous periods being offered for sale in 2006. Some estimates are that there are more than 500,000 unsold units in inventories around the country.

The slump in sales in 2004, as well as the growth in production capacity and inventories in 2005, must increase pressure on manufacturers to export wherever they can. Although the number of car makers, both wholly Chinese-owned and joint ventures, have grown rapidly in recent years, their profit figures do not perfectly reflect the vigour of their growth. Twenty-three of the major vehicle manufacturers reported declining profit figures in 2004, but four car makers acknowledged making losses.[126] There are warning signs that the domestic market is already reaching its limits and there is inertia creeping into domestic demand. One such indicator was that 450 auto dealers in Beijing had to withdraw from the industry (through choice or bankruptcy) in 2004.[127]

Cost cutting and aggressive marketing saw a jump in sales in early 2006, and China's new car sales in the first three months of the year rose 74 per cent from the same period a year earlier to 890,000 units, the official Xinhua News Agency reported in early April, citing data from the China Association of Automobile Manufacturers.[128] The official estimate of a total of 2.75 million cars sold in 2006 could very well be surpassed. There have still been some marketing failures, namely the Chinese-made BMW mentioned already and some VW models that were not well-accepted by Chinese consumers and have not sold well in competition with more sophisticated and better featured models recently available. Despite recent drawbacks, Shanghai Volkswagen will probably reach its annual sales target of 340,000, due to the continued popularity of the Passat. Of some of the other car makers, Shanghai GM had plans to make and sell 380,000 vehicles in 2006.

Official forecasts for the future, based on progress during 2006, drip optimism:

> In the first eight months of 2006, China's auto sales reached a record high of 2.369 million. Car sales of the top 10 auto manufacturers exceeded 1.661 million, accounting for 70.14 per cent of the country's total car sales. The prospects of the 2006 auto market are promising.[129]

Indeed the car industry in China may be facing an exciting future overall, but the situation of its various auto manufacturers is uneven. In 2006, many of China's older truck and bus factories established in the 1950s and 1960s continued to operate, some of them despite big losses, because of the support of local governments. There have been challenges of rising material costs and macroeconomic control.

There remained a reluctance to allow too many of these older SOEs to collapse because of the implications for unemployment and social unrest. Around 300 of such factories continue to operate. Some were turning out vehicles that remained in high demand, such as Liberation trucks and Chengdu buses, and others built vehicles which had some demand in China but which had few Western competitors, such as the three-wheeled micro-cars, and tractor/trailer workhorses.

The efforts of these older truck and bus factories, when combined with the output of the newer and technologically advanced car makers, led to the situation in 2006 where wholly Chinese-owned factories had increased their market share to 20 per cent of new vehicle sales in China. The government has encouraged local enterprises not to be content with these levels, but to aim at achieving a target of a 60 per cent market share (in relation to the Chinese domestic market) by 2010, in addition to the plans for increased exports. The balance will, of course, be met by the joint ventures and imports — and this declining share of the domestic market may be an ominous sign for the Western companies that have invested heavily in China. The global corporations such as GM and Ford that have looked to China, and to India, for continued high growth may have their hopes dashed.

The Future Path, as Seen by Chinese Car Makers

Despite the bumps on the world car sales super-highway, China's manufacturing industry has continued and will continue to develop apace and the number of wholly owned Chinese auto businesses has increased just as the number of joint ventures has increased. At the 50th anniversary of the establishment of China's automobile industry in Changchun, there was a week-long celebration centred around an auto fair that offered displays from no less than 1,000 Chinese and international car makers who presented their latest models. The auto fair was the largest that China had ever held.

As noted at the beginning of this chapter, China's annual motor vehicle production capacity — in joint-venture plants and wholly Chinese-owned plants — is expected to reach around 11 million to 12 million units in 2010, allowing for expansion plans at its major manufacturing plants and conservative estimates of growth. In order to absorb this increase, domestic demand in China would have to grow by up to 40 per cent annually. This is unlikely, and optimistic forecasts suggest demand will be no more than 7 million units in 2010. This estimate assumes an average annual growth in demand of 17 per cent, and it would result in an annual surplus in production of between 4 million to 5 million units — which would be the number of vehicles available to be exported.[130]

What of the aspirations of the wholly Chinese-owned car makers? They do not see themselves as limited to their own environs. There is no shortage of aspirants to the world stage beyond the confines of China itself. Chery Automobile Company is just one of them. In 2005 the *Detroit News* wrote of an

> agreement today between New York-based Visionary Vehicles LLC and Chery Automobile Co., one of the fastest-growing players in the fledgling Chinese auto industry. ... The deal to import up to 250,000 Chinese-made cars annually beginning in 2007 was finalized ... 'We are shooting for 250,000 vehicles the first year.' ... the Chinese auto industry is expanding at a breakneck pace, with Chery among the so-called 'young tigers' that are aggressively adding manufacturing capacity and setting their sights on overseas markets. Bricklin said that the goal is to price the vehicles 30 per cent below competing models in the U.S. market.[131]

The ultimate aim of Chery was to sell 2 million vehicles a year. However, the future of the Chery deal with Visionary Vehicles was unclear, because in October 2006 Chery and DaimlerChrysler announced their own plans to import Chery sedans into the US in 2008 under the Dodge brand to take a bigger share of the low-cost market.

Another newly established car maker, Geely, has plans to enter the US and European markets in quantity in 2008, with a modestly equipped vehicle costed at under $10,000. The goal was to sell 25,000 vehicles in the first year, rising to 100,000 cars by 2012.[132] A GM spokesperson commented that the US car maker was not concerned about the entry of the Geely into the market for they believed that it would not be competitive. However, that spokesperson had to add, 'Long term, you'd be crazy not to be looking at what China could do given what others have done.'

It is clear that the rapid growth of the Chinese car industry to 2007 has not only made it capable of taking on the world, but more importantly it has given its executives and managers the confidence to compete in the world marketplace. Automotive entrepreneur Malcolm Bricklin can be quoted once more:

> I have great confidence that they are going to be as innovative and productive as any automobile company in the world, ... They want to be a major global player. ... You know, if we don't make sure these cars are among the best in the world, we're going to get our ass handed to us,' he said. 'But if we do what we're supposed to do, this could be the deal that changes the industry.'[133]

Part Three

Research into the Chinese Automotive Industry

10 Domestic Demand

Introduction: Consumer Demand

The following chapters describe and discuss research into aspects of the automotive industry in China and this chapter considers the nature of the domestic consumer demand for cars. The intention behind this examination is to determine whether the Chinese consumer has similar demands to consumers in the West. For example, if the Chinese demand a different style of car from the West (i.e., cars like the three-wheeled micro-vans, or small work vehicles like the tractor/trailer that are illustrated in this book) then it is probable that the Chinese domestic industry will continue to meet that demand, and will not gear up to produce sophisticated cars with high levels of features. It follows that if there was a divergence in the demand for cars in China and the demand for cars in the West then vehicles mass-produced by Chinese factories would not appeal to consumers in the West and there would effectively be no threat from the growth of the Chinese industry.

This book includes research on the market for (a) luxury cars, (b) family/business cars (and particularly the Buick range of mid- to large-size cars) and (c) small cars (1.6 litre engine capacity or less). These three categories were chosen because they seem to be the largest and most crucial sectors of the car market.

The first category was chosen because observation suggested that most of the luxury and prestige cars being driven on the streets of China were imports, and research of these vehicles might provide insights into the market for foreign cars in China The category of foreign luxury cars scouts some issues of interest to Chinese society as a whole. For many years, under the strict Communist system, the people were told that foreign customs led to decadence — perhaps exemplified by the temptations to drive showy shiny cars. In the 'new' China, there is often a preference for foreign products when they can be afforded, for status reasons, but also from a belief that foreign products are superior in quality and design to the home-grown equivalents. The thinking of hard-line Communists — that local equalled good and pure and foreign was bad — has gone through an extreme wind-shift to become 'local product equals poor standard' and 'foreign means quality'. The research into the luxury, or prestige, car segment does not plan to exhaust these broader social issues — a much more extensive social study would be needed for that — but it does look at reasons why foreign cars were chosen and it profiles the purchasers/users of such cars.

The second category, Buick cars, was chosen because these were vehicles manufactured in China by a joint venture, from mainly imported components, so they included foreign design and technology in a Chinese-assembled vehicle. Moreover, the Buick, as a comparatively large vehicle with a high level of features, seemed to appeal to wealthier consumers. The Buick therefore represents affordable luxury for a much wider cross-section of Chinese professional society. The profile of Buick users will be examined.

The third category, small cars, included a range of models, some made by joint ventures and some made by wholly Chinese-owned enterprises. These small cars seem to be aimed at a mass, or popular, demand. They seemed to be affordable to a large number of people in professional or commercial employment, and hence may represent the most common type of consumer demand for cars in China, at least in the developing urban areas where wealth is growing fastest.

In the Chinese system of grading cars, economy cars are referred to as the A00-class. The next category is that of medium-grade cars, referred to as A-class; then medium-high-grade, B-class. The highest grade, which we would call luxury cars, is referred to as C-class. Most Buicks sold in China fall into the medium-high grade, or B-class. The three categories of cars chosen to be researched thus represent the full range of cars as determined by the Chinese system: C-class, A/B-class and A00-class.

The chapter will also consider the pricing of cars in China, and consumers' preferences and ability to pay market prices. The implication of this section is the setting and answering of a question: Will Chinese cars be priced competitively with the West? This question is explored with material also gathered in the research into the three classes of car and car consumers.

There are numerous factors to take into account, because the industry and the world market are huge, and indeed the Chinese domestic market is a very large and complex one. For example, the reduction in tariffs as part of the agreements surrounding WTO accession has resulted in price competition within China (although the market still retains restrictions on imports). The prices of smaller cars in particular has fallen dramatically. For example, the price of a new Nanjing Fiat in 2005 fell around 10 per cent in 2006. This price competition would bring no cheer to Western observers, for it should bring about greater cost-efficiency in the Chinese market and allow the Chinese manufacturers to reduce further the prices of the vehicles and components they export.

There are other factors that influence the market, among the more important of which are the world price of oil and availability of finance. China has for much of its history been self-sufficient in oil, but now, due to the great increase in domestic demand, it imports oil and hence is subject to some extent to the vagaries of fluctuating world oil prices for at least some of its oil consumption. Prices of fuel at suburban pumps have been rising. In recent years, China's oil imports have been increasing at the rate of 9 or 10 per cent a year, and this will probably result in a continuing preference for smaller and more fuel-efficient cars, just as it has done in the West. The domestic demand for cars will also be enhanced by the development of the finance industry in China. In 2006, there were loans issued at a zero interest rate to finance the purchase of a motor vehicle. Despite the availability of this finance, the research showed that the majority of car consumers make their purchase with cash.

Therefore, the following discussion and research findings are hedged about with provisos that they do not, and cannot, provide definitive answers to the many questions that must swirl about the future development of the car market in China. However, they do provide some indicative answers, and some suggestions about how the market is likely to develop and how Chinese demand may contribute to the growing likelihood of its dominance in world markets.

The Market for Luxury Cars

The definition of luxury cars to be used in this research refers to quality, well-equipped cars which retail in the price range 400,000 to 800,000 yuan. This high price means that such vehicles are inaccessible to all but the top one per cent of income earners. The recent history of the market for these top of the range vehicles in the area of study — the city of Qingdao — has been uneven. In 2004/05, Qingdao's luxury car market experienced a period of difficult trading, particularly in regard to European luxury cars such as the BMW and Mercedes-Benz. Over the same period of two or three years, structural changes have been taking place in the industry. Against this background of changes in the marketplace, researchers examined aspects of the luxury car market in order to draw conclusions about the changing nature of the market and of consumer demand for vehicles that are far out of reach of the ordinary Chinese employee. The research was carried out through interviews with a selected sample of owners of luxury cars and also with marketing managers of Qingdao luxury car franchises.

The luxury car market in Qingdao, and generally throughout China, has been affected by a number of factors that can be grouped under two broad headings — external factors, that is, those factors that are outside the operation of the marketplace for cars; and internal factors, aspects of the marketplace itself.

The external factors include demographic factors (changes in the population), economic factors affecting the affordability of top of the range cars (such as changes in the economic circumstances of the local people); financial factors (such as changes to the exchange rates), and regulatory factors (such as changes to import quotas). The internal market factors that will be considered include competitive strategies and the availability of substitute products.

External Factors Affecting the Market for Luxury Cars
In relation to demographic factors, since the 1980s there has been a big increase in the number of urban households. The population of the city of Qingdao and its environs expanded through natural increase and also through migration from rural areas of Shandong province, and this pattern of development was shared by hundreds of cities in China. In 2002, the population within the municipal boundaries of the city was around 5 million people, made up of around 2.6 million people in the central urban district and 2.3 million people in surrounding counties. There have also been notable economic factors which supported growth, especially the continuing economic reforms at official level which spurred private development, and investment for the Olympic Games scheduled in 2008 — a number of water sports events will be held in the aquatic facilities being built in Qingdao.

These economic factors have provided a strong impetus for the city's economic development and urban construction, and in the space of just a single generation there have been marked increases in measures of economic activity and wellbeing. In the municipal area, Qingdao's total GDP and average per capita GDP rose from 3.81 billion yuan and 650 yuan in 1978, to 178.03 billion yuan and 23,398 yuan in 2003 — a 40-fold increase in a single generation.[134] The monthly income per capita in Shandong province in 2006 was 1,041 yuan, which can be restated as an annual average income of 12,492 yuan (US$1,567 or A$1,837). This appears to be very low by world standards, but is higher than the average income in poorer areas of the country. By comparison, the annual income per capita in Qinghai province, the poorest province of China, was 8,796 yuan (US$1,103, or A$1,446). It is worth noting that due to the lower income tax structure in China, the disposable income is proportionately higher than, say, the proportion of disposable income to gross income in Australia. The disposable monthly income per capita in Shandong (2006) was 954 yuan, which represents 92 per cent of total income. These low figures explain why there was migration from the country areas to city areas, and from poorer regions to wealthier ones, despite the difficulties of changing one's place of residence under the Communist regime. The low figures also explain why goods and services in China can be provided so cheaply. If an autoworker in China can earn A$100 a week, then a wage of A$5,000 a year puts them well over the average — over two and a half times the average wage in the comparatively well-off eastern province of Shandong, in fact.

In the West, over a similar period from the late 1970s to the early 2000s, there was an inflationary impact. In China, however, the effect of inflation was not as great due to government controls on factors such as interest rates and hence much of this increase represented a real growth in income for ordinary Chinese. The reported average annual income does obscure an increasing gap between the highest and the lowest income levels and differentiation between different occupations. Those at the higher income levels have become very wealthy indeed, but even those at the lower income levels have seen significant increases in disposable income. This increase in GDP over the generation suggests that some areas of China, and the Shandong region in particular, have become much more productive and wealthy, and that consumer goods such as cars have become more affordable to many more people.

Over a more recent period, say from 2000, there have also been policy changes and amendments to government regulation at national and municipal level. These changes have been far-reaching, in part required by the demands of WTO accession, and by the opening of domestic markets to imported goods and services. For example, customs duty on some cars has decreased to 28 per cent and there was a further decrease to 25 per cent on 1 July 2006 (compared to, say, an Australian tariff of 10 per cent in 2006). However, the applicability of this tariff has been the subject of an appeal to the WTO, as noted earlier.

In relation to the Chinese car industry, the effects of reducing customs duties, cancelling quotas and implementing automatic import registration have made it easier to arrange automobile imports, which has led to the increased the supply of European luxury cars like BMW. There have also been exchange rate factors. Under pressure from trading partners, the exchange rate between the US dollar and the yuan, and also between the yuan and the euro, has been allowed to rise and fall within narrow limits, although there is still a large degree of control by the central government and the yuan cannot freely float and find its 'natural' level.

Internal Factors Affecting the Market for Luxury Cars

Since 2000, there has been increased competition from European, and also some Asian luxury vehicle manufacturers whose vehicles appeal to the higher income segment of the market. In Qingdao, brands that were rarely seen ten years ago now include BMW (in its 2006 series), Volvo, AUDI, the 2006 Mercedes-Benz series, top-tier and fully equipped SUVs made in Korea, and luxury vehicles imported from Japan. The competition that was limited only a few years ago has now become extended. General Motors, which has two joint ventures in China, has also given indications that it will expand its presence in the luxury vehicle market, building the Buick Royaume in Shanghai.[135] According to market questionnaires, many of these brands not only have high recognition, but also invoke high brand loyalty.

The marketplace is thus in a state of flux, with a number of new entrants. The SUV series made by Hyundai and Daewoo in Korea are becoming popular partly due to competitive pricing and partly because there is a large Korean expatriate community in the region, due to the proximity of the Korean peninsula and increasing Korean investment in Qingdao and Shandong. The SUV series of the two major manufacturers have proved to be attractive to Chinese consumers and they have sold well since their introduction to Qingdao in 2005. Japanese vehicles — mainly Toyota and Mazda, with equipment and finish that make them attractive to the upscale buyer — are also present in the marketplace.

There remain market risks for luxury cars. There are quotas for European cars which could be subject to arbitrary change, which may affect resale values. The number of high income earners who can afford these comparatively very expensive cars remains small, although their number continues to grow. Perhaps the biggest single internal market challenge to the foreign importers of luxury cars is the possibility of domestic manufacturers producing competitive high quality vehicles with similar levels of features and equipment.

The Research

The research was carried out by aiming for a sample size of 200 owners of luxury cars, and then asking them questions about their preferences and circumstances. These 200 people were selected as randomly as possible (although the population of owners of luxury cars was not a large one) by approaching drivers of BMW, or Volvo, or Audi, or Honda or Mercedes-Benz vehicles when they were entering or about to leave their vehicles. The drivers were asked if they were the owners and then, of course, whether they wished to participate in questionnaires related to their choice of vehicle. These questionnaires were distributed to drivers/owners in the parking areas of large supermarket complexes such as Jusco, Carrefours and Parksons, and generally completed on the spot. Two hundred and sixty-four questionnaires were distributed, but not all were returned. The research team continued to distribute questionnaires until 200 completed forms were received. The response rate of those approached was 76 per cent.

The questionnaires were distributed on several days of the week, both working days and weekends, over various times of the day. Despite best endeavours, the sample may not be entirely representative, for example, many drivers of luxury cars may not shop at the up-market supermarkets, but it should represent a fair selection.

The cars being driven by the respondents included: 44 people driving a Volvo, 42 driving a BMW, 31 driving a Mercedes-Benz, 25 people driving upscale models of Honda, 22 driving Korean SUVs and another 18 people driving an Audi model. The remainder were driving various other luxury cars, including Jaguars, Lincolns, Porsches and in one case a Cadillac.

The questionnaire was piloted before it was distributed. Before the distribution, the manager of a local dealership of imported cars was approached and asked to comment on the representativeness and suitability of the questions. After that, two owners of BMW cars were invited to test and assess the validity of questionnaires. The questionnaires were slightly amended to take into account their comments.

After the questionnaires were received and collated, two semi-structured interviews were conducted with the marketing managers of the Anhua and Furi agencies for imported luxury cars, seeking further in-depth comment on some of the issues that appeared to arise after an initial consideration of the completed questionnaires. Although the information thus obtained was subjective, it appeared to be a valid way to gather more data on the luxury car market in Qingdao, because such data were otherwise unobtainable. This market segment in Qingdao was too small to be shown separately in official municipal statistics of economic activity.

Results of the Research

The findings of the questionnaires and semi-structured interviews were presented and analysed as follows. The findings covered the three parts of the questionnaires and the semi-structured interviews. The first part of the questionnaires was intended to research consumer behaviour which influenced the market for luxury cars, the second part to assess the influence of distribution channels on the marketing of luxury cars (for the phenomenon of marketing luxury cars is comparatively new to China), and the third part explored the market prospects of luxury cars.

The questionnaires presented a profile of consumers. The questionnaire and semi-structured interview clearly showed that the proportion of male consumers to female consumers was large, approximately 7:2. Therefore, it appeared that gender had a large influence in the process of forming a purchase decision. The main consumer group in the sample was between 40 and 45 years old, and other age ranges only constituted a low percentage of the whole. The mean age range was approximately between 38 and 43 years. It is perhaps of interest that the mean age was in the forties, suggesting that those who have achieved high incomes have done so within the last 20 years. There is not a large group aged more than 45, reflecting that under China's economic system prevailing to the 1980s, there were few opportunities for men (and women) to accumulate retirement savings of such a level as to be able to afford luxury cars. Only a few younger people (i.e., younger than 35) could apparently afford to purchase such cars, and it may be assumed that many of these are able to do so with family funds, not their individual funds.

The research also sought a profile of owners by occupation. The division by occupation was not easy to compile, due to overlaps, for example, between self-employed and business managers. The definitions of the occupation groups were also drawn broadly, bearing in mind that just 20 years ago there were very very few self-employed in China under the unreformed Communist system. For those reasons, this aspect of the consumers' profile may have an inherent flaw. However, in broad terms it is useful in that it indicates that just over half of those who purchased luxury cars were in the private sector, and yet there were also a significant number of government officials who could afford to own or acquire for their own use these top of the range cars.

The largest group of consumers were the self-employed, who constituted 70 per cent of the occupation groups; professionals constituted 12 per cent, government officials accounted for 12 per cent, and institution staff made up just 6 per cent. The fact that most consumers were self-employed was borne out by the comments of the marketing managers in the course of the semi-structured interviews.

The research next considered income levels of consumers.[136] Table 10.1 shows that the group of people whose income is between 510,000 and 990,000 yuan makes up the largest proportion of luxury car owners, constituting 48 per cent of the total. The income level of more than 1,000,000 yuan constitutes 29 per cent. The groups between 210,000 to 300,000 yuan and between 310,000 to 500,000 yuan constitute 14 per cent and 9 per cent respectively.

These statistics could be reviewed alongside the statistic for average annual income in Shangdong — around 12,500 yuan. Nearly 30 per cent of luxury car purchasers have an income 80 times — 80 times — the average income of citizens of the province.

Add to that group the next group down, and 78 per cent — more than three-quarters — of the luxury car owners of Qingdao, according to the sample, have incomes more than 25 times the average GDP. Note also that government officials and professionals made up a sizeable proportion of the respondents, so senior government officials must enjoy very high comparative salaries (or else draw funds from other income sources).

Table 10.1: Annual Income of Owners of Luxury Cars

Annual income level (in 000s)	Frequency (number of responses)	Percentage
210–300	28	14.0
301–500	18	9.0
501–999	97	49.0
> 1,000	57	28.0

The research also examined reasons, or factors of major influence, for the respondents' decision to acquire a luxury car. The questionnaires asked respondents to consider such factors as personal preference, the brand name of the vehicle, the suggestion of family or friends or the dealer's promotion, and to nominate which was the most important factor in their decision to purchase. Personal preference is concerned with an individual's need for personal satisfaction—unrelated to what others think or do. Examples include self-esteem, accomplishment, freedom, or relaxation. Selecting a car on the basis of brand preference would be of interest to marketers and manufacturers, who work hard to win brand loyalty. This means that consumers in the target segment would usually choose the brand they were familiar with over other brands, perhaps because of habit or because of favourable past experience.

It could be expected that, as conspicuously consumed luxury products (especially in China where they have very high status value), luxury cars would be purchased mainly for the perceived value of the brand. This is related to the marketing concept of brand insistence, which means consumers insist on a particular product and are willing to expend some effort to obtain it.

According to the responses to the questionnaires, 'personal preference' was the major factor in the car purchase decision-making process, and accounted for 54 per cent of the total respondents. Around 40 per cent of respondents chose to record that the major influence in their decision to purchase was the brand name of the vehicle chosen. Around 4 per cent of the respondents said that the major factor was the suggestion of family or friends, and the very small remaining percentage nominated the dealer's promotion as the factor of choice.

These responses suggested that a majority of the Chinese luxury car consumers have not yet established strong brand loyalties, or habitual preferences, which is only to be expected, given the fact that the market is only recently established. This fact implies that foreign auto producers in China may have limited influence on the decision to purchase luxury cars, and that the threat of substitutes is therefore a significant one, for purchasers are not wedded to their own favourite brands.

The responses, if valid generally for Chinese purchasers, are not good news to Western manufacturers of luxury cars, for according to the feelings underlying the responses, they could not rely on establishing a loyal following for their brands. There are many obvious benefits in winning strong brand loyalty. For example, the prices of luxury goods can then be maintained at a high level and consumers will still prefer the brand; in fact they may value it even more because of the perceived status value. Also, if consumers of luxury cars tend to have high brand loyalty, then a manufacturer can project future sales more reliably, for once consumers start using a luxury brand, they usually want to be able to continue consuming that product.

It seems that foreign manufacturers would have to continue to work to build upon the 40 per cent of luxury car purchasers who were influenced by the brand name. The other factor that rated very poorly was the dealer's promotion efforts. This is also foreseeable, for purchasers of high-value cars tend to make their own decisions, and would be inclined to be critical of dealers' offerings that did not accord with their own perceptions.

The respondents were also asked about when they intended to trade in their cars for a new model. The largest group represented those people who chose to buy another car within two to three years, and most would turn their cars over within one to four years. Surprisingly few (18 per cent) planned to hold their cars for more than four years. This perhaps mirrors the high consumption levels of this very wealthy segment of the market.

The semi-structured interviews with the marketing managers of the two largest luxury car dealerships — Anhui and Furi agencies — elicited their opinion that luxury cars held 10 per cent of the overall new car market in Qingdao, particularly Mercedes-Benz and Volvo but including all high-value cars such as Hondas, SUVs and some American luxury cars. The marketing managers stated that, in their opinion, the profile of consumers indicated by the research survey — male, self-employed and in their mid-forties — was generally reflective of the market.

The marketing managers also stated that most purchasers paid cash. In their view, less than 20 per cent of new car buyers had to arrange a loan for the purchase, even given that the amount of money involved was comparatively large for a Chinese consumer. The fact that most car buyers pay cash may be put down to three reasons: those making the purchase are generally high income earners, most cars are bought through businesses (whether publicly or privately owned) and many private buyers can draw upon the assistance of family who in their case typically hold high levels of savings.

The implication of this research is that, for those Chinese who can afford it, the car purchase decision is a sophisticated one, and they have high standards, which reflect the very high comparative prices that they pay for their motor vehicle.

The Market for Medium-Sized Cars

After researching the top of the range, the next logical area to research was the mid-range of the market — the cars of medium size which were priced and targeted at the business segment and the consumers who were upwardly mobile, or else aspired to be. One of the cars in this range is General Motors' Buick sedan. It is available in China across a range of variants, one of the more common being the Regal. Such a car would be somewhat similar to the Ford Falcon or the Holden Commodore manufactured in Australia.

In Australia, a medium sized car like the Buick would probably be marketed as family size, although this term is not the same in China. In that country, the Buick is considered a business car and appears to be marketed to the upwardly mobile professional or executive who cannot afford the top of the range luxury cars.

General Motors Corporation (GM) has of course individual model brands such as Buick, Cadillac, Chevrolet, GMC, Holden, Opel, Saab, Saturn, Vauxhall and Pontiac — some fifteen major brands in all. This compares to DaimlerChrysler and Ford (eight major brands each) and Volkswagen (seven major brands). In 2005, GM senior management looked at the Chinese market and made the decision to concentrate on three brands to implement their market penetration strategy. The three brands they chose were Buick, Cadillac and Chevrolet, which have the highest unit sales totals.[137]

The brands are designed for what GM sees as the three main market segments and indeed they cover the B-class, C-class and A00-class segments. Cadillac is positioned as a luxury car, Buick is positioned as a car for business people and families, and Chevrolet models are positioned in the economy car segment. In the United States, sales of Chevrolet in the economy segment are higher in terms of units than sales of the other two brands. Despite this, in 1999, GM considered that the medium sized car — in the business segment — showed the greatest promise in China and it chose Buick in its various products to be its flagship brand to take a stake in the Chinese market.[138]

GM's choice has been a sound one, and sales of Buicks in China have been steadily increasing. In 1999 GM sold 19,790 Buicks, and in 2000 increased that substantially to 30,542 vehicles. The following year, there was another big increase in sales in both absolute and percentage terms when Buick sold 58,328 vehicles. In 2002, sales nearly doubled to 110,723 vehicles, then nearly doubled again in 2003 when GM sold 201,188 units. In 2004, a year of some economic restrictions and fewer car sales overall, Buick sold fewer units but nevertheless still achieved a healthy total of 180,990 vehicles.[139] GM clearly has a successful strategy for Buick, and that strategy, as evidenced in the Qingdao market, appears worthy of study, particularly the relationship between consumer behaviour and marketing mix.

As an example of the pricing, a Buick Excelle retails new in China for around 150,000 yuan. This is the equivalent of about US$19,000, or A\$24,700. This figure, which may look cheap to Western eyes, or to Australians shopping for a Commodore or a Falcon, nevertheless represents twelve times the 2005 yearly income of a citizen of Shangdong province.

This research project into the market for medium-sized cars in Qingdao centred around the Buick marque as a representative of all the Buick models. The research stretched over six weeks and was conducted on weekdays and weekends. It involved selecting consumers who were (a) browsing through Buick car sales outlets on one of the main city thoroughfares, Fuzhou Road, and (b) car owners/drivers of Buicks who were buying fuel in service stations on Hong Kong Road, another main city thoroughfare in Qingdao City.

The definition of 'owner' was not easy to frame, for, as is revealed in the following research, most cars were owned by corporations or government. The drivers of the Buicks were asked whether they had a right to exclusive use of the vehicle or made the decision to acquire the vehicle, and if the drivers affirmed that they fell into either/both of these categories then they were considered to be the 'owners' for practical purposes in this research, wherever the legal ownership might reside. In all, 120 questionnaires were received for analysis.

Results of the Research

The results of the research are presented below in descriptive and tabular form. Information that owners obtained about the car market in general and Buicks in particular came from a number of sources, but the main source of their information was the print media. This may reflect the choice of media of GM China's marketing people. However, the high percentage that received information about the car from other sources, especially friends, may reflect the Chinese reliance upon networking in the upper levels of officialdom and corporations:

The gender and age of Buick owners was also researched and Table 10.2 shows the age of the population, which was also heavily skewed towards males, as was the case of the luxury car owners. Of the 120 respondents, 95 were male and 25 were female. The ages of the respondents also generally reflected the age groupings of luxury car buyers. Although the definition of age groups was unfortunately not coordinated with the research into luxury cars, the age divisions are sufficiently close to allow limited comparisons.

Around one-half of the respondents who had exclusive use or legal ownership of the cars were in their forties, which reinforces the research finding concerning the age of luxury car owners, and confirms official nationwide statistics of car ownership.

Table 10.2: Age of Owners of Buick Cars in Qingdao

Age group (years)	Frequency (number of responses)	Percentage
< 30	19	16.0
30–40	34	28.0
41–50	59	49.0
> 50	8	7.0

The research also looked at the occupation of the Buick owners who responded to the questionnaire, using a simpler classification than the occupation used for the classification of luxury car owners. In relation to the occupations of the respondents, there was a higher proportion of government officials in the ranks of apparent owners, but it seemed that the ultimate purchasers were government bureaus and the vehicles were therefore technically publicly owned.

This question of the ultimate ownership continued to present a problem, but the research in relation to the age of 'owners' could not be corrected in relation to occupation, so the figures were left to stand. The following item, whether the car was in public or private ownership, was a more reliable piece of information. This next question in the questionnaire asked whether the car was legally in private or public ownership, and just 9 per cent of the Buicks owned by respondents were in private hands — 27 per cent were owned by private business corporations and 63 per cent were owned by government entities, including SOEs.

As with the research into aspects of ownership of luxury cars, this research considered the income levels of Buick owners, but nominated lower income divisions. Bearing in mind once again that the annual income per capita in Shandong province in 2006 was 12,492 yuan, the typical owner/user of a business car like the Buick was comparatively very wealthy.

With these questions relating to income, all the respondents were prepared to answer the question, with an openness about their income which is the opposite of the reticence Westerners have in discussing wages and income. The statements could not be verified, but were taken at face value.

Table 10.3: Income Levels of Buick Owners

Annual income (thousands)	Frequency (number of responses)	Percentage
< 60	19	16.0
60–120	28	23.0
121–180	67	56.0
> 180	6	5.0

Compared to the income levels of luxury car owners, there were many fewer in the topmost level, and the majority were in the 121,000 to 180,000 yuan annual income level, and no doubt many of these were the upper-echelon officials and cadres whose post and ranking entitled them to a car of this calibre. This income range was the direct equivalent of A$19,900 to A$29,600, or, putting it another way and expressing it in terms of Australia's average wage (A$56,000 in mid-2006), between 35 per cent and 53 per cent of the average wage in Australia — but comparatively very much higher in China, of course. From that perspective, a Buick priced in similar terms and exported to the Australian market would be affordable by even those Australians on the lowest wage levels.

The question on income was followed by a question about the owners' expectations about the pricing of motor vehicles like the Buick, and then a related question about whether the Buick was value for money. In the question about being satisfied with the price that had been paid for the Buick, 82 per cent felt it was value for money, while 11 per cent considered it was over-priced and 7 per cent stated that in their opinion it was under-priced.

Owners were then asked about their preferences when making the decision to acquire the vehicle either personally or through their enterprise. They were asked whether they thought that the brand, the appearance, the function or the price took precedence over other characteristics. The intention of this question was to assess how utilitarian were the motives of the consumers, or whether there were strong attractions to the brand of car, whatever its characteristics.

Table 10.4: Preferred Characteristic at Time of Purchase

Characteristic	Frequency (number of responses)	Percentage
Brand	8	8
Appearance	22	19
Function	56	46
Price	34	28

The responses to this question suggested that Chinese car consumers are mostly pragmatic, being concerned firstly with function, while concern with price not far behind. The appearance of the vehicle is less important and the brand itself comes a poor fourth. This is one more question whose answers suggest that there is not yet a high brand loyalty among Chinese consumers. This is not unexpected, given that many brands have not yet developed a strong profile, and Buick has only been marketed since 1999.

One final question in the questionnaires asked the respondents' attitude to the overall styling of the Buick and the impression it offered to the public at large. Of the respondents, 35 per cent noted that they thought the car portrayed a 'high-status', while 44 per cent thought that the styling of the car was generally impressive. A further 16 per cent of participants were not impressed by the styling and 5 per cent had no opinion.

The Market for Small Cars (1.6 Litre Engine Capacity or Less)
As mainland China is now the third-largest car market in the world after the US and Japan, there is obviously varied and strong competition in the domestic car industry after the decades of unreformed Communist rule when competition was anathema. There are around 100 large and small domestic and ten foreign/joint-venture manufacturers producing products for the small car market. Some local auto makers which have already been mentioned include Geely Automobile Holdings Ltd and Chery Automobile Co., which offer low-priced cars with small engines. Overall, consumers in the small car segment are able to select from about 25 entry-level compacts such as the Chery QQ and Honda Motors' (HMC) Fit. The domestic manufacturers appear to have a market advantage in that they are able to appeal to patriotic motives to persuade local people to buy their products. However, there are two factors which assist the foreign auto makers such as GM, Ford and the like: Chinese believe foreign cars have fewer problems than local brands, and foreign brands typically have better after-sale service.

Many of the Chinese consumers are first-time buyers, with little brand awareness and low brand loyalty, and the commitment by a middle-income urban Chinese person to purchase a car involves spending almost a year's income for even a vehicle at the lower end of the market. They are therefore, as indicated later in this research, very demanding.

Since 2000, with continuing market-economy reforms and an improvement in living standards, more private consumers, instead of government officials, were expected to buy cars, in keeping with the promise of the government articulated in 1993. It was generally expected that the ordinary wage earner would have to be satisfied with cars at the smaller end of the market, and in fact private buyers were, and are, the main focus of the country's small car market. These small cars are defined as having an engine cubic capacity of less than 1.6 litres, and this has become a benchmark when regulators consider economic and taxation measures such as the Chinese automobile consumption tax.

Sales of small cars have expanded, reflecting these expectations. According to the China Association of Automobile Manufacturers, in 2005 sales of small cars rose by 22 per cent over the equivalent period in the year before, to reach a total of 568,502 units. The overall market for cars grew by 15.6 per cent to 1.6 million units. A typical small car, such as Chery Automobile Co.'s $4,000 hatchback, more than doubled its sales to 61,633 units for the year.

Under the unreformed regime, all prices were controlled and markets restricted by the State Development Planning Commission (SDPC) as part of the procedures of running a centrally planned economy, and such regulatory habits died hard, at least in relation to domestic markets which were subject to a wide range of fees and taxes that acted to constrict the market. That situation has been changing. In July 2000, the SDPC declared that it would drop formal objections to domestic car makers being able to set prices for their products at whatever level they thought fit. The declaration was interpreted as a signal that the central government intended to liberalize prices in the domestic car market, in part to make car ownership more affordable. These government moves to free up the domestic car market have continued. In 2006, there was a reduction in the cost of fees and licences and the Ministry of Finance and the SDPC cooperated in cancelling no fewer than 238 administrative fees that applied to car consumers. There were reviews to taxation levels as well, and in the same year, the Ministry of Finance and the State Administration of Taxation also announced a 30 per cent reduction in the consumption tax on vehicles.

The Research[140]

As the small car segment of the car market is clearly crucial, and accounting for a very large number of sales, it is useful to research aspects of the market, particularly the factors which are influencing demand. Therefore, the aim of this research was to identify the factors which influence people's decisions when they buy new small cars (i.e., A00-class vehicles of less than 1.6 litres engine capacity), and to analyse the price and product strategies of the domestic manufacturers in the liberalized trading conditions.

The nature of China's domestic demand is continually changing. The requirements of small car buyers especially are changing as people's lifestyles and relationships become more diverse, and car ownership falls within the grasp of more people. The size of a family in China has become smaller, and the definition of a family in the popular consciousness is more flexible than in previous generations.[141] Many people now live alone, with limited needs for transport. People also live longer, which means that there may commonly be three generations living together, which has implications for the market demand for motor vehicles. For example, whereas once a Chinese family may have fitted easily into a three-wheeled Flower micro-car, now, if there are grandparents to be transported as well as parents and a child, a five-seater car is the minimum vehicle needed.

It is also a fact that, with improvements in their diet and health care, the average Chinese person is taller and wider than previous generations, which means new consumers might seek new vehicles which are roomier. Seating positions would also need to be higher too. Maybe it is a universal trait that everyone wants to feel big and tall, even in a small car. Other features that may be in demand are improvement in the interior configuration. For example, Japanese-designed cars such as the Honda Jazz include an interior which is spacious and versatile, with the ability to configure the back seat/load area in several different ways and folding arrangements. With all these features, the research also sought to determine whether Chinese consumers demanded a level of performance comparable to the best that Western-designed and manufactured small cars could offer.

If the answers to all these research questions indicated that the average Chinese consumer was very discerning, and demanding of high quality as well as superior design, then the implication was that the demand in this segment of the market is also sophisticated.

The research was carried out through surveys of actual and potential consumers and questions about the factors that determined the purchasing decision. Results of the research showed that fuel efficiency was the most important factor in consumers' purchase decisions, followed by the total purchase price. The style of make and model came in third, while the purchase factor that rated fourth was the safety features. These factors compare with the factors for purchase of luxury cars noted above, which did not even rate such aspects as fuel efficiency or purchase price.

The research concerned a number of factors influencing the decision to purchase a new small car. One such factor was its fuel efficiency. In Qingdao, the price of 93-octane gasoline, the most commonly used fuel in China, reached 4.98 yuan per litre in mid-2006, after being around 3.15 yuan per litre at the beginning of the year, an indicator that China, despite its levels of domestic oil production, is no longer as immune from increases in the world price of oil as it was during the Oil Shock of the 1970s.

Another factor concerned the features that small cars offered. Did Chinese consumers want a basic small car without them, or would they seek extra features? Did Chinese car buyers seek power windows and antilock brakes as standard equipment even in modestly priced models? The research materials attempted to resolve such questions, at least in relation to the potential car buying public of Qingdao.

The research was carried out through questionnaires distributed to potential purchasers of small cars. These questionnaires asked the respondents whether they planned to buy a new car within the coming year, and if they said they were, they were then asked to note and to weigh the factors that would determine their decision to purchase a car. Some of the respondents were selected at random from the general population, namely pedestrians passing through May Fourth Square, one of the main gathering points in Qingdao city, and others were approached in the business district as well as in hotels, hospitals and even some of the scenic spots.

The canvassing took place over a period of two weeks during an ordinary working period, on each day of the week. By this means, 50 completed questionnaires were received from a cross-section of respondents who answered in the affirmative when they were asked whether they had bought a small car (and were prepared to answer the questionnaire). This figure for completed questionnaires was not as high as hoped, as it was not easy to 'cold call' on members of the public and find those who had purchased a small car and who were prepared to spend time, on the spot, to answer the questionnaire.

Results of the Research

The profile of respondents who wished to purchase small cars differed markedly from the profile of purchasers of luxury cars, and this was no surprise. The respondents' gender and age is shown at Table 10.5. There were seventeen respondents aged below 30, which, due to the simplicity of having a sample size of exactly 50, amounted to a ratio of 34 per cent.

The total of respondents whose age was between 30 and 40 was eight. There were thirteen respondents aged from 41 to 50. The number of respondents aged between 51 and 60 was a little smaller than that of 30 to 40, which accounted for 14 per cent. Only five respondents were aged beyond 60. In each group, the ratio of female to male was less than, but not far from, 50 per cent.

It was notable that generally prospective purchasers of this small car were younger than the typical purchasers of larger cars, possibly reflecting lower incomes, but it was also worthy of note that there was a group of older consumers who had purchased a small car.

Table 10.5: Gender and Age of Respondents (Percentages)

Age group	Men	Women	Total
< 30	16	18	34
30–40	10	6	16
41–50	14	12	26
51–60	8	6	14
> 60	4	6	10

Another statistic that related to the profile of consumers who had purchased a small car was the source of their information about the vehicle. The research showed that most respondents knew of various models of small cars available through newspapers and magazines.

Television, although apparently an all-pervasive medium, only rated as an information source for 13 per cent of respondents. In addition, 21 per cent of respondents knew of the small car they chose to purchase from the internet — which possibly reflects the fact that the largest survey group were those under 30, who 30 also constitute the largest users of the internet. The balance of respondents learned of the car through various other sources, from word of mouth to outdoor displays.

When a minor question asked their opinion about the quality and reliability of the advertising of cars in the category, more than 50 per cent consumers considered it to be fair. Only 30 per cent of consumers considered it as good or excellent.

Table 10.6 indicates the various factors that consumers considered most important when choosing their car. It was clear that price was the first factor that came into consumers' consideration, but being nominated by just 22 per cent of the whole group, it was clearly not the dominant factor.

Other factors were nominated as being of almost equal importance to price, among them after-sales service and product reputation, both of which were rated at 18 per cent. Product quality was a little lower than these.

Table 10.6: Desirable Motor Vehicle Factors

Factors	Frequency (number of responses)	Percentage
After-sales service	9	18
Solid feel to the MV (i.e., perceived strength of the product)	4	8
Price	11	22
Reputation	9	18
Quality	8	16
Other factors	9	18

The factor described as 'perceived strength of the product' was intended to seek opinions about whether consumers felt that small cars were robust enough for some of China's poorer roads, or even for the hustle and bustle of city driving. The response was not as significant as the framers of the questionnaire believed it might be.

In another question on the intended use of the vehicle, around 62 per cent of purchasers stated that they would use the vehicle primarily for business purposes.

Results of this research showed that fuel efficiency (nominated by 39 per cent of respondents) was the most important factor in the small car purchasing decision, followed by performance (21 per cent) and the overall purchase price (18 per cent of respondents). Make and model (including special features) (12 per cent) came in fourth and then the safety features (10 per cent). As fuel prices increased in 2006, with considerable publicity about likely price rises in the future, it is perhaps understandable that nearly twice as many people ranked fuel efficiency over performance as the most important factor. The research also found that men were twice as likely as women to rank performance as the most important factor when buying a new car.

When surveyed as to their levels of satisfaction with their small car and with the service provided by the supplier of the vehicle, consumers reported high degrees of dissatisfaction, which indicates that they are discerning purchasers, as would be expected with a product that represents a comparatively high level of investment. On the other hand, some might have surmised that consumers who are able to purchase a product that had been denied to them for so long might have been happy to take whatever quality of product they are offered.

The fact that the Chinese consumer of small cars (as well the Chinese consumer of more expensive cars) is clearly a discerning one is another indicator of sophisticated consumer choice, and suggests that the behaviour of consumers is not very different from the behaviour of consumers in the West. It may be that China is becoming every bit as much a consumer society as are some societies in the West.

The research also indicated that if the market was a discerning one, demanding higher quality in style and finish, as well as value for money, then there would be market pressure on domestic manufacturers to lift their game to meet the demand in the marketplace. Improved products for the Chinese marketplace logically leads to improved products in global markets and increased competitiveness internationally from Chinese manufacturers.

The next research question asked consumers: Which aspect of your car's design and manufacture needs to be improved?

The answers indicated that the styling of the vehicle was by far the main cause of dissatisfaction, which may reflect a feeling that most small cars currently marketed in China are European designs for European tastes and did not represent Chinese preferences. There may also have been a perception that the styling was not completely up to date in all cases, but some vehicles were aging designs brought in to the Chinese market.

The response suggests that Western manufacturers that invest in joint ventures in China should be wary of local consumer tastes. If they take the response of the Chinese consumer for granted, and offer him/ her second-rate designs, they do so at peril of their profits.

There is also an implication that if the so-called global car comes to fruition, as a development of the trend towards an internationalization of production of cars such as the Ford Focus, then designers will have to take serious note of the tastes of Chinese consumers. Small car buyers clearly turned their nose up at European styles. It is not unreasonable to assume that Chinese tastes will not accord with European ideals of what is stylish, and hence if the global car is designed for what is becoming the largest segment of the world market — the Chinese market — then the designers will have to know Chinese preferences well. The inference is that they themselves should be Chinese, but this need not be so. Certainly, it will not do for designers in Stuttgart or Detroit or Melbourne to come up with their idea of a stylish car and expect the Chinese to like it or lump it. The lumps might flow both ways.

In relation to preferred features, it was also worthy of note that fuel economy was a cause of dissatisfaction, and that purchasers felt that the car was more thirsty than they had believed. This could be due to the fact that driving in city traffic in China is becoming more chaotic and less conducive to economical driving styles. The power of the car was not a comparatively serious concern, probably because few Chinese consumers appear to purchase a car for sustained driving over long trips. Many of the highways linking large centres within a province or region are toll roads, with frequent and costly charges. Inter-provincial travel by car is even rarer, and inter-country travellers make use of the good and improving airline system if they can afford it. The other option is the train, which in many cases would provide more speedy inter-city commuting than the car. So the power of the car would only be a feature sought for status purposes — and as engine size is not immediately obvious, it would not be ranked as a must-have for the new car buyer.

Attitude to after-sales service was another aspect of the purchase that aroused popular concern, and it was a factor that provided results that should also be of concern to Western manufacturers planning expansion in the Chinese market, as well as domestic producers.

Only 5 per cent of those who actually purchased a car of the A00-class thought that the services that followed up the sale were excellent, and only a further 12 per cent judged that they were satisfactory. Thirty-seven per cent of the consumers thought that after-sales service of their car was ordinary, 34 per cent were dissatisfied and 12 per cent were very dissatisfied. Part of the reason for this could be spare-parts availability, which often caused delay and incurred unexpected expenses. Some auto parts were expensive in the after-sales retail market mainly due to the fact that most of the parts had to be imported from Europe or other countries. Many of the foreign-designed vehicles sold in the domestic marketplace were assembled from a package of components in knocked-down kits, and it seemed that there was not sufficient attention given to providing sufficient numbers of spare parts for the service support market.

This is a significant finding about the quality, not so much of the car as of the service available, and suggests that it will be a problem that must be addressed by the Chinese industry. It could be the fault either of the manufacturers or of the Chinese automotive infrastructure generally, in that there are too few service outlets to meet the growing demand for new vehicles and the concomitant need for after-sales service. This area of providing parts support and back-up could be an area where wholly Chinese-owned manufacturers develop a strong advantage, in that they can make parts locally and ensure prompt and economical supply.

There were other research questions that covered a range of purchase considerations. In regard to the price that consumers wanted to pay for a small car, most (63 per cent) nominated that it should cost between 60,000 and 90,000 yuan (A$9,800–14,800). This is an interesting finding in the broader context of this book, for it indicates that the desired price range for middle-class and professional car buyers in Qingdao at least, for new cars (of the size and quality of European small cars generally), is in a well-affordable range.

Another question asked respondents to nominate the preferred seller of the cars. More than half of the respondents stated that they would like to buy their car from a 4S dealership, providing a full range of services, because of perceptions that it could supply better service. It was partly due to this common response that a later research project considered all four aspects of the 4S dealer support system.

The findings illustrated by the material above indicated that consumers of all classes of motor vehicle were discerning and were generally not satisfied with aspects of their purchase. Among the problems, 40 per cent of the respondents thought the shape and styling of their car should be improved to make it more attractive to Chinese tastes. It may be a mistake to assume that European models can be simply transferred into the Chinese environment. A cheap and basic European car may not succeed in China just because it is cheap and basic. Chinese consumers are discerning, have their own preferences, and can easily identify second-rate products.

Also the fact that nearly five out of six consumers assessed the after-sales service they received as less than good and well short of optimum implies that there are problems with sales back-up to overcome.

Conclusion: The Chinese Car Consumer

Taken as a whole, these small-scale surveys of Chinese consumers' demand for luxury, medium-sized and small cars indicates that they are discerning buyers. It is a rapidly maturing market. Moreover, the rate at which it is maturing is reminiscent of the speed with which the

Japanese motorcycle market matured in the 1960s. In the early 1950s Japanese motorcycle consumers (and car consumers for that matter) were satisfied with basic transportation, but their aspirations quickly grew. This may partly be due to a psychological factor (and this book has frequently emphasized the psychological dimension of aspirations to private car ownership). The ordinary person likes to think that he or she is continually improving their station in life and the quality and range of their possessions. When they buy their first car, the novelty fades quickly, and they seek to improve upon their personal steed, to make it a part of themselves and their maturing lifestyle. Hence, the average consumer's demand for a car is continually defining itself and changing, becoming more sophisticated. The only difference in the demand of the Chinese auto consumer is that their demands are increasing at a far greater pace than was the case for earlier generations of Western auto consumers. This is perhaps due to the fact that Chinese urban society itself is changing so very fast.

The overall conclusion about the demand for cars in China indicates that there are two broad consumer groups. One group constitutes the demand for luxury and prestige cars, and the Chinese view of what is a prestige car includes vehicles like the upper-range Buick models (referred to in China as the 'business car' range) and 4WD SUV vehicles like the Toyota Terios. The profile of consumers of prestige cars is that they are mainly male, mainly in their forties, and all in the upper income echelons. For this group, the price of luxury cars may be relatively elastic, that is, increasing prices may not greatly affect the demand for luxury cars as these consumers can afford what to ordinary wage-earning Chinese are relatively very high prices. To these consumers, a car is a status symbol as much as transportation, hence they also seek foreign-made cars of high reputation (e.g., Mercedes-Benz).

The second group of consumers constitute the demand for small cars, of the likes of the Nanjing Fiat, VW models and Citroens. Males are still in a majority in this group, but there is a significant minority of females. The majority of small car consumers are in their thirties, but there are significant minorities in their twenties, and also in their fifties. They are demanding and want a range of features and a quality finish in their car.

They have an income in the upper range of urban middle income levels, which start at a wage of around 30,000 yuan each year (US$3,750).

One common feature for both groups is that most consumers pay cash, which indicates that not only are there likely to be limited prospects in the short term for car financiers, but prices may be constricted (because consumers will be limited in what that can pay by what they or their families have saved).

The profile of the consumer of the more expensive cars has been well researched elsewhere, and this research simply confirms the earlier findings. However, these research projects overall contribute to the knowledge about the nature of the Chinese consumer demand for cars by pointing out that the demand is for cars that are of comparable quality and have features equivalent to small cars in the West. Moreover, these consumers are from a very large cohort — those with upper-middle income levels, which means that the demand for small cars is sophisticated and fast-growing.

It can be assumed that Chinese car makers will produce cars to meet this wider demand and that such cars will be very similar to those demanded in the West, but be competitively priced to be affordable by the upper ranges of the middle income level.

If foreign manufacturers establish joint ventures with a view to producing cars that are outdated and/or cheap and basic, they may get their fingers burnt. It seems that the Chinese will demand the most up-to-date and technologically advanced models on the world market and will not be impressed if offered second-rate vehicles. This demand will put pressure on domestic producers to lift their game to be globally competitive.

However, there are clearly problems with the infrastructure of the Chinese car industry, which is not surprising, seeing that it has developed so quickly. It is one thing to manufacture or import a large number of cars into China, but it is another matter to provide the myriad supporting services from after-sales service to finance and insurance services, etc. Even the question of where to park increasing numbers of privately used cars becomes a crucial issue.

The overall conclusion of the research was that Chinese consumers are indeed generally demanding, educated in emerging trends affecting the automotive industry, and expecting the best mix of features and economy they can obtain for their money.

The next chapter considers some infrastructure issues that are likely to impede the import/manufacture of large numbers of quality vehicles to supply the Chinese market.

11 Supply Factors

How Many Cars Are Needed/Wanted?

The statement of Premier Li Peng that every Chinese could own his or her own car by 2008 struck a chord with almost everyone in China. It resonated with an implied promise that by that time China would be well-developed and on a par with some Western countries.

The promise of owning a car brings with it many images, of wealth, of mobility, and of status. It also includes potent symbols of China's growing wealth and power and hence its influence on the world stage. During earlier ages, the people of China referred to their country as the Middle Kingdom, implying both that it was situated between earth and heaven, and that it was at the centre of the world. There were misunderstandings when early emissaries from Europe came to pay their respects at the Celestial Court of the Emperor and it was assumed in Chinese imperial circles that the barbarian nations were in fact offering their fealty, as was only to be expected in their eyes.

Although these are historical musings, the intent is to emphasize that the potency of the promise of car ownership should not be underestimated. Just as the image of nationhood in the United States in the 20th century was intertwined with images of car ownership, so the image on nationhood in China in the 21st century cannot be separated from car ownership.

Yet the very numbers involved in crunching statistics for the Chinese people produce daunting totals.

Playing With Some Statistics

There has already been discussion of an all-pervasive myth among Western business people that possibly goes back to the days when traders trekked the Silk Road. The myth goes this way — there are huge numbers of Chinese, and they therefore constitute a massive market for our product. If only we could get a fraction of them to want and buy our product, we will be rich beyond imagining!

It does not work that way. It is a myth, like many others of antiquity. If there is a product that appeals to the Chinese, chances are that an enterprising Chinese business person will be onto the opportunity and becoming rich while the Western business person is still trying to calculate his/her potential wealth on an abacus.

There is also a myth involving cars in China, and many Western business people perpetuate it. The myth says that the Chinese economy is ever-increasing and will be a source of wealth for the whole industrialized world and especially for Western producers who can get their product into the country's mass markets. The myth ignores real constraints of resources. Just as there are glass ceilings in some areas of employment, and barriers in others, in China there are two Great Walls. One is the construction of brick and stone that stretches across the northwest of the country and was intended to keep barbarians out. The other Great Wall is a mathematical barrier which consists of statistics of resource usage and represents a hard and fast limit to economic growth. It is the Great Wall of Reality, and operates to keep the myth-makers out.

Consider the numbers involved in car ownership in China. If every adult Chinese (say 950 million of a total population of 1.3 billion) was to own a car, and turned their cars over for a new model once every three years, this implies an annual new car market of 316 million cars per year.

The gasoline consumption of all these private drivers is awesome to contemplate. If they each drove 25,000 km per year, and the gasoline consumption of their vehicles averaged 9 km per litre, then that means the domestic gasoline demand, for private use alone, would reach 878 billion litres per year (which would near drain world production, but the question of the use of oil resources is outside the strict purview of this book).

The statistic of the total number of cars in private ownership perhaps needs trimming down. In Chapter 7 we made a rough estimate that one half of adults may be car owners. Let's refine that statistic. It could be reduced to the urban population, 36 per cent of the total population of the country, to get 470 million for the total number of city dwellers in China in 2004 (add 0.9 per cent per year for the population growth to get a 2008 figure of say 487 million people). Of this number, 73 per cent would be adults. Allow for aged people (say 10 per cent) and those who never want to drive (say another 10 per cent) and the potential number of car owners nationwide, both men and women, is still 275 million. Divide this by three for a new car only every three years and 91 million cars are needed each year.

The figure could be reduced still further to, say, take into account only the comparatively wealthy cities on the eastern seaboard, with the addition of some major inland centres such as Chongqing and Chengdu, and the potential car-owning population comes to around 210 million, implying a production demand of cars per year of around 70 million.

This is obviously a huge figure (although very conservative), and to meet the demand, existing manufacturing facilities would have to increase their current production more than 30-fold. This is challenging and not possible within the short term (say three to five years) but is not unlikely, in theory, in the longer term, provided other constraints of resource availability and especially the oil supply do not run out. So, is it likely, or even possible for a greatly increased demand for new cars in China?

Infrastructure Constraints

There are many other constraints which severely restrict domestic demand, even such a huge demand, such as issues of infrastructure development and prosaic matters such as a legal system able to handle the millions of disputes that arise from conflicts on public streets and highways. If there are such serious constraints, and assuming the Chinese motor vehicle manufacturers are strongly growth-oriented, then the growing car corporations will have to turn to exports to maintain high rates of expansion.

When motor vehicle infrastructure is mentioned, then often the first image that springs to mind is a highway. Indeed, highways may be the most important element of infrastructure that impacts upon how the motoring public use their vehicles. In China, there has been heavy investment in highway development, and it has been an integrated aspect of the development of the transportation system generally. There have been many notable achievements in the construction of highways into hitherto inaccessible parts of the country — the construction of bridges across natural obstacles, and the expansion of the railway network to complement the national highway grid. No one could deny that the Chinese people have vision and skills when it comes to engineering projects, as well as the determination to see them through to completion. Hence, the element of highway development as an element of a modern motoring infrastructure is not an issue. China has excellent intercity links, city freeways and cross-country roads. Most Chinese cities have well-developed road systems. Beijing, for example, has no fewer than nine huge ring roads (although they are often choked with traffic, and the city's residents are similarly choked by the smog and the pollutants). This book will not research the issue of highway infrastructure, because it is not likely to be a constraint upon the expanding number of cars in private ownership.

In relation to motor vehicle infrastructure, the next element that may spring to mind concerns the development of networks of service stations to provide fuel and oil. In China, refuelling stations have sprung up in numerous localities and the rapid proliferation of such enterprises is obvious to even the casual traveller.

These two major elements of motor vehicle infrastructure are important, but they have attracted the attention of the best of Chinese city planners and are being addressed. There are other elements of motor vehicle infrastructure which are equally important, although not as noticeable as these big ticket items. These elements of infrastructure include mundane functions such as repairs and servicing, parking, processes of selling second-hand vehicles and motorist support organizations.

These create issues related to infrastructure development which will affect the expansion of the domestic Chinese car market. While these issues have not received the same attention from researchers, they must be considered. The implication is this: If the Chinese domestic car market can continue to grow exponentially and has all the elements needed to absorb increased supply, then the number of cars will continue to increase at a high rate, but if there are significant restraints on the capacity of elements of motoring infrastructure besides highways, then the country will be unable to cope with a great increase in local ownership. Hence, Chinese car manufacturers will have to look to exports to continue their growth-oriented development plans. This book looks at four elements of infrastructure that may be under-estimated, yet are of crucial importance. They include: (a) repairs and servicing of motor vehicles (especially through the 4S system), (b) the development of second-hand car markets, (c) parking issues, and (d) insurance and legal issues.

The conclusion is that whereas the capacity of the Chinese to remedy problems should not be underestimated, some significant restraints will remain. In the author's view, the domestic Chinese motor vehicle industry will not be able to absorb a greatly expanded supply of vehicles in the near future.

Within five to ten years, the industry will hit limits to growth, and these limits will be related to motoring infrastructure other than highways. In the medium to longer term, if the Chinese economy is given 20 years to build the infrastructure, educate the hundreds of thousands of skilled people needed and form the associations that are part of a modern motoring sector, then it will certainly succeed. However, given the length of time needed to train people, to build parking centres in new neighbourhoods that are designed for cars and, importantly, to develop a mindset that makes driving on crowded roads socially possible — it is just not feasible to develop all that is required immediately.

Therefore, the Chinese car making industry is likely to have to turn to exports to maintain growth levels in the near to medium term.

Repairs and Servicing Issues and the 4S System

All markets require some distribution channel or channels for their products. The car industry has a complex distribution channel system because the modern motor vehicle has complex needs. The modern car cannot long survive without servicing by those with appropriate technical know-how. The servicing function represents more than half of the total profits of a well-balanced national automobile industry, with the remainder split between the profit on new vehicle sales and the profit on the sale of spare parts.

Auto industry distribution channels involve not just new vehicle sales outlets, but also the establishment of networks for the supply of spare parts and accessories, after-sale servicing, financing and insurance and a host of information services.[142] Clearly, the operation of such a network is complex, and it cannot appear overnight. When examining the motoring industry infrastructure, one crucial element which must be examined first is the distribution channel, not just of the new vehicles, but of the spare parts and the servicing it will need during its life.

The longstanding practice in China up until the 1990s and the influx of foreign joint ventures divided the manufacture and distribution of cars, trucks and buses, and their components, into two parts. Auto factories generally did not distribute automobiles directly and used completely separate distributors, but this created a wall between factories and consumers and brought a plethora of problems, such as low product quality and limited product updates to take account of changing consumer demand.[143] The traditional auto distribution channels in China were described as being of a pyramid style because there were a large number of intermediaries between producers and final consumers. Although these marketing middlemen played important roles in the operation of the Chinese auto marketplace, there were three main disadvantages. First, the large auto distribution companies could not exercise effective control of the distribution channels and the middlemen were often too small or too inefficient to adopt effective distribution strategies. Second, such a long distribution channel usually prevents improvements in efficiency and also increases the prices of the end product, because at each stage of the distribution channel there is an intermediary who has to take a slice of the profit. Third, a long distribution channel inhibits the fast and efficient transmission of information backwards and forwards. Auto companies cannot readily obtain feedback from their consumers and hence cannot make the most of market opportunities as they arise.

In the auto distribution channels that developed in the 1950s and 1960s, each member in the channel was an independent enterprise. The relationship of auto companies and channel intermediaries was the equivalent to that of sellers and buyers, instead of partners. There was a degree of competition within the system, and this could result in different prices in different regions, and impediments to the delivery of cars if some middlemen offered inducements to the manufacturers to receive favoured treatment. This system worked reasonably well when the demand for vehicles was small, and it was all from public consumers. This meant that the customer was usually a fleet operator, who would order a batch of cars for delivery at a far future date to replace wearing stock. Hence, the factory was prepared to negotiate a bulk price and delivery details that were customized for each intermediary (who might have a portfolio of a dozen clients or so). The system does not work so well when there are numerous private customers seeking early delivery of their chosen model, and those same customers are ready to shop around a number of dealers to get the best deal.

In the 2000s, the provision of after-sales service, sometimes called the 'aftermarket', has become a problem for the Chinese domestic auto industry. This is mainly because the rapid growth in sales presents challenges in providing skilled and efficient services in sufficient quantity to meet the needs of the millions of new car owners. The problem is not immediately evident as far as maintenance, long-term servicing and repairs are concerned, for new vehicles do not require as much maintenance as vehicles that are aging. When vehicles are more than three years old, maintenance requirements increase at a faster rate. The biggest section of the Chinese aftermarket involves vehicles that have been in use for four to nine years.[144]

As the after-sales service sector develops, three different models of service delivery are emerging. The one which appears to be fastest growing is the 4S system — that is, 4S stores provide the full range of services that a car customer requires. These services cover four areas which range from sales to after-sales service to spare parts to survey services (or customer information). The second model of service delivery is the single store, and the third is the automobile chain store linked to a particular brand. Each of these models has its advantages and disadvantages. Overall, the Chinese domestic aftermarket operates on a relatively high profit margin (as high as 40 per cent).[145]

The 4S model has advantages in the marketplace in that it effectively ties a customer into an ongoing relationship with the business network. It is a one-stop auto shop. The apparent disadvantages of the model relate to the size of the enterprise (and hence the investment) needed to cater to the range of customer requirements, and also the range of skills required by the employees. A large enterprise creates other problems, including financing and insuring the operation. Like feeding a voracious offspring, a 4S store needs a constant and engaged customer base and becomes vulnerable to movements in the marketplace such as the fall-off in demand as occurred in 2003.

The single-store model is also a substantial operation, but unlike the 4S model it has grown out of the traditional Chinese way of doing business — opening a store which offers a range of products for a customer to choose from. Such stores were the usual channel of distribution for Chinese manufacturers from the 1950s, when they acted as agents for the sale of vehicles to a restricted range of public sector clients who had particular needs. The model has continued, adapting to the reformed enterprise environment in China.

In open market conditions, dealers may have a licence to sell the range of cars of one or more manufacturers, at whatever price they decide. However, a single store that operates in the motor vehicle industry needs a large investment to carry the inventory required to give the customer the widest possible choice. Moreover, it may not have the strengths to offer in regard to aftermarket services. In the current auto market environment, single stores appear to be falling behind their competitors who follow different business models.

In the third common model of vehicle sales and servicing, the chain store, dealers invest in the right to sell a particular range, and contract with the manufacturer to provide them with product at a wholesale price that is the same for all the dealers. This system has been called the brand authorization sale and in China it acts to centralize the wholesale market and put dealers in different parts of sales region on the same footing. The branded chain stores, or franchises, appear to offer advantages in the marketplace because of their strong links to manufacturers. They also appeal to the buying public because they are backed by the reputation of the manufacturer they are associated with. However, in the case of this model of selling and servicing vehicles there is a disadvantage, as the law relating to the operation of franchising in China is not well developed.

Overall, 4S stores appear to be the preferred model — preferred, that is, by the industry. The manufacturers can support and to a large extent control the roll-out of new 4S stores. For that reason, they are worthy of research to assess how efficient they are, and how well-accepted by car dealers and customers. [146] An efficient aftermarket is crucial to a fast-growing motor vehicle industry.

The 4S system was introduced to China in 1999, when the foreign joint ventures were expanding and it became easier for Chinese citizens (if sufficiently well-heeled) to purchase a car.[147] Since then, the system has expanded over most of China and is one of the key factors that has enabled the explosion in car sales. In 2006, there were around 5,000 4S vehicle sales outlets. In Beijing, 133 4S outlets have been opened within a period of five years, and Chinese industry analysts have commented that the system could become the prime means of motor vehicle distribution.[148] Some 4S franchisees have become very big very quickly and dominate their markets. For example, Hainan Mazda Auto Company sold over 550,000 cars through its 4S outlets in China in 2003.[149]

There is another side of the coin, and this is another factor that makes the concept worthy of research. Some industry professionals believe that the system acts to the detriment of retailers, tying them into arrangements with manufacturers and taking away their freedom to act in the marketplace. One leading businessman who is CEO of a large dealership — the Asia Olympic Town Auto Market in Beijing — has publicly forecast that one-third of 4S franchises may be in deficit and only another third in profit, while the remaining third of 4S businesses are just keeping their heads above water in the strongly competitive market.[150]

The concept itself has caused controversy because, as it ties dealers and manufacturers and directs the prices they charge and the services they provide, the 4S system operates in restraint of trade and is therefore anti-competitive. The concerns were not so much with the actual sale but with the ongoing service monopoly that was created. In Europe, where the 4S concept took off, EU trade authorities brought in legislation in 2002 to regulate aspects of the system to reduce its monopolizing characteristics, and from 2004 took further steps to break the nexus between auto manufacturer and auto retailer.

The relevant EU legislation was intended to remove the restrictions on independent servicing and repair and end the contractual requirement that only authorized dealers could do repairs. The new regulation also provided that both independent repairers and new car retailers could act as authorized repairers within the manufacturer's network. No longer would service businesses be obliged to sell new cars. Neither could the car maker try to limit the number of authorized repairers, and the repairer's right to repair vehicles of other makes. However, all these provisions continue to operate in China, and the 4S system may therefore operate to stop the rise of the small, backyard suburban repair shop.

The situation in 2007 was that, generally, a car manufacturing company would establish one or more 4S outlets in a given area. Each 4S shop would be authorized to sell the manufacturing company's brand of cars and would be designed and built according to a common plan — not unlike the operation of a McDonald's franchise. To obtain a 4S franchise, an intending investor needed to have access to funds ranging from 10 million to 15 million yuan.[51] These businesses therefore rank as medium-sized in the Chinese retailing industry.

If the growth of small servicing and repair shops is strictly limited, then the private car owner — the mums and dads, in Australian terms — would find it more difficult, more expensive and more inconvenient to get their cars attended to when they need servicing or repairs. As a consequence, if the 4S system which is the main system of distribution does not work efficiently, then it will act as a brake on the growth of private car ownership in China.

The Research

The intention of the research project was a simple one. It was to evaluate the auto 4S system as it operated in Qingdao from three perspectives: its economics, its control and its adaptive capacities. The research itself consisted of extended semi-structured interviews with managers (some but not all of them owners) of ten 4S dealerships, half of them in the upper part of the market, that is selling cars valued at 200,000 yuan or more, and the other half retailing cars valued at less than 200,000 yuan. As an introduction to the research into 4S, 100 intending car customers at the dealerships were asked their preferences in regard to purchasing a new car.[152]

The interviews with intending car customers found that, not surprisingly, a large number preferred to purchase through a 4S dealership, but it was surprising (given that the question was being asked of customers in the 4S outlet) that nearly half would prefer to purchase their car in alternative channels.

The possible alternatives were: a car fair, a general franchiser, the 4S outlet or other sources. The car fair consists of the display of a number of brands and models in a public area, commonly a supermarket car park on a weekend. It provides the opportunity for potential consumers to look over a number of offerings and make comparisons, and such a venue seems to satisfy the Chinese preference for browsing through public markets to get a good look at all the products on offer. Car fairs are an increasingly popular venue for second-hand car sales as well as new car sales (see the following section).

A general franchiser is not linked to just one manufacturer, and buying through this type of outlet affords the customer the chance to look at more than one offering, and may also make an intending purchaser believe that a sales person could tailor a product to the customer's needs. Other sources of purchase include buying through a public agency, or, in rarer cases, arranging a direct import.

Figure 11.1 indicates these comparative preferences. Although the intending customers were not asked why they chose their preferences, it may be that the 4S outlet was a convenient place not only to buy a car but to have the peace of mind that it would be properly maintained and serviced by qualified people. This is a substantial factor in the mind of Chinese new car buyers, given that most of them would be buying a new car for the first time and would be concerned not only because of the amount of the investment but also because they would have to take on trust the expertise of the servicing agent.

Figure 11.1: Car Customers' Preferred Purchasing Channel (Percentages)

Car fair	4S Agency	General franchiser	Other source
27	51	18	4

Results of the Research

After conducting the telephone interviews with the dealership managers, the answers given were collated and summarized.

In regard to marketing processes in a 4S shop, six out of ten interviewees believed that sales of cars would be substantially higher through their franchise than outside it and hence the manufacturers benefited. A further two out of ten believed that the 4S concept contributed to only a slight increase in sales, and another two believed it resulted in reduced new car sales because they were not able to react quickly to the market demand and change the products or product mix quickly enough.

In regard to the economics of the sales, all the interviewees commented that they would like to be more flexible with pricing. Contractually, however, they were compelled to comply with levels of pricing fixed by the car manufacturers. On the other hand, manufacturers from time to time varied the wholesale pricing and thereby affected the retailers' selling margins, but there was not much the 4S franchise owners could do about this.

According to the interviewees, there was a big disadvantage in the 4S system, especially when the outlet opened, and that was the high initial cost of obtaining the franchise and building the 4S sales outlet to the manufacturers' specifications. All of the interviewees had financed their investment through loan finance. Although the initial cost may not have been large to the big manufacturers, it was a big investment to the local business person and placed financial pressure on the owner of the 4S outlet from the very first day of trading.

When the auto market was buoyant, economic operations of the 4S business and increasing sales meant that the owners were well able to repay their loans and other commitments. However, when the auto market endured a period of declining sales, owners still had to meet their financial commitments. In other words, the 4S system resulted in high fixed costs which carried with them high risks in a down-turning market, or in a market that was becoming increasingly competitive.

There was also the problem that, having made a big investment, it was not easy to void the 4S agreement. Retailers locked into the contractual agreement would suffer substantial financial penalties if they had to walk away from it due to falling sales and losses. There was a feeling that the 4S system, although advantageous to the retailer, operated more to the benefit of the big car manufacturers.

Despite the investment risks, all the managers believed that the value of the brand was an essential part of the operation and offset other disadvantages. The value of the brand appeared to be higher the larger the sales outlet was, possibly because a large operation would have a greater visibility in the marketplace. A larger outlet would also have an advantage of having more cars on site and available for sale, and hence greater adaptability and a greater flexibility to meet the varying demands of car customers. They would also benefit from more extensive promotion.

For car manufacturers, the use of the 4S system was preferred because of the control it offered, not just in sales of new vehicles, but in ongoing servicing. A business that had to invest heavily in the right to sell and service the brand was more likely to meet high standards of accredited service and acquire and maintain the technical expertise to give follow-up service to their vehicles.

As a distribution channel, the 4S system appeared to have brought benefits to a rapidly growing market in that it brought some semblance of order to the growth, ensuring ongoing technical expertise and a guarantee for consumers that their new cars would be properly serviced and repaired if needed.

However, as a system, it is biased in favour of larger scale operations and does not appear to have the flexibility to appeal to potential smaller business operators, nor does its economic model favour a more universal distribution. The conclusion must be that, as the market matures and calls for more widespread means of selling and servicing cars, the 4S system may act as a retarding factor on the development of the market unless it can be made more flexible.

The Development of Second-Hand Car Markets in China

A prosperous new car industry must be established on the basis of an efficient second-hand car market, which is the premise and guarantee of car circulation. A good second-hand car market that provides a reliable recourse for both buyers and sellers plays a vital role in resource disposition and car chains linking. However, there are problems in the development of a second-hand car market, and these may hinder the long-term development of the auto industry if left unchecked.

Before 1985, there were no second-hand car transactions because of the nature of the centrally planned market economy and the absence of private ownership. Presumably, as cars aged and wearied, they were just junked. From 1985 to 1997, there may have been some limited second-hand car sales, but it was still an era when private car ownership was very limited and there were not enough transactions to gain the attention of government regulators. By 1997, when the number of joint ventures in the country was expanding rapidly, it became evident that there would soon be a flood of new cars on the market and that a growing proportion of these would end up in private hands — indeed the promise of cars for all by 2008 demanded that private sales would have to explode sooner rather than later. This all meant that there would have to be a market for second-hand car sales, which would also facilitate the promise of cars for all, even if they were second-hand cars.

In 1998, the government addressed the need for an orderly development of a second-hand car market. The Ministry of Trade promulgated a set of regulations termed the Old Vehicle Transaction Policing Method, and since then the second-hand car market has expanded exponentially, measured by car transaction volumes, and matches growth in the new car market.

From 1998 to 2003, the volume of second-hand car business increased by more than 25 per cent each year. In 2002 the number of second-hand car transactions broke through the one million mark, and the value of those transactions amounted to 35.8 billion yuan. In 2005, the national second-hand car business volume grew 10 per cent compared with 2004.[153] Transaction volumes reached 1,450,000 units.

In 2005, there were a number of new laws promulgated with the aim of regulating and controlling aspects of the auto industry besides the sector relating to new car sales. There were new regulations about imported car components, regulations on car fuel consumption and especially regulations that governed the operations and management of second-hand car markets.

Some other laws also had an effect on second-hand markets, because they stimulated and encouraged the replacement of outmoded models. At the same time, there was an emphasis upon new consumer protection laws, and these acted to increase the ordinary shopper's confidence in the operation of second-hand car fairs and the sale of second-hand cars generally. The ordinary Chinese consumer, like the consumer in the West, wondered if he (or she) could trust a used car salesperson. For the good of the industry and the economy, they were encouraged to believe that they could.

The Research

This research reviewed the development of the second-hand car market in Qingdao, including the development of car brokers, car fairs and internet car trading.[154] In the last few years, as the Qingdao second-hand car market has developed rapidly, Shandong province has encouraged the establishment of the Shandong Second-Hand Car Association to supervise the activities of the marketplace and second-hand car circulation.

There is a local government office named the Qingdao Car Management Center which exercises a loose supervisory oversight of official and unofficial dealers.

The urban car market has a relatively stable sales pattern and most transactions take place in big second-hand car fairs, which are held periodically — normally monthly. Established companies which act as brokers or commission agents on car sales also play an essential role and there are also transactions through the internet. In the first six months of 2006, there were four large second-hand car fairs in Qingdao, and the total number of sales transacted was 13,600. One analyst predicted that in the years 2006 to 2008 the second-hand car market will be a major part of the retail milieu of the city.[155] Research techniques used included interviews of prominent second-hand car dealers, including a city official of the Qingdao Car Management Center and questionnaires addressed to potential second-hand car buyers who attended two of the large weekend car fairs. In all there were three face-to-face interviews with dealers and 40 completed questionnaires were received.

Results of the Research

As a result of the interviews with officials, the first data of the research sought to establish the various channels used by buyers and sellers of second-hand cars. The car fairs proved to be the most popular means of initiating and concluding transactions, followed by the activities of broker companies, and then the internet as a source of information. Table 11.2 presents data obtained through the Qingdao Car Management Center, and details the relative proportions of sales channels.

Table 11.2: Distribution Channels of Second-Hand Cars in Qingdao

Distribution channels	Proportion of total sales (percentages)
Second-hand car fairs	48
Broker companies	27
Internet transactions	16
Major brand car companies	7
Others	2

As an example of the operation and scale of car fairs, one of the car fairs attended was at Li village, in the northern suburbs of the municipal area of Qingdao. The second-hand car fair held there in April 2006 had more than 600 cars exhibited and more than 40 second-hand cars were sold. The fair was held each weekend, and exhibitors paid the organizers a fee to exhibit their vehicles. In the first six months of 2006, the total value of sales at the four main second-hand car fairs, like the Li village second-hand car fair, reached 210 million yuan.[156]

According to regulations governing the industry,[157] companies which broker the sales of cars can be registered even if they have limited capital. Consequently, there were many companies which were involved in running second-hand car sales as intermediaries for buyers and sellers. The brokerage companies accounted for just over a quarter of all second-hand car transactions, so it seems that more car owners preferred to sell their cars themselves at the car fairs.

Based on the information gathered from the questionnaires, there was one problem in particular that worried Chinese consumers, as it worries second-hand car buyers in the West. It is the risk of encountering a dishonest seller and getting stuck with a lemon. Of the 40 questionnaires completed, twelve respondents reported that they thought there was substantial risk in buying a second-hand car from a broker company — more so than buying one from the owner who was present at the car fair. Although the trade in second-hand cars was increasing, there was still that worry about trusting the used car salesperson.

Many consumers also felt anxious about the condition of a second-hand car, and the risk of concealment of car defects. The question arose of how they could check the car to be assured it was roadworthy. The country still has a shortage of qualified mechanics, given the rapid growth of the industry, and the ordinary citizen has not had much to do with a car. Because the society relied on public transport for so many years, few people came into intimate contact with a car, and so there remains a widespread ignorance about what to do when the vehicle needs servicing, or even when it breaks down. It is noteworthy that a major constricting factor upon the growth of private motoring is the fact that a stranded motorist, or one seeking advice on motoring matters, has relatively few avenues of cheap advice. There are some motoring support organizations growing, but their networks are not yet widespread. Some comments on the topic follow later in this chapter.

As for the internet, according to Table 11.2 detailing information from the Qingdao Car Management Center, 16 per cent of second-hand car transactions came about through use of the internet. There were a number of internet websites dedicated to the display and contact details of would-be participants in the second-hand car market.[158]

The other named category of second-hand car sales — through branded car companies — was not a major player, accounting for only 7 per cent of total sales. Franchisers, both 4S outlets and general franchisers, have the authority to sell second-hand cars that carry the brand of their franchise, but they are not general second-hand car sellers and do not generally sell any or all the car brands available in the marketplace. This means that there is not yet a common trend of trading-in an existing car for a new car of a different brand, although research on new car demand noted that purchasers intended to replace their car in three to five years. It may be that the market is still growing and the practice of trading-in is not yet established because people are still on their first new car. The Chinese car market is that new!

The other channels for second-hand car transactions that are noted are various. For example, because the purchase of even a second-hand car is a major one for Chinese citizens, some people in Qingdao were prepared to travel further afield and buy a car from another city, such as Tianjin or even Beijing.

The average price of a second-hand vehicle countrywide in 2005 was 32,800 yuan, which had grown by 5.13 per cent compared with 2004.[159] However, this average concealed different prices for trucks and cars. The demand for second-hand trucks grew, probably due to the buoyant economy, whereas the price of second-hand cars did not increase. The average price of a second-hand truck in 2005 was 27,400 yuan, an increase of 5.8 per cent over 2004; the average price for a small second-hand passenger automobile was 25,500 yuan in 2005, basically even with 2004; and the price of a second-hand luxury car was 46,600 yuan, which represented a fall of 3.12 per cent compared with 2004.[160] These figures indicate the increasing supply of second-hand cars in the market, which in turn reflects the increasing sales of new cars.

The survey questionnaires asked intending purchasers how much they wanted or expected to pay for a second-hand car. Of the 40 completed questionnaires received from respondents, 32 people replied that they were looking to purchase a second-hand car for less than 50,000 yuan, five were prepared to pay between 50,000 and 75,000, and three were seeking a particular model of car that they would purchase, if they found one, no matter how high the cost. Overall, it seemed that the prospective purchasers were mainly middle-income, and were looking for a low-priced car.

What sort of vehicles were prospective buyers looking for? Statistics on the type of cars sold in 2005 reveal that trucks accounted for 26 per cent of the total, passenger cars 30 per cent, other small vehicles (minivans, three-wheelers and the like) 42 per cent, and four-wheel-drive SUVs 2 per cent.[161]

When preferences were surveyed, of the 40 respondents to the questionnaires, 24 people said they would like to buy a small second-hand car (that is, a vehicle with an engine of less than 1.6 litre capacity). When asked their reasons, most said that it was a response to the increasing price of fuel. Most respondents also confirmed that they were seeking a car of a particular brand, rather than just looking for any small car.

Some Problems in the Second-Hand Car Market

When asked about problems they encountered in the used-car marketplace, respondents noted a number of issues. One concerned the time taken to process the transaction. For the typical small car purchase, it took around two days to complete formalities, which involved getting approvals and registering with the Management of Industry and Commerce Administration Center, the local Police Station, the Environmental Protection Department, the Bureau of Taxation and the Transportation Administration. It was a complicated process to register the change of ownership of the motor vehicle and was very time-consuming.

A second cause for frustration was that there was no system of completing a technical examination of a car before finalizing the transaction. Most second-hand cars could not be fully examined, especially in relation to their documentation, and hence intending buyers could not be entirely sure of the provenance of the vehicles.

Third, when brokerage companies were involved, the relationship and the obligations of the consumers and the company were not regulated and transparent. Where there were conflicts or disputes arising, there was no recourse but to the legal system, which was in any case expensive and took time.

A fourth major problem area concerned the national vehicle taxation revenue system. The second-hand car markets are taxed by authorities and these taxes are passed on to the consumers in the overall charges for using the markets, but the taxation regime is not unified. Different authorities have different charge standards, different forms for transaction receipts and certificates, and there are no standard regulations that apply in all markets. There is also a problem in ensuring that the property rights in the second-hand car are correctly and legally recorded after the transaction.

One other problem relates to expectations of customers and perhaps indicates cultural perceptions of what sellers should do, rather than legal requirements. Some respondents to the survey commented that they did not get ongoing service from the brokerage companies, even though the brokers had taken a considerable slice of the price of the vehicle. Some respondents noted that as second-hand cars were more likely to break down, then the sellers should have an obligation to assist with service and repairs. Even when the purchase was from an individual and there were no brokers involved, some respondents still felt that the seller had some sort of obligation to guarantee ongoing service for the vehicle.

In the short to medium term, there appear to be no real constraints upon the growth of the second-hand car markets themselves, for if the main venue for such sales are the car fairs then it is obviously possible to have them wherever there is space available. The constraints that will hamper the second-hand car markets are those that relate to the quality of cars and the inexperience of buyers. That is, as the second-hand cars get older and more battle-scarred, and need high levels of maintenance, will Chinese car buyers who have limited mechanical skills continue to buy?

The answer to this question is not clear. What does seem clear is that in China there is a division that is probably centuries old between manual workers and intellectual workers. An intellectual, or an office worker, will probably not relish having to work on his/her aging car and get their hands oily and dirty, not to mention cut and bleeding. It is more likely that they will seek a mechanic to do the work for them (which is sensible, given the generally low wages for manual work). This issue harks back to the problem raised in the preceding section — namely, will there be sufficient trained technicians to service the growing and aging number of cars in China?

Although there is not a direct constraint on the growth of the second-hand car market, there may be an indirect one in that the supply of trained mechanics may become scarcer as the cars grow older.

A Related Problem

Some of the responses of participants in the second-hand car markets raise a serious problem that confronts China's aftermarket infrastructure — the lack of competent and trusted motoring support organizations, or automobile clubs. The Chinese private car buyer faces a number of daunting challenges. Where can he or she go to get advice on the mechanical status of a vehicle prior to purchase? Who can he trust for fair and impartial advice? What happens if his vehicle breaks down in an unfamiliar patch of countryside? In the West, where there has been a long development of private support systems, most motorists can nominate a friend or family member who is knowledgeable about cars, or else a local not-for-profit motorists' support organization which will help them out or give them the information they seek. The genesis of such organizations or clubs goes back to the early years of motoring, when like-minded enthusiasts swapped information and support and the clubs grew into larger institutions that provided almost everything that a motorist would need, including roadside assistance. An example of one of the largest of such organizations is the American Automobile Club, which provides a range of support services for over 49 million members, which figure represents more than 40 per cent of all US car owners.

In China, as a result of generations when private car ownership was not permitted, the only people who have knowledge about cars are the professional drivers and mechanics employed by SOEs. This situation is changing, but it is changing slowly in most parts of China, given the size and expanse of the country. It is reasonable to suppose that the lack of support organizations will contribute to a lack of confidence in new and especially second-hand car owners and so be a drag on the rapid spread of private car ownership.

A number of clubs or organizations have sprung up in some areas where there are clusters of private car ownership. An example of this is Beijing, where a support organization known as UAA (United Automobile Association) is one of the largest motorists' support clubs, its members recognizable by a round black and yellow sticker on their cars. The association has grown quickly from its establishment barely five years ago and now has 300,000 members, with plans to expand to 5 million by 2008 and 10 million by 2010. Among the services offered are 'road rescue', as well as travel advice, information and bookings, insurance and legal services, etc., but the bulk of its revenue comes from motor vehicle servicing. Members subscribe to the UAA to receive what it has to offer, but it is not a mutual-assistance club on the model of benevolent societies in the West. It is set up to operate at a profit. The membership numbers, actual and planned, seems very large, but in the context of planned annual sales of 7 or 8 million units a year industry-wide in 2010, even this large membership will not cover more than a fraction of the new drivers and car owners unless it spreads out of the larger urban centres.

Besides associations which are focused on service, and are commercial in nature, there are some automobile sporting clubs (e.g., the Federation of Automobile Sports of the People's Republic of China) and associations which focus on travellers and their needs and hence are more in the nature of travel agencies.

Despite the proliferation of such associations in the larger cities like Beijing, finding help when he or his vehicle needs it most will remain the major problem for the private motorist. Until avenues of help and assistance are more widespread, this deficiency of infrastructure will slow the overall spread of private ownership throughout the country.

Parking Issues

Urban Chinese neighbourhoods are typically either high-rise or four-to six-storey walk-up apartment buildings. They are densely packed, compared to some Western cities, and because of the density there is very limited room to park privately owned cars. Put baldly: Chinese neighbourhoods are not designed for car-parking. There are solutions and new (and expensive) high rises include several levels of parking below ground, yet even these parking areas could not cope if every family in the block owned a car. The parking areas are intended for the very wealthy, who pay dearly for the privilege of parking their car — perhaps a price per metre equal to some 20 per cent of the per metre price of their apartment.

There are new developments that include open space, parking provisions and even golf driving ranges, but these developments (which are often gated) are aimed at the rich and designed for their needs.

In the existing middle-class residential neighbourhoods there is almost no space to dedicate for car parking. The street space is also typically narrow, and barely adequate for the flow of business vehicles, for often the ground floor of a Chinese apartment block includes a number of small businesses — groceries, restaurants and the like. Even small cars could not fit into some of the spaces available. The limited number of cars that are seen crammed into residential areas are often business vehicles, and seem to fill almost every available space.

This discussion is based upon impressions, but the impressions are all-pervasive and the author would challenge any contrary view that claims that ordinary Chinese in middle-class neighbourhoods could purchase a car and find a place to park it near their dwelling. In time, there will be multi-storey car parks, but even these could only cope with a fraction of the demand.

This lack of space for car parking constitutes a very serious constraint upon the possibility of widespread car ownership. It must impede the demand for new cars in the short to medium term.

The Research

The research into the extent of parking problems and the potential limits on parking involved surveys of households in two middle-income residential districts of Qingdao. In each district, a residential compound was chosen.[162] Such compounds are characteristic of Chinese residences, and typically consist of a half-dozen to a dozen six-storey apartment buildings with 30 to 50 apartments in each block. There would be access ways to the buildings, and some open space around them, usually with grass and small trees.

Two residential compounds were chosen, one in the Nanjing Lu area (hereafter Compound One) and one in the Xuzhou Lu area (hereafter Compound Two). Both are middle-income districts, not far from the commercial and administrative centres of the city.

Researchers made a loose estimate of the amount of space available around the apartment blocks to enable a rough calculation of the potential number of cars that could be parked in the environs. Then they canvassed the apartments, surveying the number of households and people who lived there, and their income level, and asking how many owned a car and how many aspired to own one.

Compound One

In the compound selected at 228 Nanjing Lu, there were 360 apartments (36 in each of ten blocks). At the urban rate of 2.95 persons to a household (in 2006) then this meant that 1,062 people would be expected to be living in the compound. It was not difficult to estimate how many cars could be parked around the blocks within the compound, for on a Sunday night, in virtually every space and alcove where a car could be parked ... there was a car parked! In total, 59 cars were parked in the compound at Nanjing Lu. Three of them were SUVs, four fell into the category of luxury cars, 41 were small sedan cars and the balance, 11 vehicles, were three-wheelers or micro-cars.

This total of 59 cars to 1,062 people, or 360 apartments, equalled an average car ownership of 5 per cent of people, or 16 per cent of households (assuming that the cars are privately owned and not owned by businesses — which may be a big assumption, but errs in favour of the highest rate of private car ownership, rather than the lowest). If it is also assumed that each car owner holds their car for five years (based on the research reported in chapter 5) then just 1 per cent of the people at Nanjing Lu would buy a new car each year.

The next stage of the research involved surveying the residents. This survey was conducted over three Saturday mornings. Of the 360 apartments, there were residents present in 289, and 148 agreed to answer the survey questions (a response rate of 51 per cent). The responses are summarized in Table 11.3.

Table 11.3 Car Ownership and Parking — Compound One

Question	Average response (persons)
How many people lived in the apartment (average)?	3.2
What was the income of the primary wage earner?	
< 1,000 yuan/month	18
1,000–3,000	27
3,001–5,000	60
> 5,000	43
Is there a secondary wage earner in the household?	136
Did they own a car? 'Yes' responses:	22
Did they intend to purchase a car? 'Yes':	98

Note: Six persons declined to answer, or were unable to answer, the question about income.

There appeared to be an anomaly in that there were 59 vehicles parked in the compound, although only 22 householders stated that they owned a car, and even though the response rate was half the total householders, this still means that fifteen or so cars appeared to be unclaimed. It may be that the householders preferred not to state that they owned a car, or else the vehicles were borrowed or belonged to people who lived elsewhere and were utilizing an available parking space they were not entitled to.

There are three notable statistics. First, the median income of the primary wage earner fell in the 3,001 to 5,000 yuan per month range, with an average of 3,800 yuan, which suggests that most residents fall into the occupation groups of managers or fairly senior level officials. This places them in the upper range of middle-income earners.

Second, the high rate of employment of spouses/partners indicated by the statistic that 136 out of 148 households have a secondary wage earner (92 per cent) means that these households could afford to purchase a car.

Third, the very high response rate to the question of whether they intended to purchase a car is significant, for it is indicative of the aspirations of Chinese middle-income earners. However, in the case of this residential block, where virtually all the space was taken up, there would obviously be difficulties in finding any spaces for additional cars. If every one of the aspiring residents bought a car, and that statistic was extrapolated to take account of the residents in households who were not surveyed or who did not respond to the survey, then there would be an additional 200 cars in the compound — when it was already choked by the existing 59.

Compound Two

In the compound selected at 340 Xuzhou Lu, there were 4384 apartments (48 to each of eight blocks). At the urban rate of 2.95 persons to a household this equalled 1,133 people who would be expected to be living in the compound.

It was not easy to estimate how many cars could park within this compound, because the compound was bordered on two sides by alleyways which were not walled, and which seemed to include public parking (notably by Jie Feng trucks from a nearby construction sites).

By pacing out access ways within the compound and including all the spaces on both sides of the alleyways, researchers estimated that there were around 800 metres of curb space available which, allowing eight metres per car, means that 100 cars could be parked in the vicinity and within the compound of 340 Xuzhou Lu.

This survey was conducted over three Saturday afternoons. Of the 384 apartments, there were residents present in 262 apartments, and 202 agreed to answer the survey questions (a response rate of 77 per cent). The responses are summarized in Table 11.4.

Table 11.4 Car Ownership and Parking — Compound Two

Question	Average response (persons)
How many people lived in the apartment?	3.7
What was the income of the primary wage earner?	
< 1,000 yuan/month	23
1,000–3,000	43
3,001–5,000	94
> 5,000	38
Is there a secondary wage earner in the household?	192
Did they own a car? 'Yes' responses:	14
Did they intend to purchase a car? 'Yes':	135

Note: Four persons declined to answer, or were unable to answer, the question about income.

There are three notable statistics for the responses for this compound: The median income of the primary wage earner also fell in the range of 3,001 to 5,000 yuan per month, as did the group of respondents at 228 Nanjing Lu, with a slightly lower average of 3,440 yuan, which also suggests that most residents fall into managerial of professional occupation groups in the upper range of middle-income earners. This is not unexpected, given that the residential blocks are in close proximity to the commercial centre of the city.

The respondents at this address had a higher occupancy rate than at Compound One, and the researchers noted that there seemed to be more elderly people, probably a parent, living in the apartments (which also seemed to be somewhat larger, although older, than those at 228 Nanjing Lu). There is also a high rate of employment of spouses/ partners indicated by the statistic that 192 out of 202 households have a secondary wage earner (95 per cent), which means that these households also could afford to purchase at least a small car.

The very high response rate to the question of whether they intended to purchase a car reinforces the answers to this question at Compound One. However, there is as little space for car parking in the compound at Xuzhou Lu as there is at the compound at Nanjing Lu. Unless a solution to this problem can be found, the issue of lack of parking must mean that people, even those with an above average income who can afford a car, will not be able to garage the vehicle close to their place of residence.

Infrastructure Issues — Insurance Cover and the Legal System

A major issue for the expanding motor industry is the limited motor vehicle insurance industry. Limited access to insurance, plus a legal environment that is not able to handle a great increase in motoring disputes to be adjudicated, must equal a very great constraint on continued expansion of private motoring and hence continuing demand at exponential rates.

Put simply, Chinese society and legal culture are not geared up for the legal disputes and conflicts that arise when a big increase in cars means a big increase in accidents and also in legal cases ranging from car theft to penalties for breaches of traffic laws.

In earlier years, when there were fewer vehicles on the road, if there was a traffic accident, the police attended and apportioned blame. They also determined who would pay and how much. Usually only a few hundred yuan changing hands would pay for the repairs to the basic Chinese cars, trucks or buses. In the event of an accident causing injury, then more serious penalties would apply. For example, the author was a passenger in a car when a pedestrian was struck and injured. The driver of the car was gaoled for the amount of time that the injured pedestrian spent in hospital, which was three weeks, and the car's owner, the university, was fined a set amount determined upon the average wage of the area, and this was paid to the pedestrian to compensate him for his time off work and to pay for his medical expenses. To an extent, it was a speedy though rough and ready system, but it had practical justice and was generally seen to be just by all the parties concerned.

However, when there is a greater number of cars on the road, with many inexperienced drivers, all wrestling with other road users on roads designed for far less traffic, then the number of accidents must increase. Already the rate of traffic accidents in China per number of vehicles is higher than in Europe. Inexperienced drivers are involved, but also long-time drivers who may have become accustomed to bad driving habits, such as speeding, that they got away with when there was not much traffic but which cause disaster when the roads become choked.

Also, when accidents occur with expensive cars, and the cars' owners are private individuals who cannot look to their work unit to meet the cost of the damage, and it is also unlikely that the cars are insured, then disputes must increase. Moreover, the parties are hardly likely to accept the adjudication of a local police officer making a quick judgment on the spot. The parties will take their cases to court, and it is unlikely that a court system that is already overstretched coping with increased petty crime can quickly adjust and expand to meet this new contingency. Judges need training, and that training will most likely take ten years or more.

The following research project into the workload of the Qingdao courts notes that many judges have limited experience and high workloads.

The lack of a developed legal and insurance infrastructure — when matched with inexperienced drivers — must act as a very considerable restraint upon the growth of private ownership and hence the growth of demand for motor vehicles overall.

The Insurance Industry

The insurance industry came into China in the nineteenth century. In 1949, the new government of the People's Republic, established a nation-wide insurance organization, The People's Insurance Company of China (PICC) and it played a role in the new country's construction until 1958, when the hard-line ideological attitudes of first the Great Leap Forward and then the Cultural Revolution arrested the development of the Chinese insurance industry. This hiatus lasted for 20 years until the end of 1979. The indigenous insurance industry resumed operations in 1980. In 1986, with the start of reforms, new companies were encouraged and resulted in the establishment of the China Pacific Insurance Company, Ping An Insurance Company of China and smaller insurance companies which broke the monopoly enjoyed by PICC. China Pacific Insurance was established in Shanghai and by 2000 it had grown to be one of the 200 largest insurance companies in the world, ranking 45th.[163]

In 2005, around four years after China's entry into the World Trade Organization, there were altogether 34 insurance companies part-owned by foreign investors, mainly in the life insurance and property insurance business. In addition, another 112 companies from nineteen countries and districts have established branches or offices in fourteen Chinese major cities, working for a share of the Chinese insurance market.

It is estimated that the Chinese commercial insurance industry will keep increasing at a rate of 20 to 30 per cent each year and that this trend could last for up to 20 years. By 2025, commercial property insurance premiums could be up to 2 trillion yuan. By that time, the total premiums paid in China would surpass those of the UK, Germany and France. Five per cent of the total insurance premiums paid throughout the world would be in the Chinese market and China would be the biggest insurance market at that time.

However, the industry has its constraints. Among them is a general distrust of insurance companies. According to one survey, 40 per cent of respondents stated that they could not completely trust domestic companies and were waiting until they could be covered by foreign insurance companies.[164]

Because of the form of government and society they are used to, many Chinese do not see the value of insurance products. The ordinary citizen was not likely to insure his or her household goods, but instead took steps to protect them against loss or theft. In the event of disaster, there was usually some form of government relief. Until the 1980s, few Chinese owned their own home, be it apartment or house, so there was no point in their having property insurance. What property insurance there was was only for large construction projects. The reduced need for insurance led to the demise of the industry in the 1950s.

As there have now been two generations without insurance, it is not likely that individuals will be quickly convinced of the need for insurance cover. The big expansion in insurance in the 1990s and 2000s was mainly brought about by commercial enterprises taking out cover. The low incidence of insurance for motor vehicles, especially privately owned motor vehicles, will cause problems for those involved in accidents. Such problems must influence the popularity of vehicles, although the extent of the influence is unknown and awaits further research.

Legal Infrastructure

With the expansion of the car industry and a huge increase in the number of cars on the roads, it is pertinent to inquire whether the judicial system could cope with a huge increase in legal disputes resulting from accidents involving expensive cars. It seems logical to assume that parties in an accident involving cars costing hundreds of thousands of yuan will no longer accept the adjudication of a local police officer, especially if those parties have grown accustomed to resolving disputes through courts. Once, when the country was less developed, and there was less traffic and a traffic accident might involve just scratches, or damage to a bicycle, it was reasonable to expect a police officer to sort out the incident and allocate blame so that the matter was cleared up quickly. In a world grown more modern but more complex, such a system cannot stand much longer.

What is the situation in local courts?[165] There has been recognition of the growing workload and steps have been taken to streamline procedures and introduce modern technology where possible. Before 1996, the Intermediate People's Court of Qingdao still managed legal cases with traditional judicial methods. The judicial process was completely based on handwriting and paper to record and save case information. Such methods meant that it was not easy to save, search and analyse the information and evidence required for the existing number of court cases, let alone any projected increases in the case load.

In order to standardize the judicial processes and improve judgment efficiency, the court's information base was computerized during 1997, using what was called the Court Information Management System (CIMS) designed by a local computer consultancy centre of the Intermediate People's Court of Qingdao, together with Qingdao Eastsoft Computer Technology Company. In October 1997, this system was in operation in the Intermediate People's Court of Qingdao and twelve basic People's Courts in the suburbs of Qingdao. There are four major functions in the CIMS: case management, judicial process management, judicial statistics, and electronic document transmission. From the point of a litigant filing a case to saving the case records, there were sixteen steps in the whole judicial process, including choosing the judges who would sit on the case.

The Research

The research examined how efficiently the court information system was operating, as an indicator of how it would cope with a greatly increased case load from, say, increased incidents of disputes over traffic matters. There were ten major judicial departments in the Intermediate People's Court of Qingdao, and ten judges in each department were asked to complete a questionnaire on aspects of their work, which included such matters as their experience on the court and their workload. Eighty-four judges responded.

Of the survey group, 11 judges had worked in the court for less than two years, a further 24 had two to five years' experience as a judge of the People's Court of Qingdao, 29 had six to ten years' experience and the remaining 20 respondents had sat in the court for more than ten years. This statistic indicated that a depth of experience was required and suggested that it would take some years to inculcate a high level of expertise in the judicial officers.

In relation to their workload, 23 judges (27.4 per cent) dealt with fewer than six cases per month, 54 judges (64 per cent) had seven to ten cases each month and seven judges had over ten cases to consider each month. This statistic may, on the face of it, indicate that the judges' workloads are not heavy and therefore they could accept more work, or it could indicate the contrary — that judges in China get heavily involved in each case before them and therefore it would not be easy to extend their workloads.

In relation to the judicial computer system that was intended to make the court processes more efficient, the judges were asked whether they encountered problems with the operation of the computers. They nominated four main difficulties. The first was that there remained many system bugs in the CIMS software system, even eight years after its implementation. The next major problem was that there were changes in the law, particularly after accession to the WTO, and it sometimes took more time to adjust the CIMS system than it took to amend the law. The third problem the judges described was that of miscommunication between software designers and legal practitioners. Some functions in the CIMS were not used at all and were even a hindrance to the judicial process. The fourth problem of the system concerned security. Almost all the legal administrators in Qingdao were aware of the danger of system security leaks, but they were not sufficiently conversant with the system to know what to recommend to fix the problem.

Overall, there were problems with the management side of the judicial processes in Qingdao. The judges and the legal apparatus may be able to be changed and to be streamlined to cope with greatly increased demand, but such a task would take time.

A later chapter will consider some broader issues with the legal system in China. This section has only considered the practical issues of whether the judicial system could cope with a greatly expanded workload as a result of increasing traffic disputes and infringements. The conclusion is that it is unlikely that the legal system could do so, in the short to medium term, with the greater challenge of a burgeoning workload.

12 Management

Management Issues and a Case Study

In relation to the overall theme of this book, about China's car industry producing a wave of new vehicles to overwhelm some established producers, it is pertinent to ask whether the Chinese have the executive and management skills to achieve not only quantity production (they have proved they can turn out a huge quantity of products) but also high quality products. Quality management involves a whole host of skills, as well as the display of qualities of leadership and entrepreneurial ability. So the question is, 'Can China's managers and labourforce achieve high levels of performance?'

This chapter examines some of the major issues that Chinese manufacturers face, and these include management and labour issues. The business environment in China has a number of problems, and how the vehicle manufacturing industry deals with them will have implications for the quality of management and the quality of car manufacturing processes. Chinese enterprises must overcome inefficient management and governance practices, for example the practice that directors or large corporations are usually appointed by the Communist Party and their selection is based inordinately on political factors. There are also human resource management problems, such as developing means to motivate workers and to evaluate performance standards fairly, as well as training and retaining qualified staff. Small to medium enterprises (SMEs) face particular problems, and their expansion is crucial to the establishment of motor vehicle infrastructure. The human resource management problems of Chinese SOEs include recruitment issues such as over-manning and nepotism in employee selection, poaching of skilled staff between enterprises (which sometimes results in disputes as official approvals are needed to transfer staff, even from one SOE to another, and the new employer may have to compensate the former employer). There are also issues with performance evaluation, especially at managerial level. Chinese managers are often lacking in initiative and risk-averse, not just because of the financial consequences of a failed venture, but because of the loss of face consequent upon a wrong decision.

There were a number of studies in the 1990s that indicated that many of the problems of new enterprises in China, including joint ventures, have been a result of poor human resources practices, especially in the key areas of staff retention and performance motivation, as well as in the area of management skills.[166]

This chapter discusses some of these issues, and then examines a case study of a reformed SOE — a supplier of motor vehicle electrical components in Chengdu.

Governance and Management Issues

In 2003, the *Chinese Economic Times* conducted a survey called the China Entrepreneur Investigation Project, and it included a questionnaire on the quality of management. The questionnaire was completed by managers in 3,539 large enterprises. The results indicated that most enterprise managers had not been systematically trained for modern business administration, although a majority held bachelor degrees. In almost all of the enterprises, the right of appointing and dismissing managers was controlled not by the owners but by a governmental supervising authority. The selection criteria of the relevant authority were not entirely based on efficiency and economic performance, and there were limited evaluation methods. In a majority of large enterprises, political skills were held to be as important as business skills.[167] Generally, major business strategies were impeded by political considerations, and the appointment system did not lead to the selection of the applicants with the best managerial qualities.

In no less than 30 per cent of companies with public shareholdings, shareholders cannot select the chairman or the board and the board cannot select the top levels of management.[168] Consequently, minority shareholders cannot rely on the directors and the board to protect their interests. Of more than 1,200 listed companies in China in 2004, 80 per cent to 90 per cent resulted from the restructuring of SOEs and were controlled by a parent State-Owned Enterprise which commonly dominated management.[169] The result was that directors could not ensure efficient and equitable corporate governance as it is understood in the West.

The majority of directors and managers selected were usually people with political skills, but not entrepreneurs. In most cases, they had been educated and had progressed under the old system. In the selection of directors and enterprise leaders, the method of selection was not open for employees to aspire to. An appointment as a director or senior manager carries with it high status, which is important in Chinese society. Once selected, a senior manager holds a form of official status and enjoys administrative rank in a way that seems unusual to Western observers. There seem to be parallels with past administrative systems that made high officials identifiable by the buttons on their hats.

In State-Owned Enterprises a very significant proportion of leaders hold their post by administrative order, and run enterprises according to Communist Party dictates, which are described as 'spirit, conscience and sense of duty'.[170] There is no reference here to conducting the business of the enterprise in the interests of the shareholders.

There is an additional disadvantage in this system whereby the party selects senior managers and directors, and once selected, the office-holders usually keep their positions until they retire. This includes such key positions as chair of board of directors and the general manager. Chinese Company Law does not support these practices, but they appear to be prevalent nevertheless.

In the context of the influence of the Communist Party in the operations of large companies, it is worth noting that these companies require a Party Committee, and this committee is involved in the top levels of decision-making. The Party Committee is usually supported by a Party Organization Department, which has a place within the organization structure in either the Human Resources department or the General Manager's office. It is frequently the case that officials within the Party Organization Department, although not the most visible of managers, have ultimate control over personnel above a certain rank, and this is a principle of the economic reforms referred to as 'the Party controls personnel.' For example, the senior managers will be certified and recommended for selection by the Party Organization Department.

This system means that there are limited checks and balances and virtually no external governance mechanisms. Many companies are vulnerable to insider trading, and to the activities of unscrupulous management including party officials. So common are some abuses linked to management share dealing and insider trading that the Chinese refer to a phenomenon that translates as 'age 58–59 rising'. The term refers to a pre-retirement practice in which managers of state enterprises try to take as much as they can before retiring from the company. According to the National Administrative Bureau of State-Owned Property, any transfer at below fair market prices of state assets to non-state entities, such as individuals, collectives and joint ventures, is considered to be a criminal activity and fraud of state property. Some estimates are that somewhere between 30 and 100 billion yuan of assets are defrauded from SOEs every year.[171] The scale of such fraud and its attendant corruption indicate deficiencies in areas of corporate governance. The issue of corruption will be revisited in a later chapter.

The above deficiencies in management practice and governance are obscured to an extent by the rapidly expanding economy. Where economic benefits are growing and trickling down to the lower echelons of employment, then there is unlikely to be an outcry over standards of governance and ethical management practices.

Management Constraints on SMEs

In contrast to the management of large enterprises, small to medium enterprises may have better management and control systems (because of the closer involvement of owners) but they face management problems of their own. These often constitute what are called 'internal barriers' to good performance: Some analysts consider that the main constraint faced by private enterprises is the management problem, and this management problem can be subdivided into three broad areas of management: strategic management, personnel management and formal management skills.[172] Resurgent family businesses are common in the ranks of China's new SME entrepreneurs, and these businesses especially lack modern management skills.[173] Other analysts examine the structural problems of China's relatively new private enterprises, and highlight the similar governance issue that impedes larger enterprises — namely the conflict between the role and contribution of owners and operational management duties.[174] There are also difficulties that multiply with the challenges of managing new technologies.[175]

One reason for the deficiency of management practice in China may be that for much of the early period of economic reform, the Communist government had to wrestle with its socialist ideology and define the place of the private sector, hence its determination that the private sector was a 'complement to the state-owned economy', and not supreme in itself. It was not until 1997 that the private sector was identified as an important constituent of China's economy in its own right.

The Problem/Opportunity of Guanxi

In the Chinese business context, owners and managers of enterprises have to devote much of their management time to knitting the net of *guanxi*, which term is difficult to translate. It generally means networking, entering into and discharging mutual obligations and peddling influence.

There is an inherent disadvantage to the development of *guanxi*. It can collapse with personnel changes in the network of organizations. The collapse of *guanxi* that has been laboriously built up is comparable to financial bankruptcy, and can happen just as suddenly. The business partnership between an enterprise and a consumer (organization) could be cut off by a new appointment or simply a retirement on the enterprise side. This obvious fact is often underplayed by entrepreneurs who continue to devote more time to knitting *guanxi* than to technological or management improvement. Instead of improving product quality and developing their brand reputation, they concentrate on the short-term profit that can follow effective development of local *guanxi*. They can then become vulnerable in some circumstances, for example when business decision-making is moved from a branch office to a central headquarters.

Labourforce Issues

The development of quality motor vehicles by Chinese manufacturers is also dependent upon issues related to the labourforce and the implementation of international standards of human resource management (HRM). Two labourforce issues affecting the development of quality cars are related to (a) the training and retaining of skilled employees (especially the retaining), and (b) motivating workers to achieve levels of performance.

Internationally recognized practices of human resource management were first imported into China in the early 1980s through the auspices of foreign joint-venture partners, but such practices were slow to spread to SOEs. For many years, in the State-Owned Enterprises, personnel management meant taking care of the day-to-day personnel functions such as payroll and arranging and recording leave. The existence of the SOEs meant guaranteed jobs, unchanged payment and a cradle to grave social welfare system for their workers. As a consequence, SOEs were (and many still are) overstaffed and unproductive. Another characteristic of SOEs was their poor management, attributed to the fact that managers came to their positions through bureaucratic appointment and were usually appointed by the government not according to their ability, but based on their ranking in the bureaucratic hierarchy. The large Chinese car making organizations that have grown out of the SOE milieu have brought with them, not unlike a bacillus, inefficient HR practices that are difficult to eradicate.

Chinese SOEs have experienced many reforms but there remain systematic HR problems which, for example, make it more difficult to retain skilled employees. The Labour Law of 1995 transformed workplaces (and caused much excitement when it was promulgated) but it caused some problems and brought to the fore other, hitherto-obscured, systematic flaws. Although the 1995 law allowed SOEs to determine their own wages and salaries level, they were not completely free of authorities' pressure in regard to setting rates of pay.[176] The total wage bill had to be approved by SOE governing authorities. Therefore, whatever the financial situation and the trading conditions of the Chinese SOEs, they could not usually offer their employees as a whole flexible wage rates based on productivity. There were exceptions to this rule, and it is true that generally wages have been rising by around 5 per cent a year as the labour market constricts, and the supply of labour decreases, but large Chinese enterprises do not operate in a relatively free labour environment.

The provisions of the Labour Law relating to overall wage levels have created disparities between workers of similar status in different enterprises. Joint-venture enterprises are allowed to pay higher wages, although the wage packages of SOEs and joint ventures were difficult to compare because the SOEs were still obligated to provide some social benefits.

The role and function of trade unions were defined under the law, for example in negotiating separation packages in the event of an enterprise entering bankruptcy. Employees have the right to join a trade union. However, Chinese trade unions are not considered adversarial bodies, lobbying and agitating with management on behalf of their members. There is no tradition of collective bargaining between employees and employers as there is in the West. This means that unions tend to be a part of the company structure, rather than being outside the organization. Essentially, unions in China are support bodies, more inclined to arrange cultural functions than strikes by their members. This reflects the Chinese cultural system and its Confucian antecedents and it is more an egalitarian system than an individual-reward, goal-based one. The system that results from these arrangements makes it hard to reward employees adequately and encourage high skill levels.

In addition to HR difficulties relating to the ordinary workers, there are also constraints upon the ability to promote efficient people into the top jobs. The result of a survey conducted in 1,000 SOEs revealed that 73 per cent of senior managers in these enterprises were appointed by the governing authorities,[177] which means that promotion to top levels is often reserved to the purview of local government authorities and need not result from superior performance within the enterprise. To a certain extent, the appointment system has limited the opportunities of promotion for employees and acts instead as a form of glass ceiling to the career aspirations of the best and brightest. As Chinese SOEs — and some of the large enterprises in the car industry which trace their ancestry back to them — often do not have sufficient flexibility to enhance their employees' career development, they have problems both with motivating staff and with the retention of skilled staff.

High employee turnover remains one of the biggest problems Chinese enterprises have been facing.[178] This point has been made by a number of Chinese analysts, and they recognize that management discretion in regard to the level of wages and the relative equal distribution of wage benefits are vital to the retention of skilled employees.[179] It is not that the importance of staff retention is not recognized. In the latter periods of economic reform and growth in China, there has been concern expressed about the problem of skilled employee retention, as evidenced by a high turnover of these employees as new ventures were established. Between 1998 and 2002, the net turnover among skilled employees in SOEs reached 71 per cent.[180] Among the deleterious effects reported were increases in the costs of recruitment and training, a decrease in productivity and quality of work in the workplace, a loss of technology skills and clients who follow professional and skilled employees, and effects on the morale of other employees. However, in the relative absence of results-linked wages and benefits, and with impediments to career development, the only remaining strategy open to senior management to retain staff is to emphasize company loyalty. This strategy does not work well in a market-oriented and increasingly competitive economy. In some large enterprises, management has attempted to surmount the problem of a restricted wages and benefits environment by offering innovations such as employee share programs.

Once again, it is essential to note that there are exceptions to this general situation and in joint ventures, for example, there are not the same iron-bound restrictions on setting individual wages, but overall, there remain problems with bringing flexibility into the wages system and until these problems are completely resolved, they will act as an impediment to the development of a fully skilled and efficient workforce capable of high performance. The following section considers the two inter-related issues of retaining employees and motivating their work in the context of a case study of a motor vehicle component supplier (a reformed SOE).

Case Study of Labourforce Issues — a Motor Vehicle Parts Manufacturer[181]
Located in Chengdu, Sichuan Province, in the southwest of China, the company is engaged in manufacturing electric spare parts for motorcycles and automobiles. It has experienced a series of SOE reforms since it was first established in 1966 at the time when motor vehicle manufacturing spread throughout provincial China. The company is not named here, at the request of its management, and this restriction was accepted by the researcher in order to get candid comment and opinion from senior management.

The total revenue of the company in the calendar year 2002 was 120 million yuan and it employed 1,349 management and staff. The employees included 174 men and women in positions identified as management level, and 89 professional and technical staff in positions requiring the exercise of high-level skills. The functional hierarchy was a flat one, divided into four levels. At the top level was the general manager, with two functional managers whose responsibilities were divided into operations and administration. Below this level were the department managers, who were referred to as 'senior management' within the company. The next level was comprised of section supervisors and the bottom, or junior level, was made up of employees who had no supervisory title. The HR department was staffed by a manager and five employees, mainly responsible for recruitment, payroll, training plans, promotion, retirement and leave management.

The Research
The research involved examining a number of HR practices, reviewing the records of exit interviews, surveying existing staff and then conducting

focused interviews with the general manager and HR manager. The questionnaire survey relating to job satisfaction (see Table 12.1) was conducted to measure the job satisfaction level among 123 employees, or 9 per cent of the total workforce. Six employees did not return the questionnaire, and there were 13 invalid responses (i.e., respondents who did not complete all the questions). There were thus 104 completed questionnaires returned, which represented a response rate of around 85 per cent and the equivalent of 8 per cent of all employees of the component manufacturing company.

Table 12. 1: Job Satisfaction Rates

Aspect of work	Very satisfied/Sat./Neutral/Dissat./Very dissat.
Relationships with colleagues	(one of these categories marked 'X')
Wages and salary	
Working conditions	
Promotion opportunities	
Fairness of management	
Training opportunities	
Participation in decisions	
Performance measurement	
Rewards for good work	
Company policies and management	
Company welfare policies	
Job security	
Flexibility of working hours	

The respondents were all at professional or management level, as the company management did not feel that the base level assembly-line workers would understand and fairly respond to an external survey of this nature. It is probably a fact that assembly-line workers are not commonly surveyed and examined as to their feelings and opinions, and equally a fact that they might not feel themselves able to respond candidly. However, around half of the surveys were completed by other base level staff who worked in technical and administrative positions. So there is a drawback to this survey in that it is not representative of the firm as a whole, but only of the supervisory and middle-management to senior management levels (the top level of management — the general manager and two deputy managers — did not complete the surveys either). In relation to their positions in the company hierarchy, the percentages of employees in junior, middle and senior were 51, 36 and 13 per cent, respectively. Notwithstanding the drawback, the material still seemed valuable, for an examination of the 104 respondents allowed the compilation of a profile of the supervisory levels of the labourforce of a reformed SOE operating in the motor vehicle manufacturing industry.

The respondents were categorized according to the nature of their work under two headings: technical staff (41) and management staff (63). Concerning the gender of respondents, 64 were male and 40 were female. In relation to age, 85 employees were under 40 years old, which accounted for 81 per cent of the total. The fact that four-fifths of the labourforce were in the first 20 years of their working life and just one-fifth were in their second 20 may be an indicator of a relatively young labourforce. The respondents were also well-qualified in a formal sense, more than half of them having a university degree of bachelor or above. In addition, most of them had been working in the company for more than four years, an indicator of the prevalence of full-time as opposed to part-time or casual employees whose employment would be of a short duration.

Results of the Research
Retention Rate of New Employees and Exit Interviews: The employee turnover in the company was measured by the cohort retention rate. This measure has been developed as a means to record effectively the degree of turnover of staff and managers within an enterprise.[182] For the purposes of the research project, the cohort retention rate for employees recruited to the company over twelve months between February 2002 and February 2003 was used as a sample.[183] This cohort could be divided into two categories: students who just graduated from colleges or universities, and employees who had prior working experience. The statistics presented at Figure 12.2 revealed that the total retention rate

for this cohort was only 39 per cent. This low rate implies that there were some problems of HRM existing in the company, even allowing for an assumption that recent employees may be more likely to leave, given that they were not yet wedded to a career in the industry or to the company and its values.

It should also be noted that two-thirds of the recruits were recent college/university graduates, so some or most of these would have been recruited for the skilled job categories. It could be assumed that these would be the employees whose skills would be more in demand than, say, unskilled recruits.

The low retention rate is of interest generally, for there is sometimes a perception that the workers employed under the Communist regime enter a job and hold that job for life. Under the former iron rice bowl economy, that appeared to be the case, but in the Chinese economy of the 2000s, there appears to be much more mobility in the reformed enterprises, especially among skilled employees.

Table 12.2: Retention Rate of New Employees

Period: 2/2002–2/2003	Graduates	Experienced employees	Total employees
Employees recruited as at mid-February 2002	37	19	56
Employees remaining as at mid-February 2003	14	8	22
Retention rate	38 per cent	42 per cent	39 per cent

An exit interview was conducted for employees as they left, and the reasons for their leaving were recorded. Although the matter was clearly a sensitive one, there was no reason to assume that the responses were not candid. Of the 33 employees who left, just three gave reasons that were not related to the management or practices of the company. One left because he developed a personal dislike for the industry and the other two left for other personal reasons. The other 30 who separated from the company gave more than one reason related to their duties or organizational management.

The three main reasons for leaving included lack of promotion opportunities (86 per cent), unsatisfied with salary (83 per cent) and poor or little training (72 per cent). In addition, 69 per cent of the cohort stated that they believed that the skills they had to offer or their performance were not recognized by the enterprise, which led to frustration and their decision to leave. The nature of the work, including job content, job responsibilities and workload, was regarded as a crucial reason by eighteen of the interviewees. Reflecting the candid nature of responses, more than half of the exiting employees asserted that were treated unfairly by the management or policies of the enterprise. A total of 52 per cent left because they felt that they had too few opportunities to make use of their skills or abilities. Poor welfare, poor working conditions and an inflexible schedule were also named. Only six interviewees separated from the company stating that they had suffered from poor immediate supervision or management conflict and only two deemed their departure as related to conflict with colleagues. Of all the responses, this category may be the least reliable, for Chinese workers are not usually inclined to make confronting remarks about individuals, especially when they are leaving and their comments would harm the prospects of other workers.

Survey of Job Satisfaction: In general, the rate of job satisfaction among the 104 respondents with the work factors described in the survey was not high. More than 50 per cent of the respondents chose 'dissatisfied' and 'strongly dissatisfied' in nine items. Only for one item — the working relationship with colleagues — did most employees record being satisfied or very satisfied.

Table 12.3: Job Satisfaction Data (Satisfaction Only)

Aspect of work	Satisfied/Very satisfied (percentage, rounded)
Relationships with colleagues	71
Wages and salary	35
Working conditions	27
Promotion opportunities	29
Fairness of management	43
Training opportunities	34

Participation in decisions	33
Performance measurement	48
Rewards for good work	38
Company policies and management	47
Company welfare policies	22 *
Job security	28 *
Flexibility of working hours	26 *

* Most responses to these factors recorded 'neutral', so these rates of satisfied/very satisfied were not considered of major importance to the respondents.

It can be seen from the table that the relationship between the employees was well-regarded. A total of 42.3 per cent of the respondents were satisfied with the relationship with their colleagues, and another 28.8 per cent expressed a stronger positive opinion, being very satisfied. With regard to the wages and salary factor, although 33.7 per cent were not satisfied and 19.2 per cent were strongly dissatisfied, many employees still felt satisfied, and accounted for 34.6 per cent of total respondents. There were differences in the responses of technical staff and management staff. The percentage of technical employees satisfied and strongly satisfied with their wages was 65.9, whereas 34.9 per cent of management staff deemed the salary they received to be unsatisfactory (being either dissatisfied or very dissatisfied).

In the matter of working conditions, there were small differences in the number of the employees who expressed satisfaction (26.9 per cent), dissatisfaction (29 per cent) and neither of them (i.e., responses of 'neutral') (29.8 per cent). Additionally, most respondents felt neither satisfaction nor dissatisfaction at factors such as welfare policy, job security and flexibility of work schedules, which does not allow many conclusions other than these factors were not causing problems at the manufacturer.

As regards other factors, however, the dissatisfaction rates were much higher. The lack of promotion opportunities contributed to the departure of many skilled employees, as noted in the exit interviews, and this dissatisfaction was borne out by the survey. One half of the respondents expressed their dissatisfaction and 19.2 per cent recorded strong dissatisfaction at the opportunities for promotion in the company. In addition, 47 per cent of employees who completed the survey felt that there was unfairness, or inequities, in the way work was conducted and allocated and this also contributed to the separation decisions of employees. Besides being critical of the way of their performance at work was measured, 38.5 per cent thought their efforts were little recognized and 44.2 per cent found dissatisfaction in the rewards they received for their good work. As to the policy and management of the company, although the number of dissatisfied employees (34.6 per cent) was almost same as the satisfied ones (34.1 per cent), the rate of strong dissatisfaction (21.2 per cent) was higher than the strong satisfaction rate. Moreover, at least one-third of employees were not content with the training provided by the company and the progress they made in their careers. Of the respondent group, 32.7 per cent did not record satisfaction with their opportunities for participating in decision-making, which may reflect the fact that around half of the respondents were employed at base, or junior, level.

Overall, the respondents in the survey did not seem to be very satisfied with their work, even though they were experienced employees and half had progressed to supervisory positions. The results were similar to the tenor of responses given in the records of exit interviews. Using the terms 'hygienes' and 'motivators' as propounded by Herzberg in his Two-Factor Theory, these employees who responded to the survey appeared to express their dissatisfaction at motivators more than hygiene factors.

Interviews With the Managers: The interviews with the general manager and the HR manager were conducted to gain information about the management's opinions and attitudes towards skilled-employee turnover, the retention strategies initiated and barriers to implementing other strategies.

Both the general manager and the HR manager recognized the importance of effective strategies to retain skilled employees in the company and explained that this was why they had set up a policy of conducting exit interviews. They added that most of the skilled employees who left the company were around 30 years old and had worked for about six or seven years. This meant that the skills and work experience lost to the company were costly. It also meant that one skilled employee's leaving often affected the attitudes of others, and sometimes affected staff morale.

From their analyses of the exit interviews, management judged that most skilled employees left the company because of the limited salary on offer and restricted opportunities for advancement. The general manager made a further statement that since the iron rice bowl was broken, State-Owned Enterprises lost advantages they had in guaranteeing ongoing welfare and job security. Many employees had reconciled to these changes, stated the general manager, but they then made comparisons of other factors or conditions, such as salary, working environment and training, provided in SOEs and non-state companies. Once they found better pay and conditions offered by other companies, they were more likely to leave their existing jobs.

When asked for their perceptions of employees' job satisfaction in the company, the HR manager thought it could not be high for he often heard or received complaints from employees. He claimed that many employees were dissatisfied with the salary or rewards, which they thought did not relate appropriately to their efforts. He also pointed out that employee dissatisfaction was recognized as a threat to the company's efficient operation, and a contributing cause of employee separation. Both the general manager and the HR manager thought that with the increase of foreign companies in China, these dissatisfied employees would be more likely to leave for those companies. Subsequently, they expressed concern about higher turnover among their skilled employees as China continued to expand and open its markets to foreign competitors and corporations after accession to the WTO.

Problems with the Implementation of Employee Retention Strategies
Although management had taken measures to prevent skilled employees from leaving, these measures did not cover other important factors which the employees found unsatisfactory and which led to employees' separation. The general manager and HR manager explained that there were some barriers or difficulties in implementing other strategies.

The first barrier was in being flexible in setting wages. The total wage bill had to be approved by SOE governing authorities, even though the company was operating as a private, for-profit enterprise in the motor vehicle component manufacturing industry. Moreover, he added that because of financial restrictions, it was hard for the company to provide a competitive salary and rewards structure for all its skilled employees. The HR manager agreed with this analysis, but he expressed his disagreement with the payment distribution system that was partial to technical staff, but as this policy was decided by the top management he had no authority to change it.

Despite the technical staff/management pay differential, the record of company exit interviews between 2001 and 2003 showed that among the skilled employees who left their employment with the company, 66 per cent of them were technical employees who were favoured by the differential. This was not unusual in the broader sphere, for many Chinese SOEs have suffered a loss of technical staff in recent years. For example, the number of technical staff in the large and middle-sized SOEs fell from 1.47 million in 2000 to 1.41 million the following year.[184] This is clearly an area of growing labour shortage, which may seem to be an anomaly to those who believe that China's huge population means an inexhaustible supply of labour. In reality, as has been noted elsewhere, in 2006 there are growing labour shortages in China. However, wages are only adjusting slowly to take account of this. The interview with the general manager and HR manager of the car component company revealed why wages were adjusting slowly: The large enterprises, SOEs and former SOEs, face controls in the steps they can take to increase pay levels.

When interviewed about the factors related to self-development, such as training and promotion, the HR manager said that the HR department was responsible for personnel management of 1,349 employees, and there were only six employees including himself in the department. Therefore, they did not have any specialist training resources. They usually sent their employees out of the company to receive short-term training where that training was deemed essential. This outsourcing training option was costly to the company, as a result of which it was impracticable to provide training for every employee. He added that, in order to give opportunities for more employees, an employee who had been trained usually received no further training opportunities.

With respect to promotion policies, the HR manager explained that due to the system of appointments, it was hard for an employee to reach the top levels of management even if he/she was competent for the position and had worked hard to justify their promotion. He further indicated that, both on the top level and the lower levels, promotion would depend on many complex factors such as age, longevity and even *guanxi* rather than on an aspirant's good performance or competence. Consequently, this limited real promotion prospects in the company. In addition, it was rarely possible for the company to create new higher level positions that could be filled by mid-level managers working their way up.

Performance Assessment, Motivation and Rewards

Money is still an important motivator for Chinese employees.[185] Therefore, an uncompetitive wages structure is one of the main reasons for skilled employees' leaving.

According to the records of exit interviews in the company, 82.8 per cent of its skilled employees left due to what they considered to be a relatively low salary. This was reflected in the responses to the job satisfaction survey, where 55 out of total of 104 respondents recorded dissatisfaction or strong dissatisfaction with their wages. In relation to the management sector in the company, 28.6 per cent management employees expressed strong dissatisfaction with salary.

This result is similar to a salary survey conducted in fifteen cities of China by ChinaHR.com.[186] Reponses to this survey indicated that 27.38 per cent of employees in Chinese SOEs were strongly dissatisfied with their salary. The country-wide survey also indicated that the rates of dissatisfaction with wages/salaries in wholly foreign-funded companies and joint ventures were less, being 14.6 per cent and 17.1 per cent respectively.

The survey presented comparative figures for annual average salaries in four types of enterprises (Table 12.4). It can be seen from the table that the salary provided by non state-owned enterprises is higher than that in state-owned enterprises, indicating the disadvantages that

SOEs faced in the wages/salaries they could pay to retain their skilled employees.

Table 12.4: Wage and Salary Comparisons (in Yuan)

Type of enterprise	Average annual pay	Median
Foreign companies in China	51,519	39,000
Joint ventures	45,311	36,000
Chinese private enterprises	35,726	26,900
State-Owned Enterprises	31,895	24,000

Source: Salary Survey of 2002 (ChinaHR.com)

In the past 20 years, foreign companies have attracted many technical employees from Chinese SOEs but it remains to be seen how much longer the labour structure can bear this imbalance.[187]

Opportunities for Training and Career Development
In the case study of the Chengdu auto component manufacturer, the data showed that the HR department could not devote what they considered to be appropriate resources to employees' career development. As was recorded in the records of exit interviews, 69 per cent left because of lack of recognition, 72.4 per cent owing to poor training and 86.2 per cent due to limited opportunities for promotion. In the job satisfaction survey, more than one-third of respondents recorded that they were not satisfied with the training the company provided. The company did not provide training for every employee and the training it did provide was often a short-term palliative responding to a skills shortage. This was not uncommon, for a similar situation existed in many Chinese SOEs. Research carried out in 40 SOEs found that about 20 per cent of SOEs spent just 10–30 yuan per employee on training each year, more than 30 per cent SOEs spent under 10 yuan per employee and most loss-making SOEs did not provide any training programs for their employees at all.[188]

In contrast, many Western companies give strong emphasis to training and devote considerable resources. For example, companies such as GE and Motorola allocate to training 4–5 per cent of the annual payroll expense (these are admittedly not auto manufacturing companies, for such percentages are not easy to access in published financial statistics). Putting a dollar figure on these statistics, the average annual amount that Motorola invests in training amounts to approximately US$600 million. Expressing this in terms of training hours, each employee in Motorola receives about 40 hours' training every year.[189]

These policies compare with the Chengdu component manufacturing company, where the HR manager had to admit that it was difficult for a trained employee to have training in the one company for a second time. With limited training programs, it is likely that Chinese SOEs will continue to find it difficult to retain their skilled employees, let alone expand their skilled workforces, without radical changes to their point of view — which may come about as a result of competitive pressure from joint ventures in China and the introduction of Western ideas about the value of extended training.

Promotion Opportunities

Another severe problem that existed in the surveyed company, and with which 50 per cent of the respondents to the survey expressed dissatisfaction, was the lack of opportunities for promotion. One writer found similar results (albeit some time ago), when he surveyed employees in six Chinese SOEs and found that they were dissatisfied with their prospects for advancement and promotion.[190]

The first part of the problem related to the available channels for promotion. These were narrow and influenced by concepts of promotion by seniority as much as promotion by merit. As the HR manager explained in the interview on this subject, usually an employee cannot be promoted until he/she reached a certain age and had completed a certain number of years' service. However, even if an employee did meet requirements for good quality performance, as well as sound ability, he/she may still be unsuccessful in achieving promotion. As a result, these promotion policies, not uncommon in Chinese SOEs, lead to skilled young employees feeling dissatisfied, and 'voting with their feet' to search out a more rewarding job that offered greater prospects.

Secondly, under the promotion system as it operated in the Chengdu company, nepotism was a trump card over skills. The HR manager explained that it was not difficult to find several generations of an extended family working in the one SOE, and this was especially true for an industrial enterprise. Therefore, a complex *guanxi* net, made stronger by family bonds, existed in many Chinese SOEs. Although in the case study under examination, the HR manager would not give details on the importance of nepotism in promotion, this point is supported by the literature on the subject. As some analysts explain, in the eyes of those assessing candidates for a promotion position, employees may look unqualified if they have little *guanxi* even though in reality they may be good performers.[191]

As a third point, there is often limited space for advancement in the traditional manufacturing enterprises. The HR manager in the company under review explained that, due to the slow growth of the company, few new positions had been produced, and there were no possible vacancies at top management level. As a result, many employees concluded that the space for their advancement was limited, or even non-existent.

The job satisfaction survey, review of exit interviews and interviews with the general manager and the HR manager indicated that company management was aware of the HR weaknesses and problems in the company, and recognized the barriers and difficulties which can hardly be overcome in a short term. Those barriers and difficulties mainly lie in the organizational structures and practices inherited from the Chinese SOE system. The large, and not-so-large, enterprises that have grown out of the SOEs do not have sufficient funds to remedy the pay, training and promotion conditions that cause dissatisfaction for their employees. The problem is a deep-seated one.

After China's entry to the WTO, the problem has been exacerbated, as there has been greatly increased demand for qualified personnel, especially by foreign companies which can offer higher salaries. It has been impossible for many of the SOEs and former SOEs to raise wages to stem the outflow of skilled labour, and this has been an inhibiting factor in the growth of big manufacturing enterprises in the auto manufacturing industry.[192] The problems cannot be overcome quickly. They will be overcome in time, but in the meantime they will delay somewhat, but not halt, the flood of quality manufactured goods.

Conclusion

So what is the answer to the question posed in the opening section of this chapter, namely, 'Can China's managers and labourforce achieve high levels of performance?' The answer is a qualified 'yes', based upon the ability of the Chinese to pick up advanced concepts quickly and then apply them. In such a large population, there is a massive pool of talent and those who stand out as the best and brightest are the best and brightest indeed. In addition, the Chinese labourforce, when utilizing up-to-date technology, has a productivity equal to any other labourforce in the world.

These are the human advantages. The human disadvantage is the presence of poor management practices at many levels that impede the best and brightest from coming to the top and earning a fair reward for their effort.

In addition to these human aspects, there are systemic disadvantages and serious flaws in the Chinese system of governance and reporting. These flaws must impact upon the potential to raise significant domestic and foreign capital in the long term. In the short term, Blind Freddie and his dog could rush into any business venture anywhere, but only in the long term, when dividends are flowing regularly, do investors persist and invest further.

On balance, however, China's managers and labourforce will indeed achieve high levels of performance in the near future.

It is of interest to note that, just as the major auto manufacturing companies in the US and western Europe have systemic labourforce problems, mainly related to heritage costs, so the Chinese companies also have deep-seated labourforce problems that are a heritage of the practices of the centrally planned socialist government of the 1950s to 1970s.

13 Summary and Implications

The research detailed in this part of the book addressed aspects of supply and demand of automotive industry infrastructure in China with nine research projects that addressed issues under four broad headings:

1. The Nature of Domestic Consumer Demand in China

The conclusion of the research was that Chinese consumers, at least in urban areas, appeared to share preferences with consumers in the West. This led to two conclusions. The first is that Chinese consumers, at least in urban areas, have a demand for vehicle size, styling, features and sophistication similar to that of consumers in the West. The second conclusion is that the Chinese car industry would probably not be directed at the production of basic vehicles, à la the three-wheeler models, but would instead aim at producing motor vehicles that were similar to the products of Western manufacturers. The production of small commercial vehicles like the auto-rickshaw may become the specialty of certain manufacturing enterprises, and these products are likely to find markets in regions of Africa or Asia, but not in the US or Europe. The biggest vehicle manufacturers — the Chinese flagship enterprises — will compete in the same markets as do the other big global auto firms like GM and VW, and in time offer similar products.

2. The Pricing of Cars in China

This research addressed the question: Will Chinese cars be priced competitively with the West? It indicated that, subject to taxing arrangements, the price of a car in China, in absolute terms, was comparable to the price of a car in the West (e.g., a Toyota Corona equivalent cost 40,000 to 50,000 yuan). Of course, given the disparate income levels in China and the West, this does not mean that a car such as a Toyota Corona is as affordable to a Chinese citizen as it is to, say, an American or Australian citizen.

From this flowed two conclusions. First, cars will remain relatively expensive to Chinese consumers (hence limiting domestic demand and forcing manufacturers to turn to exports if they wish to continue with their 'growth fixation' — as of course they will). Second, Chinese manufacturers can price their products at levels that could substantially undercut the price of cars in the West. The issue of the under-valuation of the yuan has been mentioned as contributing to the problems of the global marketplace and a major cause of the Chinese building up a huge trade surplus with the West and threatening a financial imbalance with developed and developing countries. This book is not intended to cover all the issues of the global currency system, other than to note that the under-valuation of the yuan is a factor in what is a tilted playing field.

3. Issues Related to Infrastructure That May Affect the Expansion of the Domestic Chinese Market

The implications of this research can be briefly stated. If the Chinese domestic market continues to grow exponentially, then this may absorb increased production, but if there are significant restraints on local ownership, then Chinese manufacturers will look to exports to continue their expansion. The original research looked at issues of infrastructure, and came to the conclusion that whereas the capacity of the Chinese to remedy problems should not be underestimated, some significant restraints on their domestic supply and demand will remain. In fact, even if all other factors remained the same, the industry is likely to have to turn to exports to maintain growth levels.

Putting an infrastructure issue such as servicing simply, to underscore its importance to the 'so what' factor, if there are few cars in an economy and you sell a million new cars, there is initially a limited requirement for servicing. However, as those cars age, and as there are increasing accidents (and China has a high accident rate, not surprisingly given the congestion of its cities and the relative inexperience of its many new drivers) then there is a growing need for a service and repair network. Such a network cannot appear overnight, for mechanics must be trained, and shops must open on suburban streets for local residents to get their vehicle serviced/repaired. This is only now growing into a major constraint factor on the growth of private car ownership in China. There are also requirements for such mundane things as parking and insurance cover — but although these may be mundane they are nevertheless important for the development of a well-rounded industry.

The requirement for an advanced infrastructure is probably the greatest restraint on the Chinese car market, and has not yet come to the fore in analysis and discussion because the phenomenon of private car ownership is still relatively new.

4. Issues Related to the Development of a Skilled and Efficient Labourforce

If Chinese workers are to be competitive with Western workers, they will require good management, training, a wages structure that rewards effort and motivates workers, and performance evaluation to ensure high standards of performance. A case study of a motor vehicle component manufacturer, a State-Owned Enterprise, examined some management, governance and labour issues that impacted upon improving performance. It came to the conclusion that although there were systemic disadvantages that should not be underestimated, the management of the big auto corporations could compete with international players and take a hand of poker at any global table.

Conclusion: A Flawed but Effective System

Although this book propounds a thesis that the Chinese car industry will expand rapidly in the near future and take a dominant position in world markets, it is not suggested that this expansion will be without its problems, or that the Chinese industrial state is an all-conquering monolith. The Chinese economy remains a hybrid — neither completely free market nor completely socialist — and it has very serious contradictions and impediments to its operation on a macro as well as the micro level. There are controls in almost all aspects of business. Some of these controls are evident, for example the wages and benefits of most employees which are set within the parameters of Labour Laws. Other controls, such as the existence of Party Committees in large enterprises, are not so evident.

The ease with which controls may be exercised in the community generally was evident during the SARS epidemic of 2003. The author's university, Sichuan University, is among the oldest and largest in China. It could operate almost as a self-contained community of 50,000, with its own educational services, as well as canteens and residentials for staff and students, and ancillary services such as health, education, police and emergency services, and also supermarkets, childcare and sporting venues. The university is surrounded by high walls with the traditional four gates in the east, west, north and south. Each gate is manned by two or three security guards, who up until early 2003 usually sat hatless in the sun or dozed in their bunks in the security hut, nodding occasionally to those who passed through the gates. When the SARS epidemic hit, the flow of visitors was checked overnight. Staff and students were issued with identifying badges. The guards were made over, with belts polished and badges shiny and demeanour changed instantly. Tables were set up at the gates to channel visitors, and everyone who wished to pass in or out of the university was stopped, questioned closely, and more often than not turned away. The new regimen lasted long after the SARS crisis had passed, almost as if force of habit kept the strict controls in place. Such a rapid and effective response to a public health problem, in a large semi-open institution like a large university, was an indicator of the degree of control that could be quickly and effectively imposed by the authorities over large organizations.

When I commented once that daily life seemed more relaxed and open than it had been in the 1980s, people stated firmly that, 'You foreigners see only one level. You come and go, and do not understand what really flows beneath the surface.'[193] The degree of control in Chinese society should not be underestimated, just as its economic challenge should not be underestimated.

Another serious flaw in the Chinese system is the pressure exerted against nonconformity and creativity. Remaining with the university example, a common term for students was 'stuffed ducks', meaning that they were simply pumped full of the one and correct line of thought, wound up and gently propelled out the gates. Curriculums and teaching in non-scientific faculties are not of high standard. Higher education faces challenges in meeting the demands for skilled and independent thinkers to take their place in driving the reformed Chinese economy.

So the way forward to creating a world-beating economy will not be an easy one. However, as has been stated, the ability of the Chinese should never be underestimated. Despite the sometimes-overbearing controls, and also the corruption that will be mentioned in a later chapter, many Chinese entrepreneurs exercise extreme ingenuity in getting around the controls and the bottlenecks in the system.

In summary, the Chinese economic system has its flaws which will put obstacles in the path of developing industry, and hinder the development of a performance-oriented labourforce making quality products, but these flaws are offset by the advantages of a cheap and disciplined labourforce operating within a particularly large and controlled domestic marketplace. Notwithstanding its flaws, the Chinese economic challenge to Western economies and Western car makers is a serious one and the debate should now be concerned with the speed with which Chinese car makers become globally competitive, not whether they are able to.

Part Four
Strategies for the Global Marketplace
14 Protecting Domestic Industry

The Economic Benefits of Cheap Products

The challenge posed to the automotive industry by the growing Chinese operations is not necessarily harmful to all players, and although this book reviews the threat posed to local industry by China's growth, it does not take the stance that this must result in all doom and gloom. A consumer's being able to choose a cheap quality Chinese-made car in preference to a more expensive locally or US-made car has benefits. There are certainly winners in this situation, and first among them are the consumers who get a choice of low-priced products.

To return to a fish-based metaphor, like the 'prawn test' of the Prologue, we could illustrate the point with the example of a consumer who wants a fish. He or she can purchase fishing equipment and bait and trot down to a river or seaside to cast their line into the water and see what they can catch. Alternatively, they could go to a fish shop and select a fish from the products on display. It would be cheaper (because they do not have to purchase their own equipment), and less time-consuming, for them to go to the shop. But then they would forego another benefit they perceive to be of value — the enjoyment of catching their own fish.

There is no moral dimension to their choice of catching their own fish or taking the cheaper option of buying one from someone else.

According to Adam Smith, in classical economic theory an influx of cheap products into a marketplace creates winners and losers. The winners are the consumers, who benefit from being able to buy cheaper goods, and producers who are able to produce the product at a cheaper price. The losers are those existing producers whose cost structures or profit margins may be higher than those of a new competitor. In the economic model of a perfect market, the producers are forced to become more competitive and more efficient so they can match the products of the new entrant. They either reduce their costs or their profit margin, or both, or find better technology or more efficient processes in order to compete with the new player in the market. If the existing producers are not able to achieve cost or efficiency savings to match their competitor, then they go out of business — swept away by the operation of what Adam Smith called the 'unseen hand' of perfect competition of supply and demand in the marketplace. End of story. The market has found an equilibrium where the most efficient and cheapest producer has brought products into a market at the cheapest possible price and there is a balance of supply and demand. The best players have won. The consumers have won. The 'unseen hand' has achieved the best possible use of resources.

There are, however, three points to make out of this scenario, and they concern those who suffer serious loss. The first point is that the existing producers who have failed to compete efficiently have suffered through the loss of their business and investment. This is capitalism, and is not really a problem. The second point is that the people who worked for the existing producers have lost their jobs and livelihoods. This is no problem either, if there is mobility of labour, which means that they can readily find new jobs with their skills and abilities, or can adapt and re-learn new skills. It is, however, a big problem if the workers are not able to adapt for various reasons, are not able to move to where the new jobs are, or if the market for their skills is shrinking and there are no new opportunities for them.

The third point concerns the new entrant to the market. What if they have achieved their market advantage by having wages and conditions that are set at an artificially low level by means of strict labour controls? And what if they further protect their pricing advantage by means of a controlled rate for the exchange of their currency? This does not result in a free market, but in an injustice. We use the phrase level playing field to describe a free market, where all competitors in the market play to the same conditions. If the field is tilted by the imposition of unfair advantages, so some players must run uphill, and the ball naturally runs downhill to the other side's advantage, we see a clear lack of fairness.

To change the metaphor from the playing field to the racing track, we should not put too much lead in the saddlebags of a good horse so that it has no chance against a lightly weighted rival.

The world car industry is showing signs of unfair competition, for one at least of the players — who will soon be one of the biggest players — has the field tilted in their favour. To be sure, consumers will benefit from cheaper products, but society as a whole must measure whether the increased benefits for some outweigh the loss of benefits for another.

There seems to be a need for a balance. There are values on either hand. There is an economic good on one hand, namely:

#1 — Low-priced products for consumers.

There is, on the other hand, another economic good, namely:

#2 — A fairly paid manufacturing labourforce.

If the marketplace is unfairly tilted too far in one direction and is therefore no longer a free market, then society, through its leadership (government), needs to intervene in the marketplace to achieve a compromise, that can be expressed by a middle way — a *via media*. Society and all its members could benefit if the following balance is achieved:

Slightly higher prices for products + a slightly smaller labourforce

New and potentially cheaper products that enter the marketplace should have a charge imposed (that offsets any unfair advantage), so consumers pay a little more, but this impost means that there is a degree of protection for the local labourforce when it is in competition with an overseas labourforce. There is thus a balance of economic goods, but this can only be achieved by interfering in the free operation of the marketplace with one or a number of protective measures.

Protection Strategies

The discussion of development of industries, maximizing benefits, competition, and global free trade keeps coming back to a central issue — protection of jobs and industries within countries and regions.

Governments and regulatory authorities can act to achieve what they perceive to be a fair balance of economic goods within their national or regional markets by following a number of strategies involving rules on the quantity of goods imported (quotas) or special taxes on imports (tariffs). Note that some of the following protective measures, including tariffs and quotas, are not well accepted globally, and various world organizations (such as the gathering of states referred to as the Doha group, after the place they met) are working to reduce such measures to achieve more open world trade. However, even those states which are agitating for a reduction in tariffs and quotas in many fields maintain very high protection measures in some sectors of their own economies — such as the protection for agricultural products in the US, the EU and Japan.

To use a metaphor once again, a tariff can be like an old watchdog who prowls the boundaries of his territory, warning off intruders, and only allowing strangers to visit at their peril. They have to tiptoe around him in fear of receiving a nasty nip. The old watchdog is useful and necessary, but when he is old he becomes somewhat mangy and maybe odoriferous and no one wants to pat him anymore. However, it would be a nuisance to go through the task of getting rid of him. His owners prefer to leave him to himself, sleeping noisily on an old sack or blanket by the door, or prowling the boundaries as he has done by long habit. He may be unloved, even scorned by the neighbours, but he can still fulfil a useful task even if no one wants to talk too much about it.

It must be emphasized that measures that are imposed to protect an economy are not necessarily bad. Protection such as tariffs and quotas have been commonly used to shelter nascent domestic industries, or to protect the development of essential industries such as those of defence or health or food production, or even to protect crucial industries that are suffering from unemployment. Major corporations themselves can lobby for and benefit from protection measures in their home turf, because such measures can act to keep the competition out. Also, corporations, like cunning old dogs begging for the best spot on the carpet instead of a sack, are often strong enough to negotiate exemptions and benefits for themselves under a regime of protectionism. It is not commonly said, but it is true, that global corporations are not entirely averse to a spot of protection here and there.

However, since the middle of the 20th century, there has generally been a freeing-up of world trade and excessive protective measures have been held to be disadvantageous to the development of free markets and hence neither desirable nor acceptable in most circumstances of world trade. A number of agreements between countries and groups of countries, starting with the General Agreement on Tariffs and Trade of 1948, have led to a reciprocal reduction of trade barriers. The European Union grew out of an agreement to liberalize trade in Europe that resulted in a grouping called the European Economic Community. The international movement to liberalize trade gathered force in the latter years of the century and was linked with the concept of globalization — the free movement of goods and services across countries which would result in very large markets which would benefit the peoples of the world.

Different Types of Trade Barriers

Tariffs and quotas are two of the more common means of protection, but there are many other overt and less-overt, or direct and indirect, measures that a government can take to restrict imports by imposing disadvantages on imported goods and services to make it easier for domestically produced goods to compete. Such means can include legalistic provisions that make it hard for imported products to be registered for use in a country. There can be quarantine provisions that are too strict. For example, there are restrictions on the importation of apples into Australia from New Zealand based on the risks of a disease called fire blight, which New Zealand producers claim are overstated and simply amount to disguised protection.

There are unstated barriers such as appeals to nationalism and community loyalty like those said to be strong in Japan, where local people will prefer to buy locally produced products either from patriotic motives or from a genuine belief that locally produced products must be better. The products of 'foreigners' may be held in suspicion. In Australia, there are sometimes marketing campaigns along the lines of 'Buy

Australian' or exhortations for local customers to buy products labelled 'Made in Australia'. A word sometimes used to express such nationalism in business is autarky — a feeling that a national or regional community should be as self-sufficient as possible in terms of trade and production because outside interests may act to their disadvantage, or take out of the community more than it receives through the fair exercise of trade.

There are other effective barriers of language and culture. Countries with a unique language can use this to create a trade barrier against foreign products, for example in the realm of entertainment, in relation to products such as movies and books. This type of barrier can act in two directions, however, as local citizens, especially the young, turn away from local products in favour of international products that appear to be more worldly and exciting.

Another form of trade barrier that effectively results in protection against imports is the barrier of excessive bureaucracy. For example, France is said to have protected its electronic industry for years by requiring importers of new electronic products to obtain import permissions that were only available from one small office in a rural area. The delays caused by lack of staff sometimes amounted to years.

One more effective barrier to a free trade in goods and services can be found in the operation of a country's legal system. If the legal system is both archaic and difficult to understand, as well as not exercised fairly between parties, then foreign investors will be put in a disadvantageous position. This is the current situation in China. There are cases where international corporations and individuals have been clearly disadvantaged in the operation of the Chinese legal system. The following chapter expands this discussion and brings in case studies of less than impartial treatment of local and international parties before the courts of China. Although the provisions of WTO agreements demand that the legal and financial systems of member countries must be transparent and impartial, it takes time to change a massive and cumbersome legal system. Until China's system is so changed, it acts as a very effective barrier to the widespread entry of foreign traders, particularly small to medium-sized businesses who cannot exert any political clout within the system.

In the context of trade barriers being used on a reciprocal basis to make the global playing field more even, we could now consider some means to offset disadvantages in the world trading system created by direct and indirect protective measures.

Instituting a Charge on Imports to Achieve a Level Playing Field — Wage Equalization Theory (WET)

The Moral Basis for a Special Charge on Imports

The thesis of this book is simple. The expansion of the Chinese car industry and the factors of supply and demand mean that it must become a major player in the global marketplace. A prevailing set of economic theories, loosely tied under the heading of globalization, directs that world trade should be free trade, and that the rigours of a free marketplace will ensure that the most efficient and equitable distribution of the world's resources will result, with the maximum common wealth of all.

However, theories of global free trade cannot stand up if a major player is not bound by the same rules as other players — if, in fact, they set their own rules in relation to the pricing of their labour and they insulate that pricing by only permitting a limited float of their currency. If foreign competitors were allowed unfettered entry into their own growing markets, then these imbalances would be partly corrected. But the barriers of culture and history have resulted in economic barriers to new entrants into China's domestic markets. These take the form of inequitable legal systems and endemic corruption.

If free trade cannot stand, then there is a moral and legal argument to impose measures to level up an uneven competitive field. This book has advanced certain conclusions based upon a range of research into aspects of the car industry in China, so it is only logical to put forward a possible response to the problems that will be caused by a tsunami-like flood of cheap imports. One such response could be a measure fairly aimed at the inequitable wages imbalance through a charge that redressed that imbalance. The measure could be based on what this author terms Wages Equalization Theory — hence it may be called a WET charge. It would be intended to allow some survivors to float when the economic tsunami hits.

The need for such a levelling factor can be illustrated by considering a small boat anchored in a current. The boat represents a national economy in the current of global trade. The boat can be anchored from one end, perhaps the bow, by a tie to world capital markets. In the world, we could say that there are common standards of capital, in the sense that world currencies, as media of exchange, are closely tied to one another, and the slightest movement each day can be known and assessed in the marketplace of capital. So we know the exact price of capital, and the interest rates which reflect the availability of that capital. The other end of the boat, the opposite of the capital end, is the labour end. This end is not controllable, in the sense that the world does not have common standards for the value of labour. Indeed, labour is almost infinitely complex, reflecting different values, different productivity, even different social and cultural mores on what is and what is not labour.[194] The point is that the stern of the boat swings widely in the current even as waves lap and splash against the hull. In order to make comparisons between economies, to assess whether market access and competition is fair and equitable, analysts need standards of wages and they are not easy to compile. If there was such a standard, then the boat could be anchored at bow and stern and its place in the current made stable so that its position could be compared with other boats.

The cost of labour should be equalized, for in theory, in a global free market there must be transparency and free movement of labour and capital. There must be a balance to obtain equilibrium in the marketplace. All things should be in balance. It is said that there can never be a one-armed economist, for they are fond of saying, 'On the one hand, this ... and on the other hand — that'. There must be a balance — equity — in the marketplace, or else the marketplace cannot operate fairly for all concerned.

For that reason, a Wages Equalization Theory is proposed, as a device to level the world economic playing field when it comes to fairly comparing wage levels. The use of such a theory can allow a fair assessment of the degree to which the field needs to be tilted to return it to a semblance of normality. Then, to level the field so that domestic products can more fairly compete with cheaper imports, a charge could be imposed upon those imports.

Such a charge would not be a tariff, because a tariff is usually based upon a nation's internal economic factors and the word, in common usage, refers to a table of fixed charges or a duty on a class of imports.[195] A WET charge on the imports of goods from one country to another would be calculated on the relative imbalances of wages in both countries expressed in terms of a standard — say the US dollar, or the euro — and the relative productivity of labour. Hence, there is a case that such a charge would not breach general undertakings made under WTO regulations.

Calculating the WET Charge

The theory can be stated like this:

Where a country (A) does not permit the equalization of its wages to global standards by free market forces, that is, by the application of WTO principles and being fully open to free trade through a free exchange of its currency on world markets, then another country (B) may impose a charge on country A's imports intended to correct the anomaly created by the disparity in wage values, and thereby partly restore an equitable trading position between the two countries.

In the case of motor vehicles, the charge, levied as a percentage of the total cost of the vehicle, could be calculated using three elements. The first element would be the percentage cost of labour to the total cost of the product. As this theory is intended to be applied to products that are globally traded, in order to correct an unfair wage and currency imbalance, it uses a standard cost and the proportion of labour costs is the best comparison to hand. For example, the labour cost of a motor vehicle could be a standard figure for a car of a certain model which is manufactured in a similar form in a number of countries. The labour cost percentage of such a car would not be difficult to assess, even when the exact details would be commercial in confidence. A fair estimate of the percentage would be sufficient for the calculation. A small car may be known to require 30 hours of labour to assemble, and wages costs may be known to be around US$60 an hour, so the assembly-line labour component of that vehicle costs US$1,800 (and of course there are additional supervisory and management labour costs etc. included in what are called 'labour overhead' costs). If a vehicle is imported and its declared manufacturing cost is US$7,200,[196] then the assessed labour cost, or the 'nominal labour cost', could be 25 per cent. A higher figure could be calculated to take into account labour costs that relate to other than assembly line labour, but for the purposes of this discussion, take 25 per cent as a labour figure.

The second element is the average wage per person working in that sector of the manufacturing industry in the country of origin, or in the region of origin (say a province or state within the national boundaries). This statistic also is usually available or able to be estimated from data collected by the statistics authorities of the country. This average wage, where stated in local currency, should be converted to a common world currency (say the US dollar, or the euro, or a new Asian currency unit being discussed at the Asian Development Bank). The third element is the average wage per person in that sector of the manufacturing industry in Australia, and this also is converted to a common world currency (say the US dollar, or the euro).

The three elements are combined by multiplying the labour percentage by a factor obtained by one minus the proportion of the average wage in the sector of the country of origin (in US dollars) over the proportion of the average wage in the sector in Australia (in US dollars). The result is that the charge is calculated on two out of three statistics that are influenced by economic policy in the country of origin. The charge is variable depending on the degree of inequity in the country of export, or, in other words, the degree to which they have tilted a supposedly level playing field in their favour.

The elements of the WET charge can be more clearly stated as a formula:

Wage Equalization Charge as per cent of vehicle cost $= a \% \left(1 - b/c\right)$
where a equals the percentage cost of labour to the total cost of the product, b equals the average wage per person in the relevant sector in the country of origin of the imports converted to a common world currency (say the US dollar, or the euro), and c equals the average wage per person in the relevant sector in Australia converted to a common world currency (say the US dollar, or the euro).

287

The calculation is based upon the regional wage in the relevant sector of industry, not the nation of origin as a whole, so that the figure is not unduly skewed by, say, very low agricultural wages. The wages figures in both country of origin and Australia are expressed in a common currency that is a worldwide yardstick, so that the calculation will iron out problems caused by fixed exchange rates. If the currency in the country of origin is undervalued, thus giving its exporters an unfair advantage, then the result will be that the WET charge will be higher. The closer the exporting country's currency is to a fair freely traded market value, the more the WET charge will be reduced.

If the wage rates in the exporting and importing country reach parity, then the factor b/c will be one, and within the brackets the calculation will be $(1 - 1)$, which equals zero. Hence the WET charge would be zero. This emphasizes that WET theory is only intended to take account of variations in wage rates for workers in different countries carrying out the same work.

The formula also takes into account the varying productivity of labour, and a developing country with low labour productivity is not penalized. If the workforce in the exporting country becomes more productive, then factor a will be affected. The comparative cost of labour involved in assembling the product will decrease, and so the WET charge will also decrease. The country that will be penalized through this formula is the country whose labourforce achieves productivity levels similar to those of the Australian labourforce, yet that has wages and benefit levels less than those of Australia.

If economists could find a perfect world, with perfect free trade in open global markets, then as labour becomes more productive in that world, by the laws of comparative economics, wages rise to a level that is common throughout the marketplace. However, in an imperfect world, workers' wages can be kept lower than they should be, and be prevented from rising to a common level in a number of ways. If there are only a few large employers in the labour market (as is the case with the auto industry) then the major players can keep wages down, provided there is a continuing supply of new labour prepared to work at those low levels. In China, there are signs of labour growth reaching its limits, which means that real wages should rise — but the process will take years. The car industry in the West does not have enough years to wait, so there is a need for a WET charge now. The following three examples indicate how it is calculated in various changing circumstances.

Example 1: Take the example of an imported car with a labour cost of US$1,092 in a total manufactured cost of US$7,000, which means a labour cost percentage of 15.6 per cent. If that vehicle should come from a country which does not allow its currency to float freely in the world currency system, then WET would apply. Assume that the car requires 30 hours to build in that country, where the average wage is US$1.50 per hour (at the fixed rate of exchange). In Australia, workers are more productive and build the vehicle in 25 hours and their average hourly wage rate (with all on-costs etc.) is A$40 or US$30 (to use round figures).

The **WET charge** (on the total cost of the vehicle) is calculated as follows:

15.6 per cent x $(1 - 30 \times 1.50/25 \times 30)$
=   15.6 per cent x $(1 - 45/750)$
=   15.6 per cent x (0.94)
=   14.7 per cent
=   14.7 per cent of US$7,000 = **US$1,029 (WET)** + US$7,000
= US$8,029 (total imported cost)

Example 2: The following example shows how the WET charge would be less if the country of origin had a wage rate closer to that of Australia. Consider the labour cost is US$1,800 in a total manufactured cost of US$7,200 or 25 per cent. If that vehicle should come from a country which does not allow its currency to float freely in the world currency system, but follows a currency regime that results in an exchange rate to the dollar closer to that of Australia, then the following calculation could be made. Assume that the car still requires 30 hours to build in that country, but the average wage is US$20 per hour (at the fixed rate of exchange). In Australia, the figures stay the same, namely, that workers are more productive and build the vehicle in 25 hours and their average wage rate (with all on-costs etc.) is A$40 or US$30 (to use round figures).

The WET charge (on the total cost of the vehicle) is calculated as follows:

25 per cent x $(1 - 30 \times 20/25 \times 30)$

= 25 per cent x $(1 - 600/750)$

= 25 per cent x (0.20)

= 5.0 per cent

= 5.0 per cent of US$7,200 = **US$360 (WET)** + US$7,200 = US$7,560 (total imported cost)

The end result is a minimal additional charge, even though their wage rate is only two-thirds of the Australian.

Example 3: Now amend the example once more, assuming that the country of origin has improved its productivity overall, which results in both a lower labour cost percentage and less time to build the vehicle. Assume that the imported car has a labour cost of US$1,000 in a total manufactured cost of US$6,700 or 15 per cent (i.e., a similar labour percentage to example 1 because although productivity is higher, the cost per hour is much higher as well — but the benefit in terms of a reduced WET charge is much more). If that vehicle should come from a country which does not allow its currency to float freely in the world currency system, then WET would apply. Assume that the car requires the same labour input as in Australia, namely 25 hours to build the vehicle in that country, where the average wage is US$20 (at the fixed rate of exchange). In Australia, workers are just as productive and build the vehicle in 25 hours and their average wage rate (with all on-costs, etc.) is A$40 or US$30 (to use round figures).

The WET charge (on the total cost of the vehicle) is calculated as follows:

15 per cent x $(1 - 25 \times 20/25 \times 30)$

= 15 per cent x $(1 - 500/750)$

= 15 per cent x (0.33)

= 5.0 per cent

= 5.0 per cent of US$6,700 = **US$335 (WET)** + US$6,700 = US$7,035 (Total Imported Cost)

In this third example, there is a clear benefit in the form of reduced

WET to 'reward' the country of origin for not only having wage rates closer to those of Australia, but also improving its productivity, and the consumer still benefits from a lower price for a new car.

WET theory is intended to be applied to the car industry, because in that industry direct comparisons are possible and not difficult, but it should in justice be applied across all the manufacturing sectors where domestic industries are operating at an unfair disadvantage. Clearly in the worldwide car industry there will be workers working in plants in different countries assembling virtually identical models, as a result of which clear and valid comparisons can be made. That is the case where disparities in wage rates should not, in justice, give a very great advantage to one party where wages may be depressed through the influence of historical or political factors.

Globalization is meant to be about worldwide equity in free and fair markets. It must include the concept that workers who do the same job in different parts of the world should receive comparable wages. If they do not, it is not unfair to establish a mechanism to help correct the problem.

Objections to WET

There are six main objections to Wage Equalization Theory, or questions that may be asked of it.

1. The definition of wage can vary from place to place. For example, in China it may include non-cash benefits, such as subsidized housing or even food rations. In Australia and other Western countries, the total wage cost includes what are termed on-costs such as superannuation (pension) benefits, health benefits and the like, as well as additional wage-like benefits such as allowances to reimburse commuter travel, etc. Because of these differences, some may say that comparing wages cannot be done, because it would be a case of comparing two unlike items, such as apples and grapes.

The answer to this objection to WET charges is that, as global trade interaction continues, there is a growing convergence of practices and benefits. In a worldwide industry such as the automotive industry, it is not difficult to assess employee emoluments to find common ground on which to compare them.

2. The cost of living may be lower in other countries and hence their wages will naturally be lower. In such a case, it is only reasonable that the labour costs will undercut those of producers in the West.

The answer to this objection is that if the cost of living in these countries is lower, then that cost differential should be reflected in the country's exchange rate, provided the exchange rate is completely free and floating. Movements in the exchange rate for the currency against world currencies such as the US dollar or the euro should take account of this. As time passes, and a country's cost of living changes due to increased productivity or maybe increased inflation, then its currency exchange rate will fluctuate to reflect these changes.

3. What happens when there is a wide variation in labour productivity rates, due to availability and use of advanced technology? For example, the time needed to assemble a given, identical model of car, may vary from say 12 hours in Germany to 15 hours in Poland to 18 hours in the United Kingdom to 20+ hours in the Philippines. How does WET take account of that?

WET does not necessitate using the highest productivity figure as a benchmark. Indeed, it is not intended as a benchmark measure, but as a measure to remove inequity. The figure for productivity in Australia could be used, and the productivity of overseas producers tabulated against that. WET encourages improvements in productivity beyond certain levels, so, for example, if production in another country is higher than that in Australia, even though wages are kept lower and controlled through fixed exchange rates, WET will still work to reward productivity increases. Such increases would reduce the WET charge by reducing a in the equation.

4. What about those countries in early stages of industrial development whose labourforce has very low productivity and also low wages?

Exceptions can always be made to an impost on imports, but WET at least enables public decision-makers to quantify the cost of their decision, and forces them to justify their actions.

5. Is it valid to have a numerator based on a fixed currency and a

denominator based on the freely floating Australian dollar?

The answer is that in this case it is, because the calculation is intended to inform as much as to level the field. The application of WET indicates the extent to which undervalued wages impact upon the competitiveness of imported goods.

6. How does WET allow for daily currency fluctuations?

The answer is that the WET charge could be adjusted for each consignment over a period, based on currency exchange rates at the beginning of the period, or it could be recalculated from time to time (say annually or quarterly).

A Final Word on Protection Measures: Can Government Afford Not to Intervene?

There are some strong themes in the credo of those who support a 'free market'. One of those is the insistence on 'non-intervention', of leaving everything to the invisible forces of the free market. At the other extreme are those who argue that there is a need for a strong centrally planned economy. Somewhere in the middle is the answer, with a compromise driven by the need for an efficient and affordable answer that goes along with a recognition that not every aspect of society can be reduced to an economic argument. Some things are too valuable for economics to measure.

In 2004 the US Senate passed a package of measures to favour its own manufacturers. One of those measures was the use of public procurement — that government contracts would give absolute priority to domestically produced goods and services. While some may argue that this can be more expensive for the taxpayer, the riposte is that failing enterprises in the home country result in extra expense for the taxpayer one way or another anyway.

In 2007, there is not much enthusiasm in the West for governments to get involved in the operation of global trade and so-called free markets. The forces of globalization are given free play.

In the US, where the huge car makers, GM and Ford, are under stress from the pressure of pension and health care costs, there are few signs of the government wanting to be a party to addressing the problems. This may be because of the market philosophy of those in power, but it is also because many foreign companies have established a presence in local manufacturing. Their names include Nissan, Honda, Mercedes-Benz and Hyundai. In 2006, out of a total of 64 major auto plants in the US, one-quarter — sixteen plants — are owned and managed by foreign car makers. These figures also mean that around a quarter of employment in the auto industry is through foreign firms — that is, around 110,000 employees out of around 450,000.

The oil crisis of the 1970s led to a rapid expansion of the importation of cars into the United States. At that time, the US car industry was able to extract government assistance, because the rise in oil prices helped tip the US economy into recession, along with many other world economies. The global economy generally suffered high interest rates and inflation. Japan was developing its economic muscle and was a real threat in the global marketplace. Ten years later, in the 1980s, there were continuing high levels of imported motor vehicles, so much so that Chrysler looked as if it might go under. There was government intervention once again, and a publicly funded rescue package saved Chrysler. There were also tough negotiations and arm-twisting by the Reagan administration behind closed doors, as evidenced by the Japanese companies accepting voluntary restraints and agreeing to establish plants in the US to sustain local employment in the auto industry. The foreign-owned plants also agreed to source a proportion of their car components through US companies.

It may be an irony that the success of these foreign plants in the US increased the pressure on US companies in the long-term, for it removed the ability of GM and Ford to cry out that they had to be protected to conserve US jobs. Other companies are now providing US jobs as well. In the 2000s therefore, there is a clear reluctance to intervene, but can governments afford not to intervene when a greater challenge arises?

What if the auto industry in Australia collapses entirely? It is not beyond the realms of possibility that all cars in Australia could be sourced from overseas. Australian manufacturers could not even compete in the area of making components, for low-cost Chinese operations could undercut them every day in terms of quality and price.

Has the local industry in Australia a right to survive? For much of its history, Australian governments believed so, and provided high levels of protection in the form of tariffs, quotas and other protective measures. Will it even consider doing the same today? The answer to this point appears to be 'no'. This means that, first under the pressure of Chinese imported components, and second under the pressure of whole cars imported, the domestic Australian motor vehicle manufacturing industry will not survive. The period of its dying may be five years or up to ten years, but it will certainly die without government intervention in the form of enhanced protection and other measures after 2010, when tariff protection is reduced to just 5 per cent.

15 Will Globalization Work Both Ways?

The Question of a Quid Pro Quo

A previous chapter raised the issue of a country's legal environment being an effective barrier to the free movement of goods and services into that country from overseas. The issue becomes crucial when businesses, faced with challenges from a region with lower costs and wage structures, seek to meet the challenges by relocating their operations to that region. Most of the previous discussion has considered the manufacturing industry within the operation of the world economy, and especially within the principles of developing global trade according to the requirements of the World Trade Organization agreement.

The prospect of manufactured goods flooding into Australia and other Western countries and decimating local economies is, in theory, offset by the ability of Western countries to offer their own goods and services in the Chinese marketplace. When cheap quality cars and car components from China have resulted in Australia's car-manufacturing industry having to close because it is no longer competitive, then Australians can concentrate on other areas where they have a 'comparative advantage' in the global marketplace. An example of where Australians have superior services to offer could be its legal services, or its insurance services. As a country, we can offset the economic loss of a car industry by expanding the international income we earn through the export of services expertise.

For example, in 2007, Australia was negotiating a free trade agreement with China that would grant China further access for its manufacturing exports in return for Australian access to China's services and agricultural markets. There has been concern expressed in Australia about whether such an agreement will be fair and open-handed. The concerns of the South Australian state government in relation to the import of cars and car components has been mentioned earlier. Such concerns are in fact widespread, and only 24 per cent of Australian manufacturers support a free trade agreement with China.[197]

The concerns are based on their conviction that not only is the playing field uneven, but that it may remain that way. Up to 2007, tariff barriers have worked in China's favour, for Australia had duty-free access to China for just 8 per cent of its tariff lines, while China had duty-free access to Australia for 48 per cent of its tariff lines. An even-handed free trade agreement would also require China to address other issues that impede access to its markets by foreign businesses, for example, its legal and financial processes. Under existing arrangements, Australians and other Westerners are impeded from setting up new businesses, not so much by the classical instruments of protection such as tariffs and quotas — although these exist — but through such things as the operation of restrictive and inequitable financial rules and a legal system that is biased against foreigners.

It has already been commented that one flaw in globalization as it is practised in 2007 is that there is no level playing field in regard to comparative wages, but there is another crucial flaw in globalization as it is applied to China and countries trading goods and services into China. The Chinese legal system simply does not provide such a field for those seeking to set up businesses in the country. This chapter takes up the issue of China's legal system and adds comments on the associated problem of corruption of officials.

It is vital for any investor, before making any investment, to research the legislative and policy environment of the country within which he or she (or it, in the case of a corporation) wishes to invest. China has a legal environment which is very different from those of Western countries, from European traditions of law and from the Anglo-Saxon tradition of law. For foreign investors to be able to succeed in China's market, they need to understand the parameters and practices of its legal system — and it is not easy to gain this understanding.

This chapter describes the Chinese legal environment and the relationship between its various players. There are substantial defects in the Chinese legal environment which to a large extent counteract the hoped-for benefits of foreign investment. Until these defects are remedied root and branch by all levels of the Chinese legislative structure, there will not be a level field for those who wish to invest in developing goods and services in the country. The field is tilted too far to the benefit of the home team.

Background[198]

For centuries, China and its economy operated under a legal system based upon feudalism. There have of course been substantial legal reforms, even since the republic was established in 1912, and since the Communist government took power in 1949, but there remains a raft of practices, regulations and national, provincial, municipal and district legislation that floats on the sea of everyday activity, occasionally with leaks here and there which are sometimes patched and sometimes not.

The reform process that started in the late 1970s, and that was described in the first chapter, included measures to provide a new legal background for foreign investment. One of these measures — the law called The Law of the People's Republic of China on Chinese-Foreign Equity Joint Ventures — has been mentioned. Since 1979, there has been a flood of foreign investment, and within ten years there were no fewer than 150,000 joint ventures between foreign companies and individuals and Chinese partners. At the end of 2004, activities brought about by foreign investment accounted for around 34 per cent of GDP.[199] However, the legal culture and environment that exists in the main still results in foreign investors encountering more barriers and difficulties than their Chinese counterparts.

On the one hand, foreign investment brings advanced ideology and technology to China, but on the other hand it also brings what many Chinese regard as negative influences, for example, when multinational enterprises flex their economic muscle to lobby and influence government policies (even though the Chinese themselves excel at this through their *guanxi* practices). For another example, some parties in China fear that large multinationals may use their advantages in efficiency and technology to create monopolies in some sectors of the economy.[200]

To an extent, the Chinese government is caught in a cleft stick, for it has agreed by treaty to revise its relevant laws and regulations to meet the requirements of the WTO Accession Agreement.[201] According to the commitments made, the Chinese government will revise its relevant laws and regulations so that those domestic laws and regulations become consistent with the requirements of the WTO Agreement. Under the terms of the agreement, China was obliged to overhaul a wide range of laws, regulations, policies and governmental practices. Whether this process will be carried out smoothly and thoroughly is problematical.[202]

It is possible to comb through sheaves of national laws and revise them where it is obviously necessary. But it is not always as easy to judge where the laws and regulations need to be revised, and the actual implementation of those changes is more important but much more difficult than the revisions. As one Chinese writer has stated: 'The existence of provisions exists in one hand, and the enforcement of law exists on the other hand. [In China], some legal provisions might not be put into effect in reality and remain a mere scrap of paper. There is usually some distance between the social reality and the legal provisions.'[203] For example, the Chinese government gave commitments to continue to enhance its enforcement of laws relating to intellectual property and promised that appropriate cases would be referred to relevant authorities for prosecution under the criminal law provisions. In fact, most intellectual property enforcement in China has been carried out through administrative actions, which mean that the rights-holders are seldom compensated for the loss they have suffered through the theft of their intellectual rights. Despite the WTO provisions and agreements to pursue the issue, copyright piracy and trademark counterfeiting have increased rather than decreased, as will be discussed in the next chapter.

In practice, many foreign investors are confused by the Chinese legal environment and legal culture. Though they may understand some of the background of Chinese culture, the difference between East and

West, especially in regard to legal systems, is sometimes not so much a gap but a crevasse. Westerners find it hard to grasp the essence of the Chinese legal culture, which is as much legal ideology as legal culture. They find it hard to understand how a judge may weigh up a case and not be influenced by precedent, or even by the interpretation of law by other judges in his or her jurisdiction. Legal systems based on the common law of England, including the USA and Commonwealth countries, are bound by a general principle of law described as *stare decisis*, which requires that like cases be decided in like fashion. For example, in Australia, in the prominent case of Mabo (No. 2), Justice Brennan declared that the High Court could not depart from old English precedent 'where the departure would fracture what I have called the skeleton of principle. The Court is even more reluctant to depart from earlier decisions of its own.'[204] The maintenance of a predictable legal system is, in the common law, predicated on this system of adherence to precedent. Cases which turn on the interpretation of statutes are managed similarly, by applying the rule of precedent to previous interpretations as well as instituting the general principle of interpretation. An example is the Australian Acts Interpretation Act 1901, which describes the meaning which is to be given to common phrases and concepts, and limits the materials a judge can use to interpret other phrases.

The situation in regard to precedent is different in China, and this is just one area where foreign investors and litigants often misunderstand the Chinese legal system. There are a number of writers and analysts who give sound advice on how to adapt to China and its foreign investment environment,[205] but few of them discuss at length the Chinese legal environment. There are urgent issues in relation to contract-making, enforcement and the law, inequities in the justice system, and the negative impact upon foreign investors generally.

One notable case involving an Australian falling foul of Chinese law concerned an Australian-Chinese businessman named James Peng. Mr Peng founded a company in China during the mid-period of reforms in the late 1980s and in 1993 he was involved in a commercial dispute with his Chinese partners. Instead of the dispute being resolved by a court, he found himself arrested on a charge of corruption based upon dubious evidence. He was held for six years and only released after the Australian government applied diplomatic pressure on his behalf, but he lost all of his investment in the Chinese business venture.

The Legal Environment and Foreign Investment

The legal environment within which foreign investment takes place is an important factor in developing a sustainable market economy integrated into global trade, because it should guarantee a fair conditions for all concerned. The importance of the legal environment to investment has been well-noted by analysts, for example: 'Differences in legal systems can have an important impact on the attractiveness of a country as an investment site and/or market'.[206]

As of 2007, the Chinese legal environment is a multi-layered one. According to the Constitution of the People's Republic of China, all the powers of state belong to the people and the organizations by which the people exercise their powers are the National People's Congress and its Standing Committee.[207] At the local levels, these legal powers are exercised through organs such as the People's Court and the Procuratorate. This is the environment in its stated theory, but not all aspects of the legal environment have been systematized or standardized. There are some areas where there are conflicts between administrative regulations and departmental rules (and these may also contravene national laws). Local regulations also may run counter to national laws.[208] These defects in the existing legal system have had the result that some of the laws concerning foreign investment cannot be effectively enforced. Some of the problems identified include the localization of judicial power, the uneven training and performance of judges and the lack of sufficient judicial supervision.[209]

The multiple layers of China's legislative and regulatory system are not dissimilar to most Western systems. What appears to be different is the means by which the potential conflict of laws between separate levels is governed. In Australia, for example, it is a constitutional issue. Section 109 of the Australian constitution provides that a law passed by a state is invalid to the extent that it is in conflict with a Commonwealth law. Another aspect of conflicting laws is set out in the body of rules known as 'private international law,' which consists of cases and statutory rules which describe how disputes which have elements of foreign law involved will be managed in domestic courts in each Western country.

The system of law as it develops in any country is linked with its history and customs. 'Understanding the legal environment of a country allows insight into the moral and philosophical mindsets of the citizens.'[210] The ideology of contemporary Chinese is deeply influenced by the Confucian legal culture and feudal mentalities. One of China's foremost social scientists has attributed the deep-seated flaws in the legal system to the current circumstances of Chinese culture and society. 'China, in which the traditional thoughts about litigation are obstinately observed by folks, is still a provincial society in transition so that the modern judiciary cannot be carried out completely.'[211] That is, the traditional Chinese legal mentality is rooted in the values, lifestyles and behaviours of Chinese society, and cannot be quickly changed even under the pressure of global economics. A French jurist, Rene David, has addressed this point, when he noted that lawmakers can pass legislation to annul some system by placing their signature on a revocation order — but they cannot change longstanding customs and practices, especially those based in religious beliefs, in a short time.[212]

To put this situation in a few words, in China under the current legal environment, sometimes a judgment depends on the litigant's identity, post, status and social relationships, and not on the statutes or on facts which are presented.[213]

The attitude that Australians should have in regards to the Chinese legal system was stated simply by the President of the Australia China Business Council: 'People cannot assume that the same legal principles that they are accustomed to here at home will apply in China.'[214]

Foreign Investors' Legal Concerns

Clearly a difficult situation arises if foreign investors are treated differently under the law and even excluded from the governance of laws which regulate general enterprises. The inequality of different legal petitioners is not sustainable in a globally reactive society.[215]

The concerns of foreign investors about the operations of the Chinese legal environment can be placed under several headings. One analyst has listed these concerns. They include: the predictability, feasibility and consistency of foreign investment laws; the improper collection of fees and fines, and the inappropriate and intrusive inspection of the activities of foreign companies; excessive government interference in the activities of foreign corporations; the need for the maintenance and extension of an open and fair market environment; the need for an incorruptible and efficient exercise of government oversight where appropriate; and the maintenance of a sound and efficient administrative environment for foreign investment.[216]

To expand this discussion of the problems facing foreign investors, some specific areas need to be detailed.

Perceptions About Commercial Contracts in China
Formal commercial contracts are always necessary when publicly owned corporations invest in another country. The days of agreements made and enforced on a handshake are long gone (if they ever really existed outside the world of anecdotes). A contract is a document that is intended to define clearly a set of rules that reflects the way in which an investment is to be conducted. The way that these rules are expressed reflects the etiquette, traditions, values, communication and the negotiating styles of different people. Sometimes a successful global investment depends on how flexible the investor is recognizing and respecting the culture of other people.[217] The role of a commercial contract in China is seen differently by the Chinese. It is not necessarily a hard-and-fast agreement with every detail of the relationship spelt out in black and white. It therefore becomes an issue for foreign investors determining how to protect their legal rights and interests in a legal (and cultural) environment where contracts are perceived to be different beasts from what they are in the West. Expressing the situation baldly, in China contracts cannot always be relied upon.

A contract, in law, as it is commonly understood in the West, 'is a document that specifies the conditions under which an exchange is to occur, and details the rights and obligations of the parties.'[218] However, according to Chinese law, 'A contract refers to an agreement establishing, modifying, and terminating the civil rights and obligations between subjects of equal footing, that is, between natural persons, legal persons or other organizations'[219] In China, a contract established according to the law shall be under the protection of law, which seems clear and simple, provided the exercise of the law is equally clear and simple in the event of a dispute — but this is not necessarily the case. Foreign investors certainly concentrate on the details of a contract, and they may have abundant experience in making contracts, but this does not ensure that their interests are protected effectively. There is a wholly different Chinese perception of contracts and business dealing. To the Chinese, 'Business transactions are made on the strength not of contracts but of personal agreements. Transactions are purely private, and are neither verifiable nor enforceable in the public sphere'[220] The contract is the beginning of a relationship, not its determinant.

Compared with Western understanding, this is a sea change, but it is entirely logical and rational from another point of view. If the other point of view sees business dealings as part of a relationship, and not just the handing over of goods or services for other goods or services, then it is logical to state that, 'Transactions are purely private, and are neither verifiable nor enforceable in the public sphere'. In the West, business transactions may be between individual traders or companies that pass like ships in the night, but in China this is not so: Business transactions are between those who get in the same boat for the voyage.

An interesting aspect of contract law which is under-developed in China concerns what in the West is called trade practices. Most Australian legal jurisdictions have a form of Trade Practices Act, which makes particular limitations on how companies can contract transactions (no misleading or deceptive conduct, etc., or the contract will be set aside), as well as corporate regulation through the relevant Corporations Act and other rules, such as requiring some contracts to be evidenced in writing if they are to be enforceable.

Case Study — the Jialilai Case

The different concepts of what was entailed by a contractual agreement in China came out in the Jialilai case which went through the Chinese courts.[221] In 1995, the Jialilai (Hong Kong) company entered into a Sino-foreign joint venture with two Chinese partners, the Beijing Second Commercial Group Company (BSCG) and Beijing Heng Ye company, after conducting due diligence and entering into appropriate contracts. Jialilai took 60 per cent of the shareholding. The joint venture was to develop plastic mouldings. However, on 25 September 2001, BSCG submitted a request to the corporations regulator in Beijing, the Beijing Commercial Bureau, to exclude Jialilai Company as a shareholder — effectively taking over the foreign investor's shareholding. Their motives may have included the fact that they received up-to-date moulding technology from the Hong Kong partner, and wanted to convert this technology to their exclusive use.

This application to the corporate regulator was clearly outside the provisions of China's Company Law, but the Beijing Commercial Bureau approved BSCG's application and struck Jialilai Company from the shareholders' register of the venture. By this stroke of the pen, Jialilai was deprived of its part-ownership of around 1 billion yuan in property assets. This matter was later referred to as the 'Beijing gate scandal' and was reported in the overseas press. As a consequence, Jialilai took action through the courts to protect their interests, and after the legal processes had run their course the legal appeal authority, the State Council, required the Beijing Commercial Bureau to reverse its decision. That has been done, but the question of compensation remained unresolved. The implications of the case were that contracts could not be relied upon, but neither could the corporations regulator be trusted to provide a fair and equitable resolution of a contractual dispute.

The disappointing experience of some joint ventures has had the result that in the new millennium, instead of joint ventures, wholly owned foreign enterprises (WOFEs) have become the main vehicles of foreign investment in China.[222] Such enterprises offer a more certain management environment.

Making a contract in China, or in any cross-cultural situation for that matter, can be more difficult than concluding a contract in a domestic operation.[223] Chinese business people do see a contract differently, and they tend not to treat each stage of the contract-making process in a legalistic fashion. In the Chinese view, to be too legalistic may spoil a friendship, for good friends should trust each other. When drawing up a contract, not all the details may be listed. For example, this means that when disputes arise, the parties will use their *guanxi* to deal with the arguments and so maintain the overall relationship.

It is also a common practice to make overstated commitments. In the West, if parties aspiring to a contract overstate their likely contributions and the possible goals of the contrasting parties, there is a tendency to cry 'false pretence'. However, in the Chinese cultural environment, it is not uncommon for business people to put what they see as the best possible gloss on the deal under consideration. If the other party is a foreigner, then the tendency of the Chinese party to exaggerate is more common, but it is not intended to be misleading in a legal sense.

The tendency for overstatement leads to other problems. One such problem is the ability to check the creditworthiness, or the asset backing, of a prospective partner or business associate. Clearly, in business it is necessary to check the credit and reputation of a prospective partner carefully. Every investor will undertake research into the bona fides of a partner of a proposed joint venture. However, in the Chinese business environment it is very difficult to conduct a reliable credit check or to get correct information about an enterprise, let alone full details of all the stakeholders in that enterprise. The availability and reliability of business information also varies across China, depending upon the region where a prospective investor plans to do business. One source asserts that it is easier to establish the credentials of Chinese enterprises and business personnel in the eastern coastal regions than in the western and far western areas of the country.[224]

Despite the fact that a foreign party to a contract may be at a disadvantage in a contractual dispute, it is still essential that that party keeps to the terms of the contract. Any breakdown in the relationship should be dealt with squarely within the provisions of the contract — for example, if there are clauses relating to the provision of goods or funds or services if matters are under dispute. This was an important provision in the Beijing Jeep affair, when the American partner realized that their Chinese counterparts were using funds due to the Americans to fund other aspects of their business.

When a dispute does arise and cannot be readily resolved, then in China, even more so than in the West, the aggrieved parties should take all reasonable measures to resolve the dispute without having to resort to the legal system. Lawsuits may not bring any benefits but only increase the losses. Even if foreign investors dispute a contract, take the issue to court and have it resolved in their favour, it can happen that the decisions of the tribunal or law court cannot be enforced. The issue of inequities in enforcing the law is considered below.

There is another reason why parties in dispute should only take legal action as a last recourse. That reason is that often, when a contract is negotiated, especially a large contract, and especially one involving a foreign player, government officials may have a stake in it. Many officials openly take part in the negotiation of investments. Those officials may be among those making overstated promises, in order to demonstrate their influence and their *guanxi*. For that reason, if the contract should later emerge in a court of law, there is every likelihood that the officials involved will put the weight of a heavy thumb on the delicate scales of justice and tip it more in the favour of the Chinese parties.

To conclude this section on the vagaries of contract dispute resolution in China, as just one impediment to a level global playing field, it should be stated that the comments made here are not intended as advice to prospective investors. Aspiring investors attracted by the shining possibilities offered by China's huge marketplace (which opportunities sometimes shimmer like mirages in a dry desert) should seek out their own sources of advice. There exist specific books on making contracts in China and legal counsel should be a necessity.

Inequities in the Administration of Justice in China
Investments May be Subject to the Whims of Officials
In China, the exercise of judicial power tends to be localized. What results is a form of protectionism — of their turf and of the interests of their district. The president and the vice-president of the local court are appointed by the local party hierarchy, and moreover there is a party committee which oversights the way judges exercise their role. There is

also a flaw in this local control of the judiciary, in that judges may not be well-qualified and trained for their role.

Local and departmental protectionism are so serious that they mean that the local courts often do not exercise their judicial power independently and the result is that many judgments cannot be enforced. Because the local power organizations produce and supervise the officers of the local courts and appoint all the local judges,[225] there is a clear possibility of ineffectual justice. In addition, rights of appeal are not always clear-cut. In Australia, a right of appeal is provided for if a judge has not applied or has (mistakenly or deliberately) misapplied a law, and the appellate court will be bound to overturn the decision, but it is the culture of compliance which maintains the system. In China, the system of appeals is cumbersome and not always transparent.

The First Parkson (Qingdao) Company is wholly owned by a larger company called the Golden Lion Group, which is one of the largest enterprises in Qingdao. In 1996, Parkson contracted with Qingdao Zhengjin Group Company to process codfish. When disputes arose, First Parkson took their case to the Qingdao Arbitration Committee in December 1999. Zhengjin Group is a very large company, ranking seventh in the list of all private companies in Qingdao, and contributes a large amount of taxes to the local government, which contribution brings with it a certain influence with public officials. It was not until four years later, in December 2003, that the Committee gave a decision in favour of First Parkson and directed that Zhengjin Group should pay compensation of 5 million yuan to First Parkson, in recompense for a disputed quantity of codfish. However, Zhengjin Group made no attempt at payment, and in May 2004 Parkson went to Chengyang People's Court to enforce the arbitration, but by 2006 there had still been no action to enforce the judgment of the Arbitration Committee.[226]

This case is one example of how government officials may determine the future of a dispute concerning a foreign enterprise. In China, as indeed elsewhere in the world, politics has an influence on commercial affairs and investors have to monitor political trends.[227]

Another example of political influence in the justice system goes back to 1992, when a businessman from Hong Kong named He invested in a new factory in Shenyang, in Liaoning Province. The new investment grew and was profitable, but then there was a change in the top ranks of officialdom. The new mayor insisted that the factory had to be closed. Mr He, unhappy but persistent, then established a joint venture in Yujiang county, Jiangxi Province, where he had a good relationship with the county mayor. However, two years later, once again officeholders changed and the new mayor declined to support Mr He's venture. Once again, a facility was forced to close, without compensation for the factory owners.[228]

The nub of the problem is that foreign investors spend time, effort and funds in building up *guanxi* with local mayors and other officials, but are vulnerable if those officials do not respect the implied agreements they make, and there is no recourse to law because judges may be part of the same network.

Inconsistencies With Decrees and Policies

Another minefield for foreign investors is a consequence of the fact that local decrees are a part of the body of the Chinese law system even though they may be inconsistent with national law and regulations. The biggest problem is that the decrees can be revised by local government officials even if they result in damage to foreign investors. The following case illustrates this point.

In March 2000, the Huijin Company (an enterprise that was ultimately UK-owned) invested 270 million yuan to set up the Changchun Huijin Sewage Disposal Company in a joint venture with the similarly named Changchun Sewage Disposal Company. In order to facilitate the operation of this large joint venture, the Changchun city government promulgated a decree that set up the parameters of its operations and defined the management methods and work conditions that would be used in the venture. However, just two years later, the city government abolished the decree. This effectively resulted in uncertainty in management and work operations, and the business ground to a halt. Huijin Company suffered twice — first through their economic losses and then through losing their lawsuit in a local court which ruled against them, even though in doing so the court contradicted provincial laws. In bald terms, it seems impossible to win a case against a local city government when that case has to be prosecuted through a local court.[229]

Court Judgments Cannot Always be Enforced

In China, although a judgment may be made in favour of one party, there is no guarantee that that judgment will be enforced. Even at the highest levels — the high court of each province — barely one-half of the judgments are enforced impartially by court officials. This is one more factor that undermines foreign investors' confidence in the Chinese legal system.

In 1998, Guangdong Acefood Industrial Company entered into a conciliation process with Qingdao Dazhong Food Company, some of whose funds were already held by the court in trust. According to the terms of the conciliation resolution, Dazhong Company was required to pay around three-quarters of a million yuan to Guangdong Acefood in addition to the money already held.

By the end of 2003, Guangdong Acefood had still not received any money from Dazhong Company, and meanwhile part of the money which had been held in trust was able to be withdrawn by Dazhong. Then the manager of Dazhong Company disappeared. Guangdong Acefood not only missed out on its compensation but suffered a further loss of monies owed to it. The case could not be pursued further because Dazhong Company had no more assets.[230]

The WTO Agreement and the Chinese Legal Environment

According to commitments made when China was admitted to the WTO, the government was obligated to revise domestic laws and enact new ones so that its legal system would be fully in compliance with the WTO Agreement. This meant that the Chinese government assumed a responsibility to ensure that all China's laws, regulations and other measures, including those of local government, would conform to the obligations assumed in the agreement.[231] Amending national laws and regulations appears straightforward, but the task of repealing or revising thousands of central, provincial and municipal government notices and circulars will not be easy. China has amended more than 3,000 regulations relating to trade, but there are thousands more to go. Hence the legal environment will remain difficult for foreign investors seeking to enter China and compete on equal terms with domestic companies and individuals.

In China, local governments include provincial governments, cities, counties and townships. Local regulations, rules and other measures may be issued at local government levels acting within their constitutional powers and functions. What creates a problem for foreign investors is that those local regulations, rules and other local measures are often inconsistent with China's WTO obligations, not to mention the fact that often they are interpreted in favour of local parties and enforced corruptly.

The next section considers the associated problem of corruption. Together, the problems of an unfair legal system, codes of practice and a corrupt business environment mean that foreign parties do not have the opportunity to market their goods and services in China and thereby offset disadvantages they themselves experience when the world playing field is tilted by wage and currency distortions.

Corruption and Globalization

Associated with the problem of an inequitable application of justice in the legal environment, there is the problem of corruption in public officials. In China, corruption of governmental officials and the leaders of State-Owned Enterprises is discussed in political and academic circles and its impact upon the structures of the state at all levels is recognized.[232] Even judges have been caught up in corruption, and the presidents of the local court systems of the provinces of Hunan and Guangdong were punished for corrupt activity in 2004.

The opening up of China's economy resulted in a big increase in corrupt activity. Public officials were not highly paid, and in fact Communist ideology directed that they should be unselfish servants of the people and be paid no more than what the average managerial worker received. Hence, some officials became responsible for huge investments and organizations with big revenues and valuable properties, and they wheeled and dealed with foreign and local entrepreneurs, but the system did not reward their efforts with merit-based pay. It became a practice to supplement their income through various means. The practice of *guanxi* reinforced this situation, because the practice of building and maintaining special relationships readily aided the exchange of payments and other favours.

Corruption includes activities such as embezzling, smuggling, bribery, theft of public property and many more. The two most common corrupt activities in the 1990s and early 2000s were *nuoyong gongkuan* (purloining public property) and *tanwu shouhui* (seeking bribes or special favours for family or friends). One writer who has researched corruption in Chinese business listed four types of activities which are examples of *nuoyong gongkuan*.[233] They included: public officials establishing private companies to invest in shares and bonds and covering up the proceeds of corruption by declaring that the origins of their wealth are due to their business dealings; public officials transferring the proceeds of corrupt dealing into companies controlled by relatives or confidantes; managers of State-Owned Enterprises creating a web of transactions to funnel corrupt payments back to their own benefit; and public officials and managers of state-owned companies colluding with foreign firms to overbid for contracts to supply goods or services.

These practices amount to what has been described by more than one source as 'systemic corruption'.[234] This systemic corruption has been maintained because it is so widespread — which means that lower level officials could not be prosecuted because they could accuse higher level officials of doing much the same thing.

Systemic corruption is clearly a major impediment to business, because, leaving aside the moral and criminal aspects, it skews investment towards those who are well-connected, not those who offer the best and most efficient product. The whole economic framework can become distorted, honest businesses are discouraged and profits are creamed off by the corrupt. One analyst has estimated that between 13 and 17 per cent of China's GDP was lost to corrupt activity during the 1990s.[235] Corruption is clearly a problem of such size that corrupt payments have an impact on capital movements to and from China as illicit capital flows into black markets or out of the country into safe havens.[236] The total volume of money laundering in China is said to amount to over 200 billion yuan every year.[237] One study found that only 10–20 per cent of corrupt actions are brought to light, and of the public officials charged with corruption, only around 6 per cent receive criminal sanctions.[238]

This problem impacts upon the application of globalization principles because all classes of investors are not treated the same. The already uneven field is made even more uneven for some players because of corrupt decision-making and approvals.

The widespread corrupt practices in China in the 1980s and 1990s were seldom publicly acknowledged, but a series of illegal activities have more recently erupted into the media and into public consciousness. In 2000, wide publicity was given to a crackdown on fraud and corruption, and a senior member of the Central Committee and a provincial vice-governor were executed after being found guilty of corrupt activity. In 2001, there were rumours of a major fraud involving management of a leading power company. Then there were street protests in Beijing over an investment scam which cost thousands of people their savings. In the following year, the head of one of China's largest banks, the Bank of Construction, Wang Xuebing, was dismissed for fraud, but that fraud was publicized largely because Wang had first come under investigation by US Treasury officials while he was head of the New York branch of the Bank of China. These scandals were dwarfed by a major one involving officials turning a blind eye to smuggling in the city of Xiamen. A deputy minister in charge of public security was sentenced to death for his part in the corrupt activity. In another case, a vice-chairman of the National People's Congress, Cheng Kejie, was executed for gouging around US$6 million in kickbacks from land developers.

In 2002, President Jiang Zemin, in his final report to the national Party Congress, publicly recognized the damage that corruption was doing, not just to China's image, but to the relationship between governed and government in China.

Normally, details of corruption and fraud by top-level officials, even statistics on fraud, have been kept secret, but in recent years this attitude has been changing as senior members of the government appreciate the damage to China's image that is caused by public perceptions of corruption. As a result, there have been ongoing efforts to reduce corruption, especially since the 2008 Olympic Games were awarded to Beijing. As part of the organizing for the games, Beijing city officials have promised a 'sunshine' policy — that is, letting the light fall on previously shady activity in an effort to get clean government. The issue was important for the Beijing government because no less a figure than the Mayor of Beijing, Chen Xitong (who was also a member of the governing politburo) had been gaoled for embezzlement.

Despite these official efforts, corruption remains a widespread problem and a challenge to foreign businesses seeking to establish or expand operations in China. High-level corruption scandals continue to be revealed. In September 2006, the Shanghai party secretary, Chen Liangyu, was placed under arrest after an investigation found that he had been involved in a major scam involving pension funds.

This book does not advance the suggestion that corruption is worse in China than in all other countries, nor that corruption in all its forms is absent from Western countries, because the activities within the management of Enron and WorldCom would swiftly give the lie to such a proposition. Instead, this book proposes that corruption in China is enough of a problem to concern international investors. The issue has relevance to this discussion of the impact of Chinese-produced motor vehicles on Australia and the West because it is one that affects the competitive advantage of Chinese corporations. If WTO principles demand that Western countries open their markets to manufactured goods even at risk to their domestic manufacturing sectors, then it is part of the deal that China's markets are concomitantly free and open, and that the legal system treats all parties with — it seems superfluous to say — justice.

If there is such a degree of corruption in China's economy that foreign competitors are put at a disadvantage, then this reduces the moral and ethical imperative for Western countries to allow less restrictive imports of China's products.

16 Related Issues

Some issues have been lightly touched upon in discussion in previous pages, but deserve more detailed comment. For example, the depletion of the world's oil resources and consequent rise in the oil price have impacted upon consumer consciousness and brought about changing preferences for smaller and more fuel-efficient cars. Also, the expansion of Chinese industry, along with the accelerating expansion of Indian industry, has created so great a demand for all types of raw resources that some analysts are now asking when — not whether — the limits of resource usage will be reached.

The Constraints of Oil Production and Pricing

China has been fortunate in having its own sources of oil products to fuel its rapid growth from the 1980s. The current explored reserves of crude oil in China are around 2.5 billion tons. However, there have been no new oilfields or expanded facilities coming on stream, and since 1993 most of China's oil production facilities have maintained their production rates, so the output of crude oil in China will not grow in the next five to ten years. The country's output of crude oil will remain at the level of 160–170 million tons, but as the fields become exhausted, crude oil output in China will decrease after 2010.

Although the rate of domestic oil production in China has remained virtually static since 1993, the demand for oil and petroleum products has continued to increase exponentially, keeping pace with the country's growth rates. As a result, China has reached a stage of having to import oil to meet the shortfall between domestic supply and domestic demand, and its reliance upon imports has risen from 6.6 per cent of total consumption in 1995 to 45 per cent of total consumption in 2005. The International Energy Authority estimates that the country will be reliant upon imports to meet 61 per cent of its total oil consumption in 2010, and 76.9 per cent of its total oil consumption in 2020. There are estimates that the demand in 2010 will be around 380 million tons — double the demand of the late 1990s. Moreover, this increased demand must also result in ever-increasing world prices for crude oil in the long term, whatever may be the short-term fluctuations.

In 2007, the oil price in China is fixed by government, which means that, in the short term at least, there may not be increases in the price of fuel for the domestic consumer to force down demand. However, the price is already comparatively high, which explains the attraction of the smaller fuel-efficient vehicles noted in the previous chapters. The Chinese car industry is generally geared up to meet the needs of consumers who demand smaller cars, which means that it is also in an advantageous position if the world's car consumers continue to turn to smaller cars in response to the long-term prospects of an increasing oil price.

The situation in regard to the world demand for oil will not change for the better. In the past, the car industry in the West was 'rescued' from high oil prices when supply was increased and the price of crude oil fell in the 1990s. The car industry could continue to build and sell gas-guzzlers for ten years more. The price of crude oil cannot fall again, because of China's increasing thirst (and the growing thirst of India). In the 1990s, China was not yet a major player, and supplied the bulk of its oil needs from domestic sources. In 2006, the country was at a turning point in relation to labour supply and demand, and in relation to the development of its car industry. It will encounter another turning point in 2008 when the bulk of its oil, not just a percentage, must be sourced from overseas. At such a time, not only will China be an elephant (or dragon) in the room as far as international oil markets are concerned, but it will be an elephant growing to more than mammoth size.

The Long-Term Capacity of the World Car Industry and Resource Limits

The situation with supply and demand for oil is a strong reminder that the current practices of the motor vehicle industry in regard to resources, both in production and operation, are not sustainable. There are simply not enough resources in the world to permit the growth of car-ownership and use in many countries around the world. Certainly there is not enough oil to permit many other economies to reach levels of oil consumption comparable to those of the United States in 2007.

Some analysts have clearly stated that the world could not survive every Chinese person owning a car. Lester Brown, president of the Earth Policy Institute, presented estimates of future Chinese consumption. In *Plan B 2.0* Brown stated that if China's economy continued to grow at the rate of 8 per cent a year, by 2031 the per capita income of its 1.45 billion people would equal that of the United States in 2004. According to a report in the *Washington Post*: 'This means that if the Chinese match America's rate of three cars for every four people, they will have 1.1 billion vehicles, nearly 40 per cent more than the world's current fleet. And if China consumes oil at the same per capita rate as the United States, it will use 99 million barrels of oil a day by 2031, well over total current world oil production. In other words, if the Chinese consume at current US rates, there won't be enough of anything left for the rest of the world.'[239]

Brown's basic point was that China's overwhelming demand for commodities would fracture current models for economic growth. As he put it, 'The Western economic model — the fossil-fuel-based, automobile-centred, throwaway economy — will not work for China's 1.45 billion people in 2031.'[240]

It may be that, given human ingenuity, future cars may be made of plastic or nylon and powered by hydrogen. If that comes to pass, then there may still be a future for private personalized transport.

Safety and Regulatory Issues

There is an issue with Chinese-designed cars (as opposed to foreign designs licence-built in China) being able to meet engineering and safety standards in foreign jurisdictions. The engineering requirements in one export market — say, the United States — may differ from other markets in Europe, and this causes problems for producers. However, the problems in obtaining the relevant compliances would not be insuperable ones, and would be resolved by changes on the manufacturing line.

In the unlikely event of any authority seeking to use safety and engineering requirements unreasonably to restrict access to a market, then that would be a breach of the principles of the WTO and the aggrieved party would have grounds to lodge a complaint with the organization.

There is an equally strong motive to ensure that national regulatory bodies do not overstep their authority on this issue. If China's cars should be restricted unduly in entering the markets of another country, then the Chinese government may very well reciprocate. So, for example, if a French bureaucratic organ created unrealistic obstacles to the entry of Chinese-designed cars into the French market, it is not outside the bounds of probability that the Chinese bureaucracy would create equal problems for Renault or Peugeot in China.

That scenario only applies when regulations are used in an inequitable manner. Global corporations and national regulators generally know all the accepted rules, and are prepared to play by those rules by, for example, recognizing that there may be different standards for such issues as emission controls in different regions. As a general rule, auto designers would seek to meet the highest levels of standards so that their designs are acceptable in those jurisdictions and also in jurisdictions that may have settled for lower standards.

The matter of different national regulations and standards is an issue for exporters, but changing the product to meet those standards may only be a matter of a few months' work for a minor re-design.

The Issue of Intellectual Property Rights

One problem which continues to impede the development of the Chinese domestic auto industry, and the provision of advanced technology to joint-venture enterprises, is the security of intellectual property. Foreign companies will be reluctant to commit heavy investment in an environment where their processes and designs can be copied and there is ineffective sanction. As an example, in 2003 GM went public with its dispute with Chery Automobile Company over a breach of intellectual property concerning the design of a GM car. The American car maker complained that the Chinese company had copied GM's Daewoo Matiz. Chery denied the accusation, but the fact remained that its QQ hatchback had a strong resemblance to the GM design, and, to rub salt into the wound, the QQ outsold the Matiz.[241] In December 2005, GM said it would take Chery to a Chinese court in a case expected to draw worldwide attention. However, it is problematical how much protection GM will receive. It may be that the wide attention that will be focused on the case will ensure that the Chinese courts feel under scrutiny and pressure. GM has already been unsuccessful in getting official action to be taken against its local rival: 'GM complained to government officials in Beijing [about Chery's QQ copying a GM design], but authorities took no action against Chery.'[242] GM has since withdrawn their suit from Chinese courts.

The question of copying designs is not new. It applied also to the development of the early models of Japan's car industry when it was in its establishment phase. The Nissan type 70 of 1937 was copied from an American design. The Datson Roadster of 1931 was a copied Austin 7. Mitsubishi's Model A of 1917 was a Fiat Zero. The first Toyota models were based upon American designs until the production of the Toyota BA of 1940, which was very similar to the Volvo PV60. China's car industry, following a broadly similar path to that of Japan's also utilized foreign design expertise through means such as licences and joint ventures.

In the 1930s and 1950s, perhaps there was not the same emphasis upon protection of intellectual property because the prevailing technology was not so complex. In the early 21st century, car designs and manufacturing technology have become more complex and technical and the investment in intellectual property is correspondingly higher. The gambler playing for pennies rightly resents a peek into his hand, but when the gambler has a wad of cash on the table, he naturally fights harder to protect his stake.

There are intellectual property rights violations all over the world, of course, but by far the greatest number of such breaches occur in China — perhaps 70 per cent of pirated goods such as manufactured items and CDs, etc., originate in China. It seems that many manufacturers in China, including some in the car industry, are pushing to the limits and beyond what is permissible in regard to using the intellectual property of others. It is a major problem. Some US sources claim that breaches of intellectual copyright and brand piracy cost American businesses US$250 billion each year.

Not only US car makers suffer through breaches of intellectual property rights. Fiat of Italy is also assessing whether a new car from Great Wall Motors called the Peri is a clone of the Fiat Panda (which is ironic, given that the name Panda is quintessentially Chinese).

The issue is a serious one, for it results in a major distortion of the level playing field if some players are spared the research, design and development costs of a product because they simply steal the ideas of other players. A free and fair market needs exchange of information, but not commercially developed proprietary information. In an age where products are increasingly complex, the costs and benefits of technology are continually growing, and designs can be more valuable than manufactured goods.

The Chinese government is taking action over the issue, and has prepared a two-year plan to get on top of the pirates and thieves. There have been well-publicized busts of illegally copied products, especially in the south of the country, but it remains to be seen how much the government cracks down on the big corporations rather than the backyard operators. The issue will certainly have an impact upon the development of new car models by the wholly Chinese-owned manufacturers.

The Names of Chinese Cars

This is a comparatively minor issue, but cultural preferences of consumers are often reflected in the names of motor vehicles. Car makers wanted to convey a sense of power and purpose in the names they chose for their organizations, such as Jaguar and Rover. In the US, manufacturers seemed more often to elect to bear the names of their founders, as in Ford and Chrysler, or else have an over-arching name like General Motors. In the 1950s, cars with names like Thunderbird or Cougar appealed to a spirit of confidence and triumph. In the 1970s, a name like Commodore implied authority and self-assuredness, not to mention wealth and status. In the 2000s, there were names which, for some reason, appealed to us and implied elegance, for example, Kluger and Madison.

The Japanese auto manufacturers are generally named after their founders, and for all concerned it was useful that these names, like Honda and Toyota, sounded snappy as well as being euphonic. Names sound crisp and business-like. In contrast, the name of a major Chinese car maker — Dong Feng — does not rattle off the Western tongue in the same way, even though the name, East Wind, is attractive to the Chinese.

The Chinese obviously have different social constructs from peoples in the West, and those differences were borne out in the names they chose for bicycles manufactured from the 1950s, such as the Purple Flower or the Noble Bamboo. Such names receive, and almost invite, derision in the West. But such considerations are irrelevant for the Chinese, who have every right to call their products whatever name appeals to them. However, the naming of Asian-made cars intended to be sold in Western markets will create a momentary problem. The Cedric (by Nissan) is common on Chinese roads, but the name of the car still draws wry smiles in Australia from when it was first introduced in the '60s — as does its contemporary, the Gloria. Similarly, Mazda's Bongo van did not inspire respect. The name of one of China's biggest car makers — FAW — may also need a marketing makeover, as will Chery and Geely. Once the vehicles are re-named, however, and those names enter the common consciousness of the Western consumer, then the market will more readily accept them. Then Chinese cars will have truly arrived.

17 Conclusion

Future Development Patterns

The earlier chapters looked at aspects of the patterns of development of national automotive industries as they had been spread out in swirling patterns on the sandboard of history. We can revisit the topic of patterns of development, and draw out conclusions for what the car making industries of the future may look like.

Development of the Chinese car industry is around 30 years behind the pattern of development of the Japanese industry, mainly because China's period of isolation from world trade was longer than Japan's. The pivotal event in Japan's recent economic history was the surrender in 1945, after which its manufacturing industries were opened to the technology and expertise of the West and could enter world trading markets. China's recent history included two pivotal events — the Communist takeover in 1949 that closed the country, and the death of Mao Zedong in 1976 that led to it being opened again to the world and to world trade. The approximately 30 years separating 1945 from 1976 represent the distance between the stages of development of the car industries of the Asian neighbours.

Japan received an influx of expertise and technology in the 1950s and by the late 1970s had become a large-scale exporter. China received its influx of expertise and technology in the 1980s, so, assuming a similar pattern of development, China should achieve a status as a major force on world export markets by the end of the current decade. It looks as if it will certainly do that.

Let us return to the question of how many cars China will have the capacity and the inclination to export by 2010. In the introductory chapter, it was suggested that the gap between domestic production and domestic demand could be around 4 million cars out of a total Chinese production of 12 million. These estimates were based on the use of econometrics. Existing trends to 2005/06 were extrapolated for a further five-year period.

Now approach the question differently, by running an eye over the patterns of industrial development. The national automotive industries of Japan and Brazil and Korea, to mention just a few, have all seen their path to prosperity running through increasing levels of exports. Virtually every country recognized that for their automotive sector to develop to its full potential, with all the concomitant national benefits, it was necessary to refocus the industry and aim for increased exports. For example, in the 1970s, Brazil aimed at achieving a level of exports no less than 40 per cent of its national production, and although there were missed targets and shortfalls, it did achieve this level of exports by 2005. South Korea's car industry has aimed even higher, seeking to export a majority of its national production. There is nothing new in this philosophy of export-driven growth, for Ford and GM pursued such policies aggressively as far back as the 1920s, when they spread to many countries of the world. Japan began its major export drive from 1968, and by the late 1970s had achieved its goal of exporting around half its total production.

Brazil, Korea and Japan increased their levels of exports while at the same time enjoying what were effectively high levels of protection. But while they reached export goals of 40 per cent or more of national production (a similar level to the UK's export proportion of 1960), there is one difference between those industries in the recent past and the Chinese industry now. China has committed to WTO principles and in this different trading environment should not try to exercise the same degree of protection that Brazil, Korea and Japan enjoyed. However, as has been argued, legal and cultural issues can amount to de facto protection, and limited currency exchange adds to effective protection levels. There has also been debate about the application of some WTO agreed tariffs. For example, is a package containing the parts of a car equal to a whole car and thus subject to whole-car tariffs? The Chinese have asserted it is and exercised tariffs applicable to whole cars, whereas the importers (with the backing of their own national authorities) dispute this. In reality, the Chinese car industry does still enjoy effective protection and the benefits of an uneven playing field.

It seems entirely logical to assert that the strategists of the Chinese car industry should follow the example of other countries and also seek to export around 40 per cent of national production, or, given the Chinese emphasis upon raising prosperity by exports, an even higher percentage. In 2010, given that existing trends of increasing production continue and the Chinese auto makers turn out 12 million vehicles in that year, and given that they may aim at a level of exports of around 40 per cent of total production, then the target for exports would be as high as 12,000,000 x 40 per cent, or 4.8 million vehicles. Even if just (!) 4 million vehicles are exported, this is 33 per cent of total production, and a quite reasonable figure.

By addressing the question of how many Chinese autos are likely to hit the market from this different viewpoint, by a comparative study of the pattern of development of other national industries, the figure is about the same as that of the analysts discussed earlier in this book.

We may extend the statistics for a timeline even further than the analysts dared, past 2010 to 2015 or 2020. In 2015, if Chinese production has doubled again, they will be producing over 20 million cars a year — and if half are for export, that is a surge of 10 million cars on the markets every year. Ten million cars means a greater number of exports alone than the total US production of 2015 (given US production continues to decline, or even stabilizes at around 2007 levels). By 2020, China could be producing 40 million cars a year, and by then would be the dominant world producer, threatened only by Japan/Korea and India. Brazil, Russia and eastern European combined would be not far away. Car making in the West would long since have been pushed to the sidelines, crippled by high costs and the pensions for their employees of the 1980s. Some analysts predict a world motor vehicle market of 110 million vehicles a year in 20 years.[243] By that year, on existing trends,

China could be producing a major proportion of them. The number of cars able to be produced seems to be limited only by resources, although the number of cars able to be absorbed by consumer markets and used seems limited by pollution and infrastructure issues like those addressed in the research projects described in this book.

The year 2020 is not that far into the future. Any babies born in 2007 will then be entering their teenage years, and in the manner of teenagers everywhere, they will be thinking about their first car, even asking a parent for the money to buy their own metal steed in just another year or two. It seems likely that the car that they will want to buy will be a Chinese-made vehicle.

In some households, the words may be heard, 'C'mon, Dad, will you help me buy a Geely? The one with the big 1.5 litre engine? It can fit in the basement next to our Chery.'

Will the Chinese-made car of 2020 be technologically advanced? The current situation regarding the global manufacturing industry is following established patterns of development. One aspect of those patterns of auto industry growth is that vehicle manufacturing always goes from low-tech to high-tech. In the history of industrialization, manufacturing sectors have typically started with low-tech, commodity-type products, then advanced to more sophisticated goods over time, as the skills of their workforce and their designers grew.

In the case of the Japanese motorcycle manufacturers in the 1960s, they started with small and basic designs, developed from machines that were mopeds. Those designs developed in complexity into modern high-tech machines.

The major car companies that opened joint ventures in China started with basic cars, but had to quickly move to produce current models with the latest features. Take the example of Ford's large facility in Chongqing, a joint venture with the Chongqing Chang'an Automobile Company. Ford built the new manufacturing assembly line in 2001 on the model of one of its factories in the Philippines and planned to produce 20,000 cars a year based on a small, basic design also produced in India. Barely three years later, in response to the growing sophistication of the demand (confirmed by the research reported on in this book) Ford opened a second line, but this one incorporated the most advanced technology and was identical to a Ford factory operating in western Germany. The second line produced the Ford Focus, and when it reached peak operating capacity in June 2006, Ford was on track to meet its target production level of 200,000 vehicles per year.[244]

Volkswagen learnt the same lesson. It could not win a large part of the Chinese car market by simply setting up its obsolescent assembly lines in China and producing older models no longer saleable in the West. Honda marketed its current version of the Civic in China shortly after the same model entered the market in the West. Toyota produces the latest model of the Prius in China.

Chinese car makers will certainly advance down the same track, especially since the Chinese consumer so clearly demands motor vehicles that are the equivalent of those available in the West. Any suggestion that the Chinese will not be able to meet the sophisticated standards of Western consumers carries with it an assumption of inherent inferiority in Chinese abilities and capacities. This would be a foolish and short-sighted suggestion. The first Chinese-made car for sale in the United States may have been the tiny electric-powered ZX40, but it was only the harbinger of what was to come. The Chinese will certainly aim for the highest standards. The Chinese vice-director of manufacturing at the Ford factory in Chongqing, Li Jianping, was quoted as saying, 'I want to learn from Germany and then improve on it.'[245]

The pattern of development of the Chinese industry in the 2010s will probably parallel that of the Japanese in the 1980s and '90s. Besides a huge increase in production quantity, the quality and innovation of design will also improve, notwithstanding the flaws in the Chinese management system described in an earlier chapter.

In the 2000s, the parallels between patterns of development are clear to read. But while the Japanese car assault of the 1970s was repulsed by strong Western manufacturers, will the industry in the West in the 2000s able to repulse a new assault by a different growing Asian giant? Thirty years ago the Western auto industry was strong. In fact, it was hitting its peak in the United States. The Oil Shock of 1973 shook the industry, but it recovered.

It is, however, one more of many ironies that in the strength of the US and European industries of the 1960s and 1970s was sown the bacillus that would sicken and weaken them by the 2000s. When the US industry were world beaters, they negotiated the generous health and retirement benefits that would come to cripple them when their workforce had aged and come to the point of drawing on those benefits.

It is said that one of the differences between business leaders in the East and business leaders in the West is that Easterners consider that the 'long-term' is 20 or 30 years, whereas Westerners consider that the 'long-term' means three years or five years. These are all massive generalizations, of course, but underneath them is perhaps a kernel of wisdom: Asians tend to look further down the track than Europeans. In the case of the US industry pension benefits, those who framed those policies were not taking full account of the inevitable consequences which, to them at least, were far in the future.

Revisiting the Example of the Motorcycle Industry

The extended case study of the motorcycle industry will not be repeated here, but three factors from the study can be recapped, because they provide fuel for thought. The parallels between the motorcycle industry in the West during the 1960s and 1970s and the car industry in the West in the 2000s are extremely strong.

The first factor was that the West's motorcycle manufacturers badly underestimated the threat they were faced with. This was understandable to a point, because Japan was a distant country, and in the 1960s not well known other than as an adversary in the late war. The management of many old and well-respected firms in the UK and US were not only ignorant of Japan, but when the possibility of Japanese motorcycles being imported into their home markets was mooted they were smug and contemptuous, dismissing the possibility with a metaphorical wave of the hand.

The second factor concerned the image of the first Japanese motorcycles to come onto the market. They were said to be cheap and plastic, and scorned by manufacturers, commentators and so-called industry experts. This judgment was culpable, because it was based upon prejudice rather than detailed evaluation of the new products and thorough market research. It was proved that the Japanese knew their markets far better than those who had worked in those markets for years, doing little more than seeing things as they wanted to see them.

The fact that Honda and Yamaha and Suzuki and Kawasaki became so well-established was, in the end, not because they were cheap and nasty, but because they were reliable and sometimes cheaper than their rivals. The key to the Japanese success was the quality of their management, which led to their quality of product. The Western manufacturers seemed congenitally unable to accept that their products were becoming second-class. The problem was not that the Japanese bikes were 'cheap and nasty', but that some Western bikes were 'expensive and nasty'.

The third factor was that the Japanese were not satisfied with carving out a small part of the market for themselves, perhaps in the segment of low-capacity commuter bikes. This was their strength in Japan, and it could have been assumed that that was where they would concentrate their forces, leaving the medium and large size bikes to the Westerners who would maintain their prestige and their profits.

But the Japanese had a hunger, and that hunger was not just for profit and sales but to prove they were a force. It is sometimes tempting to wonder about the motivation of the likes of Honda and Takegawa — whether they were motivated by a desire to reinstate their nation's image as an important player upon the world stage, and influential in world affairs. Whatever their underlying motivation, the fact was that once in the marketplace they were astute enough to aim for dominance, and talented enough to achieve it.

The Weaknesses of Parts of the Car Industry in 2007

The car industry in the West easily repulsed the challenge of Japanese car makers in the 1960s and 1970s, but it seems that they will not as easily repulse the challenge of Chinese car makers. There is a big difference between the Japanese car makers of the 1960s and 1970s and the Chinese of the 2000s. Thirty years ago, the Japanese industry was developing mainly through its own resources — pulling itself up by its own bootstraps.

In the 2000s, the Chinese have an advantage because through the numerous joint ventures that have been established by auto makers from all over the world, they have been introduced to the best practices and technology of the West. Anyone who assumes the Chinese will not learn, and not learn quickly, from the examples in front of them is foolish, and maybe as prejudiced as some of the motorcycle manufacturers of the 1960s.

It is likely that few joint ventures will export products from their facilities in China that will decimate their own home markets, but it is certain that the flow of car components will rapidly increase. The threat of whole cars fully assembled in China and exported to the West comes from the developing wholly Chinese-owned companies that are taking strides to obtain the very latest in technology. They are able to obtain such technology not only through the joint ventures in China, but also through the acquisition of loss-making corporations in Europe.

The worldwide weakness of the car industry is giving these corporations an advantage. When Chinese companies are able to buy up Western operations, as Nanjing Auto was able to buy Rover-MG in the UK, then they expand their skill base and have access to plant and equipment. Admittedly some of that plant and equipment may not be top-drawer, but nevertheless it can be usefully operated, and improved upon, in China.

In the joint ventures, the foreign partners have generally learnt that it was the wrong strategy to set up obsolescent assembly lines in China, and in those operations they have adjusted the strategy and have installed state of the art equipment. In conjunction with the market advantages that the Chinese enjoy through their low wages and undervalued currency, the advantage of current technology adds to their potential ability to dominate the marketplace.

The 'unseen hand' that Smith postulated should act to correct market anomalies, and the theory may work in perfect markets. But global markets are not perfect. Classical economics may work well in theory, but in practice the participants in the marketplace have to get down and dirty and do not always play fair.

Where are the 'hungry managers' in the world's car manufacturers?

The answer to this question cannot be better summarized than through the following quote:

> Established in 1997 in Anhui Province's Wuhu Economy and Technology Development Zone, Chery has boosted its share of China's market to 4 per cent, from 0.3 per cent in 2000. It now sells four cars — the Fengyun, Qiyun and Son of East sedans, and the QQ. Next year, it plans to launch a sport utility vehicle, a new sedan and a crossover. Michael Dunne, president of consulting firm Automotive Resources Asia Ltd, classifies Chery as one of China's 'young tigers,' or hungry new auto makers.[246]

Some wave away the threat posed to the market by Chinese-manufactured cars, even though they have the examples of Chinese dominance in other areas of manufacturing, such as textiles, and household commodities. The same people, and others, dismiss the quality of Chinese-made cars without giving much consideration to the possibility that the Chinese can learn to make better cars.

This research has noted the constraints upon quality, notably in the areas of efficient company governance and performance assessment and motivation of employees. However, these factors can be addressed, and the Chinese will find their own way to achieve the efficiency of operations that enables quality production. In relation to the question about whether the Chinese will seek to be dominant in the world car market, the answer is that they are business people born and bred, and market skills are in their bones and marrow. Napoleon once airily dismissed the British as being a 'nation of shopkeepers' — and sometimes it seems that that appellation could be used of the Chinese too. Napoleon also spoke of the Chinese nation as a slumbering dragon that was best left undisturbed, because when it awoke, it would rock the world.

Playing with Numbers Again

In earlier chapters, we have looked at statistics, including the beguiling statistics of China's potential marketplace. In this final chapter, we could refocus our gaze on statistics in Australia. What are some numbers that relate to the flood of Chinese cars, and what effect will they have?

Australians purchase around 950,000 new cars each year (although the bulk of them are bought by business or government — family people do not often buy family cars, partly because they do not get the benefit of tax deductions). We could assume that in the first years of the coming tsunami of Chinese cars, there could be 200,000 vehicles — Chinese designed and manufactured by wholly Chinese-owned corporations. For simplicity of analysis, we will leave out of the number-playing the matter of cheap car components and imports either wholly or partly manufactured by the joint-venture operations in China. Those 200,000 Chinese cars could be composed of $6,000 small cars, $10,000–$12,000 Toyota Camry equivalents, and $18,000–$20,000 Falcon and Commodore equivalents (probably looking a lot like Buicks).

The 'cake' of the new car market will expand, because these cheap prices will tempt many buyers who would otherwise settle for a second-hand car. We might assume an expanded cake of, say, one million cars (discounting existing trends of steadily increasing new car sales anyway). The Chinese imports will probably not affect the top end of the market, the luxury and prestige cars, or the well-equipped SUVs. They will, however, have an impact upon the lower ends of the market. Those 200,000 cars will probably take a market share of 20 per cent — 25 per cent of the bottom ranges. So the cake may expand, but the share of that expanded local cake held by Australian car makers will be less overall.

It may be argued that it need not be the death knell for the local industry just because they lose around 20 per cent of their market share. This is a fair argument, but the impact of the Chinese imports will not be most severe in the area of market share. The impact of Chinese imports will have its greatest impact upon the pricing of new motor vehicles. The car yards of many Australian cities are clustered on major highways, rows of cars with bonnets up for all the world like cormorants upon branches with their wings outstretched. Toyota and Ford and Holden yards are open to inspection by the passing crowd one after another. Imagine if, within that row of car dealers touting for business, there is a Geely dealer offering cars that are a fraction of the price of those offered by the dealers on either side. The price of each car on the lot, in figures 300 mm high, is what turns the heads of the passers-by. That is price pressure.

It is price pressure, rather than the volume of cars sold, that will kill domestic car manufacturers. If local manufacturers are struggling in comparative good times, they will not be able to survive the impact of slashing their new car prices by 15, 20 or 25 per cent to compete with the new kids on the block.

This is the reason that this book argues, not for quotas, but for a WET charge or similar that will act to offset the unfair advantage that Chinese manufacturers enjoy as lower-cost producers protected by an undervalued currency (not to mention effective social and cultural barriers that protect their indigenous industry).

Consequences of the Death of Local Car Manufacturing

Some writers refuse to write about hypothetical situations. After all, who has a crystal ball to foresee the future? Futurology is an inexact science compared, say, to the science of examining and analysing trends which underpins econometrics. When we take the statistics of China's developing car industry, and apply reasonable assumptions of supply and demand, we can come to a series of valid conclusions about the likelihood of a number of cars hitting the world market. However, when we wish to consider the consequences of that flood of cars, then the discussion inevitably has some inexactitude. Despite the risk of such inexactitude — a certain 'squashiness' of conclusions, one might say — in order to scout some issues, and to provoke thought about the implications of the end of Australian car manufacturing, the following points could be made:

1. The Economic Impact

The economic impact of the end of Australian car manufacturing would probably be minimal country-wide, and there could even be a net benefit through the availability of cheaper cars offsetting the loss of employment.

There would be a loss of jobs, but the net job loss may be small, considering that Australian auto plants have been reducing headcount on the factory floor for some time. Some jobs would remain in a few local assembly plants, and there would probably still be a network of small suppliers of components such as windscreens. In some regions, for example South Australia, there would be a notable economic impact if plants closed, with a multiplier effect throughout local communities, but even this impact would be reduced over time.

The Australian manufacturing industry has been in decline for a long time, but alternative job opportunities have arisen for the population as a whole. It will certainly be the case that some individuals will suffer economically, especially those who are not able to transfer to other regions of low employment, due to age or social ties or lack of training. Despite the decline of manufacturing, job growth overall has continued to rise over past decades.

The critics of automobile tariffs, such as those noted in chapter 2, would insist that jobs growth would continue, despite the demise of car manufacturing, and the economy overall would be more efficient as the services sector expanded.

2. The Social Impact

Although the economic loss might be minor, the social costs could be high. Among those costs would be a loss of national esteem that our nation's manufacturing enterprises, built up over generations, should be lost in just a decade, to an industry in a distant nation who until recently we considered a developing country. The sense of loss would be strong and obvious every day for people would notice the scarcity of two Australian icons — the Holden and the Falcon — on Australian streets. On occasions of iconic sporting events such as the Bathurst 1000, the absence of these two cars (except for vintage events) would be particularly galling. Would there be a sense that Australians had been cheated somehow and then a backlash against Asian interests? Quite likely. Moreover, this backlash would not be felt in high-income areas of cities where consumers purchase BMWs or Alpha-Romeos, but it would be felt in outer suburbs, regional cities and small towns where the Falcon or Holden were more common. There would be resentment that our way of life had been apparently downgraded because other countries did not play fairly on the world trade playing field. In other words, they cheated and we lost our car industry.

In earlier discussion of the growth of Australia's car industry, there were references to the feel-good factor that contributed to local support for home-grown cars. This feel-good factor should not be dismissed, for it has taken hold in the national psyche. There is a similar place for the car in the American psyche. The car reflects its driver's personality and view of life. It is partly for this reason that US-designed cars tend to be large and expansive. The personality factor is also evidenced in the choice of large four-wheel-drive vehicles by those who live in inner suburbs and have no practical use for a Land Cruiser or a Nissan Patrol or something similar. A hulking SUV — sometimes called the 'Toorak Tractor' (or, in the UK, the 'Chelsea Tractor') — conveys a sense of strength and power. People often, perhaps most often, choose their personal vehicle with their heart rather than their brain.

If a reader should disagree on the impact of the feel-good factor, and its diminution or loss in the event of a flood of Chinese cars swamping Australia's industry, then simply ask a city friend who owns a four-wheel drive whether they would happily select a new car from a range of three-wheeled models (which would be much more economical and manoeuvrable in the inner city). Would they agree or would they splutter, 'No way!'?

A second area of social loss may be in the restricted choice of types of cars Australian consumers have to choose from. Most of the cars on offer for the ordinary consumer who wants a family car would be of similar shape and design to one of the half-dozen or so of those designed by the big Chinese producers and a few others. There would not be a choice of cars specifically designed for Australian conditions anymore. Instead, the cars would be globally designed and manufactured. The vehicles on offer would mostly be smaller cars, and being designed by overseas designers, in a radically different culture, may not appeal to an Australian sense of taste. There would be fewer V8s and large-engined cars, because these are not popular in Asian markets, where the fuel-sipper is more valued than the fuel-guzzler. A statistic of how fast the car accelerated from 0 to 100 kph would not be of great moment to most global car consumers.

Australians would also be unlikely to choose a replacement for the Great Aussie Ute. There will be SUVs, four-wheel drives like the Ford

Explorer, for these sell well in Asia. But Asians do not usually select a ute for their usual private transportation. Utes and small trucks will be designed for commercial use, where utilitarian values far outweigh overtly masculine expressions. Globally designed utes are unlikely to have chromed features.

3. The Environmental Impact

The imported cars on offer would probably be more environmentally friendly than larger models. Fewer resources would be used in their manufacture, and there might be greater utilization of alternative materials. The superior fuel economy of a Geely compared to a Falcon would mean less harm to the environment because there would be a lower input (of fuel) and lower output (of emissions).

4. Impact on Defence Preparedness

The local car manufacturing industry has, in the past, been an essential part of a nation's defence effort. Local manufacturers can turn their assembly lines and the skills of their workers to the building of arms and munitions. This aspect of local manufacturing is not as significant in the 21st century as it was in the mid-20th, because modern arms are so complex and sophisticated that they are now far divorced from the car assembly line. There are parallels in technology, and there is Australian defence equipment (such as the Bushmaster fighting vehicles) that is derived from automotive manufacturers, but generally a country's defence effort is no longer closely tied to the strength of its domestic auto industry.

The Final Word

After this brief discussion of the consequences of the flood of cheap cars, the final conclusion of this book can be stated briefly. The country can make a choice between two options. The choice may not have a serious economic impact, and does not have a moral dimension, but it does have a serious and far-reaching impact upon Australian life and the Australian psyche.

Our impact in the world is limited. If all the world was considered to

335

be just a single nation, Australia would be like a small, somewhat-isolated outback town. In the town there would be a factory or two, turning out products that the town's residents prefer. However, as communications improve, there are more and more products coming into the town from the big cities. If no action is taken, the town's small factories will have to close and the workers find other work, if they can. The town's residents are proud of their small community and their lifestyle. However, their lifestyle cannot continue unchanged. The residents have just two real options. Either they accept the flow of products from the big cities which change their lifestyle or they act to protect their locals' interests.

The options for Australia can be summed up as follows:
Australia, through its government, has an option of changing policies and putting various protective measures in place to offset the disadvantages of an uneven field. These measures would be dismantled as that field is returned to a more level state if China, and also India, allowed their currencies to float absolutely freely and allowed wages and benefits of the labourforces to rise to meet Western standards.

Or Australia, again through its government, has an option of keeping to the plan to reduce tariffs on automotive imports to 5 per cent by 2010. The consequence must be that the industry — struggling to keep its head above waters in the good times — will be swamped when a flood of Chinese cars hits world markets at that time. Under this option, there could be no more Australian-designed cars manufactured in quantity for Australian tastes and conditions.

So the choice is a simple one:

Either Option #1 — Review policies and maintain protective measures, and so maintain some domestic car manufacturing capacity.

Or Option #2 — Maintain current policies and move towards the death of the car manufacturing industry.

The choice has to be confronted, because an economic tsunami is coming and cannot be ignored.

Appendix 1
Chinese Population and Income Statistics

Population Statistics
Total population 1,307,989,000 (2004)
Gross national annual income per capita (2004) US$1,290
Population under 18 (2004) 358,887,000 (27 per cent)
Population growth rate (1990–2004) 0.9 per cent
Growth in GDP per capita (1990–2004) 8.4 per cent
Urban population (2000) 36 per cent
Average household size (2006) 2.95 people

Financial Statistics
Exchange rates as at 24 August 2006:
7.97 yuan = 1 US dollar
6.08 yuan = 1 AUS dollar
Monthly total income per capita (yuan) (National) (2006) = 998 yuan
Annual total in yuan   11,976 yuan
Annual total in US dollars   US$1,502
Annual total in AUS dollars   A$1,969
Monthly income per capita in Shandong province (2006) = 1,041 yuan
Annual total in yuan   12,492 Y
Annual total in US dollars   US$1,567
Annual total in AUS dollars   A$1,837
By comparison, the monthly income per capita in Qinghai province, the poorest province of China (2006) = 730 yuan

Annual total in yuan   8,796 yuan
Annual total in US dollars   US$1,103
Annual total in AUS dollars   A$1,446
Disposable Income per capita in Shandong (2006)
= 954 yuan (92 per cent of total income)
Annual total in yuan   11,448 yuan
Annual total in US dollars   US$1,436
Annual total in AUS dollars   A$1,882
Income disparity
20 per cent of low-income group in China's cities receive 2.7 per cent of total income

Sources: UNICEF; Chinese National Statistics Bureau; Chinese Embassy Release, 'China's Urban Income Gap Widens to Alarming Level', 2 June 2006.

Appendix 2
Features of the reformed Chinese Labour Laws

- Employees to have the right to choose their employment.
- Employees have the right to be paid for their work, and to have rest and protection in the workplace.
- Employees to have the right to holidays from work.
- Employees to have the right to receive training at their place of work.
- Minimum wage levels to be determined by local government authority.
- Employer and employee to set out written contracts specifying pay and conditions and contract termination provisions.
- An eight-hour working day.
- A 44-hour working week (on average) with at least one day off a week.
- Women to have equal working rights with men.
- No discrimination on the basis of race, nationality, sex or religion.
- No employment of children under 16.

Bibliography

Auffhammer, M., 'China's Market For Cars', *International Area Studies Program*, Department of Agricultural and Resource Economics, University of California — Berkeley, 2006.

Australian Bureau of Statistics, *2005 Yearbook*, Reference 1301.0, Canberra, 2004.

Automobile Distribution Channels 2005, http://esoftbank.com.cn [accessed 30 May 2006].

Bak, M., and Jackson, T., 'Foreign Companies and Chinese Workers: Employee Motivation in the People's Republic of China', *Journal of Organizational Change Management*, Vol. 11, No. 4, 1998.

Banham, R., *The Ford Century: Ford Motor Company and the Innovations That Shaped the World*, Artisan, New York, 2002.

Barnett, A., and Clough, R. (eds), *Modernizing China: Post Mao Reform and Development*, Westview Press, Colorado, 1986.

Batchelor, R., *Henry Ford, Mass Production, Modernism, and Design*, Manchester University Press, Manchester, 1994.

Beatty, M., *Studebaker: Less Than They Promised*, And Books, South Bend, 1984.

Becker, J., *The Hungry Ghosts: Mao's Secret Famine*, Free Press, London, 1996.

Bjoerkman, I., and Lu, Y., 'Human Resource Management Practices in Foreign Invested Enterprises in China: What Has Been Learned?', in Stewart, S., and Carver, A., (eds), *Advances in Chinese Industrial Studies*, JAI Press, Connecticut, 1997.

Brinkley, D., *Wheels for the World: Henry Ford, his Company, and a Century of Progress, 1903–2003*, Viking, New York, 2003.

Brown, L., *The Future of the Automobile in an Oil-Short World*, Worldwatch

Institute, Washington, 1979.

Cao, Z., *Annual Report on China's Economy in 2002*, Lanzhou University Press, Lanzhou, 2003.

Chaney, L.H., and Martin, J.S., *Intercultural Business Communication*, Prentice-Hall, New York, 2002.

Chang, H., *The New Features of Foreign Investment in China*, Law Press, Beijing, 2005.

Cheliang, C., *What's the Problem: BMW in Crisis*, http://auto.china.com [accessed 23 January 2005].

Chen, Q., and Jin, Z., 'Cong Juren Jituan Weiji Tan Duoyuanhua Jingying', *Zhongwai Guanli*, Vol. 7, No. 9, 1997.

Chen, X.P., 'Zhongguo Qiye Mianlin de Liu Da Wenti' [The Six Big Problems That Chinese Enterprises are Facing], *Management*, Vol. 28, No. 3, 2001.

Chen, X.P., and Farh, J.L., 'Transformational and Transactional Leader Behaviors in Chinese Organizations: Differential Effects in the People's Republic of China and Taiwan', in Mobley, W.H., and McCall, M. (eds), *Advances in Global Leadership*, Vol. 2, Elsevier, Amsterdam, 2001.

Chen, Y., *Zhongguo Guoyou Qiye: Lishi, Gaige, Qianjin* [State-Owned Enterprises in China: History, Reform, and Prospects], Sanlian Publishing House, Shanghai, 2001.

Cheney, S., *From Horse to Horsepower*, Rigby, Adelaide, 1965.

Child, J., *Management in China During the Age of Reform*, Cambridge University Press, Cambridge, 1994.

China Daily, 'Chinese Dealers Face Uncertain Future', http://www.china.org. cn [accessed 11 May 2006].

China Daily, 'China's SOE Reforms Succeeding in 2000', http://english. peopledaily.com.cn [accessed 19 May 2003].

China Human Resources Commission, *Salary Survey 2002*, http://salary. chinahr.com [accessed 23 April 2004].

China's Auto Market Guide 2005: Complete Guide to China's Automotive Industry, http://www.baidu.com [accessed 21 March 2006].

Chinese Auto Industry Analysis Report 2003, http://www.ecm.com.cn [accessed 8 June 2006].

Chinese Enterprises Association, *Guoqi Gaizhi Renzhong Daoyuan* [Chinese SOE System Reform], http://www.lzisti.net.cn [accessed 25 June 2003].

Company Law, Article 64, Legal System Publishing House, Beijing, 2002.

Contract Law of the People's Republic of China (Adopted at the Second Session of the Ninth People's Congress in Beijing on March 15, 1999), Article 2.

David, R., *International Company Law*, Quebec Law Press, Quebec, 1984.

Davis, D., *Conspicuous Production: Automobiles and Elites in Detroit, 1899–1933*, Temple University Press, Philadelphia, 1988.

Ding, D., *A Survey of the Foreign Investment Environment in Middle-Western Region*, http://www.yuxi.net.cn [accessed 20 May 2006].

Ding, D., *Qiyejia Chengzhang Zhidu Lun* [Development of the Entrepreneur System], Shanghai Economics University, Shanghai, 2000.

Dregni, E., and Miller, K., *Ads That Put America on Wheels*, Motorbooks International, Wisconsin, 1996.

Du, W.J., 'Guanyu Guoqi Rencai Liushi de Sikao' [Concern About the Brain Drain in SOEs], *Beijing Review*, Vol. 46, No. 7, 2001.

Ealey, L., *Global Automotive Retailing: A New Perspective*, Economist Intelligence Unit, London, 1998.

Eckermann, E., *World History of the Automobile*, Society of Automotive Engineers, Philadelphia, 2001.

Epstein, R., *The Automobile Industry: Its Economic and Commercial Development*, Arno Press, New York, 1972.

Fang, C., and Wang, D., 'Employment Growth, Labour Scarcity and the Nature of China's Trade Expansion', in Garnaut, R., and Song L. (eds), *The Turning Point of the Chinese Economy*, Asia Pacific Press, Canberra, 2006.

Farber, D., *Sloane Rules: Alfred P. Sloane and the Triumph of General Motors*, University of Chicago Press, Chicago, 2002.

Farh, J.L., and Cheng, B.S. (2000), 'A Cultural Analysis of Paternalistic Leadership in Chinese Organizations', in Li, J.T., Tsui, A.S., and Weldon, E. (eds), *Management and Organizations in the Chinese Context*, Macmillan, Basingstoke, 2000.

Fei Xiaotong, *Shehuixue Wenji* [An Anthology of Sociology], Tianjin People's Publishing House, Tianjin, 1985.

Gan, D., *Research Into Chinese Family Businesses*, Chinese People's Press, Beijing, 2002.

Garnaut, R., *The Origins of Successful Economic Reform in China*, Tenth Anniversary of the China Center for Economic Research, Peking University, Beijing, 16–17 September 2004.

Garnaut, R., Huang, Y., and Lardy, N. (eds), *The Turning Point in China's Economic Development*, Asia Pacific Press, Canberra, 2006.

Garnaut, R., and Song, L. (eds), *China 2002: WTO Entry and World Recession*, Asia Pacific Press, Canberra, 2002.

Genat, R., *The American Car Dealership*, MBI Publishing Co., Wisconsin, 1999.

Georgano, G., and Andersen, T. (eds), *The New Encyclopedia of Motorcars: 1885 to the Present*, Dutton, New York, 1982.

Gernet, J., *A History of Chinese Civilization*, Cambridge University Press, Cambridge, 1985.

GM News, General Motors Corporation, Detroit.

Goodman, D., and Segal, G. (eds), *China in the Nineties: Crisis Management and Beyond*, Clarendon Press, Oxford, 1991.

Groves, T., Hong, Y., McMillan, J., and Naughton, B., 'Autonomy and Incentives in Chinese State Enterprises', *Quarterly Journal of Economics*, Vol. 109, No. 1, 2005.

Gudis, C., *Billboards, Automobiles, and the American Landscape*, Routledge, New York, 2004.

Guo, H.Y., 'Economic Perspectives on Anti-Money Laundering', *China Finance*, Vol. 3, 2003.

Guo, S., 'China SOEs and an Adjustment of Ownership', *Towards 2020*, Policy and Law Division of the State Development and Planning Committee under the State Council, China Price Press, Beijing, 1998.

Guo, X., 'Entrepreneurship, Construction and Economic Development in China', *Shanghai Management Science*, No. 2, 1999.

He, Y., 'Guoqi Rencai Liushi Tanto' [Discussion on the Brain Drain in Chinese SOEs], *China Economic Weekly*, Vol. 24, No. 4, 2002.

He, Z., *A Study of the Foreign Investment Environment*, Nanjing University Press, Nanjing, 2005.

Hill, C.W., *International Business: Competing in the Global Marketplace*, McGraw-Hill, New York, 1998.

Hu, A., *Great Transformations in China: Challenges and Opportunities*, Center for China Studies, Beijing, 2000.

Hu, A.G., 'Zhongguo Guoqi Chulu Fenxi' [The Future for Chinese SOEs], *China Review*, Vol. 1, No. 1, 1998.

Hu, M., *The General Situation of the Automobile Market in China*, 2005, http://www.sachina.cn [accessed 13 June 2006].

Huang, W., *Warnings: Localized Money Laundering is Legalizing Corruption in China*, http://news.163.com [accessed 25 June 2003].

Huashang web, *A Summary of China's Motor Vehicle Industry in 2004*, http://car.huash.com [accessed 23 January 2005].

Hudson, G., *Europe and China*, Edward Arnold & Co., London, 1931.

Ignatius, D., 'Weather the "Red Storm"', *Washington Post*, 19 April 2006.

Jiannjong, G., *A Comment on Reform of State-Owned Enterprises in China: Why 'Grasp the Big and Set Free the Small'*, 2000, accessed at http://www.dsis.org.tw.

Jin, P., *Hequ Hecong: Dangdai Zhongguo De Guo You Qiye Wenti* [Where to Go: Problems of the State-Owned Enterprises in Contemporary China],

China Jinri Publishing House, Beijing, 1997.

Karla, C., and Shippey, J., *International Contracts*, Shanghai Foreign Language Education Press, Shanghai, 2000.

Kimes, B., (ed.), *Packard: A History of the Motor Car and the Company*, Princeton Publishing, Princeton, 1978.

Kirsch, D., *Electric Vehicles and the Burden of History*, Rutgers University Press, New Jersey, 2000.

Langworth, R., *The Complete History of Chrysler Corporation, 1924–1985*, Beekman House, New York, 1985.

Lasch, C., *The True and Only Heaven: Progress and Its Critics*. Norton, New York, 1991.

Latham, C., and Agresta, D., *Dodge Dynasty: The Car and the Family That Rocked Detroit*, Harcourt Brace Jovanovich, San Diego, 1989.

Li, Y., 'Gongping Yu Xiaolu' [Fairness and Efficiency], *China Human Resource Development*, Vol. 129, No. 3, 2001.

Liang, N., *Gongsi Zhili Jiegou: Zhongguo De Shijiang Yu Meiguo De Jingyan*, Chinese People's Publishing House, Beijing, 1998.

Lichtenstein, N., and Meyer, S. (eds), *On the Line: Essays in the History of Auto Work*, University of Illinois Press, Illinois, 1989.

Lin, J., 'Zhixian Jixiao Pingguo Wenti Tanxi' [Discussion of the Problems of Line Performance Appraisal], *China Human Resource Development*, Vol. 151, No. 1, 2003.

Locket, M., 'China's Special Economic Zones: The Cultural and Managerial Challenges', *Journal of General Management*, Vol. 12, No. 3, 1987.

Lopez, J., *The Commercial Revolution of the Middle Ages, 950–1350*, University of Cambridge Press, Cambridge, 1976.

Lu, M., 'The Behavior of Chinese Professional Managers and the Influence of Management Education', *Management World*, No. 6, 1999.

Luck, P., *Australian Icons: Things That Make Us What We Are*, William Heinemann Australia, Melbourne, 1992.

Luo, S., and Wang, A., *China Law and Practice: WTO Mandated Legal Reform: China's Next Revolution*, http://www.chinalawandpractice.com [accessed 9 May 2006].

Mackerras, C., Taneja, P., and Young, G., *China Since 1978: Reform, Modernization and Socialism With Chinese Characteristics*, Longman Cheshire, Melbourne, 1994.

Mackerras, C., and Yorke, A., *The Cambridge Handbook of Contemporary China*, Cambridge University Press, Cambridge, 1991.

Mann, J., *Beijing Jeep: The Short Unhappy Romance of American Business in China*, Simon & Schuster, New York, 1989.

May, G. (ed.), *The Automobile Industry, 1896–1920*, Facts on File, New York, 1990.

May, G., (ed.), *The Automobile Industry, 1920–1980*, Facts on File, New York, 1989.

Min, X., 'Ruguo Jinshen Bu Neng Dedao Manzu' [If Expectations for Promotion Cannot be Met], *China Human Resource Development*, Vol. 137, No. 11, 2001.

Mu, Y., *Auto Distribution Channels Stressed by Auto Companies*, 2004, http://www.southcn.com [accessed 14 May 2005].

Nan, Y., *A Crisis of Administrative Ability: The Jaialilai Case*, 2005, http://www.chinaelections.org [accessed 26 April 2006].

Nanjing Fiat Inc., *Introducing our Product*, 2006, http://www.Fiat.com.cn [accessed 3 June 2006].

National Statistics Bureau, *Statistics of Foreign Investment in China for 2004*, 2005, http://media.163.com [accessed 29 April 2006].

Odaka, K. (ed.), *The Motor Vehicle Industry in Asia*, Singapore University Press, Singapore, 1983.

Organization for Economic Corporation and Development, *Principles of Corporate Governance*, 1999, http://www.encycogov.com [accessed 29 April 2006].

Qin, Y.J., 'Chinese Auto Market Distribution Approach and Distribution Channel Analyses', *ShangHai Auto*, 42-6, 1999.

Qu Tongzu, *Chinese Law and Chinese Society*, Chung Hwa Book Company, Beijing, 1984.

Ren, X., *Gaojishu Qiye Chanpin Zhanlue Guanli*, Tianjin University Press, Tianjin, 2000.

Schnapp, J.B. (project director), *Corporate Strategies of the Automotive Manufacturers*, Lexington Books, Lexington, 1979.

Shao, Z., *Changsha 4S Shops: Embarrassing Excitement*, 2004, http://www.jjbhn.com [accessed May 17 2005].

Shippey, K., *International Contracts*, World Trade Press, New York, 2002.

Shook, R.L., *Honda: An American Success Story*, Prentice-Hall, New York, 1988.

Song, J., and Huan, J., *An Analysis of Different Regions of Foreign Investment in China*, 2003, http://news.sina.com.cn [accessed 23 May 2006].

Strange, S., *Mad Money: When Markets Outgrow Governments*, University of Michigan Press, Ann Arbor, 1998.

Stubbs, P., *The Australian Motor Industry: A Study in Protection and Growth*, Cheshire, Melbourne, 1972.

Sukhdial, A.S., Chakraborty, G., and Steger, E.K., *Measuring Values Can*

Sharpen Segmentation in the Luxury Auto Market, http://www.questia.com [accessed 25 March 2006].

Tan, C., and Lin, W., 'Yuangong De Zuzhi Chengnuo Jiqi Sikao' [Employees' Organizational Commitment], *China Human Resource Development*, Vol. 151, No. 1, 2003.

Terrill, R., *The New Chinese Empire and What it Means for the World*, UNSW Press, Sydney, 2003.

Tien, H., and Chu, Y. (eds), *China Under Jiang Zemin*, Lynne Rienner, Colorado, 2000.

Tierney, C., 'Chinese Car Maker Ambitious, Controversial — GM Has Accused Chery Automobile Co. of Copying Chevy Design, Plans to Sue', *Detroit News*, July 2006.

Toyota Automotive, *Annual Report 2005*.

Vlasic, B., 'First Chinese Cars to hit US Shores', *Detroit News*, December 2005.

Voice of Germany, *BMW's Joint Venture With Huachen Inc.; BMW Cars Will be Made in China*, 2004, http://www.china.org.cn [accessed 23 January 2005].

Wall, S., and Rees, B., *International Business*, Prentice-Hall, New York, 2004.

Wang, F., *Auto Distributors' Revolution*, 2005, http://auto.people.com.cn [accessed 8 May 2005].

Wang, G., *Qiye Zhili Jiegou yu Qiyejia Xuanze* [Corporate Governance and Selection of Entrepreneurs], Economic Management Publishing House, Beijing, 2002.

Wang, J., 'Toushi Qiye Rencai Liushi' [Analysing the Brain Drain in SOEs], *Chengdu Youth Paper*, 20 December 2002.

Wang, Y., *Research Into the Law Relating to FDI in China*, Law Press, Beijing, 2002.

Wang, Z., and Satow, T., 'Leadership Styles and Organizational Effectiveness in Chinese–Japanese Joint Ventures', *Journal of Managerial Psychology*, Vol. 9, No. 4, 1994.

Webb, A., 'China and the M&A Boom', *Accounting and Business*, February 2003.

Womack, J., *The Machine That Changed the World: The Massachusetts Institute of Technology 5-Million Dollar 5-Year Report on the Future of the Automobile Industry*, Rawson Associates, New York, October 1990.

Wu, X., *Auto 4S Shop Case Analysis*, 2005, http://www.glr163.com [accessed 20 April 2005].

Xiao, K., 'NPC Deputy Warns of Brain Drain After WTO Entry: Localization of Employees Has Become a Trend in Multinationals', *China*

Daily, 11 March 2002.

Xie, J., *Guyuan Liudong Guanli* [Employee Turnover Management], Nankai University Press, Tianjin. 2001.

Xie, J., Wang, Y., and Zhang, Z., *Qiye Guyuan Liushi* [Employee Turnover in Enterprises], Economic Management Press, Beijing, 1999.

Yan, D., and Warner, M., *Sino-Foreign Joint Ventures Versus Wholly Foreign-Owned Enterprises in the People's Republic of China*, Research Papers in Management Studies, University of Cambridge, October 2001.

Yang, Y., 'Guoqi Rencai Liushi Yuanyin Fenxi' [Analysis of the Brain Drain in Chinese SOEs], *Worker's Daily*, 24 March 2003.

Yates, B., *The Decline and Fall of the American Automobile Industry*, Empire Books, New York, 1983.

Young, J., *By Foot to China*, Radiopress, Tokyo, 1984.

Zhan, Z., *Law Disputes Related to Foreign Invested Enterprises*, 2005, http:// www.chinaelections.org [accessed 26 April 2006].

Zhang, L., *China-Made BMW on Sale Countrywide Today*, 2003, http:// business.sohu.com [accessed 23 January 2005].

Zhang, W., *Qiye Lilun yu Zhongguo Qiye Gaige* [Theory of Enterprises and the Reform of Chinese Enterprises], Beijing University, Beijing, 2002.

Zhang, Y., and Ren, X., *Management Barriers to Small Business Growth*, Tianjin University Press, Tianjin, 2002.

Zhang, Z., and Fu, Q., *Money Laundering and Anti-Money Laundering*, Economic Daily Press, Beijing, 2003.

Zhao, S., 'Guoyou Qiye Fazhan Yu Renli Ziben Touzi' [The Development of SOEs and the Investment of Human Capital], *People's Forum*, Vol. 67, No. 3, 1998.

Zheng, Q., *The Chinese Judicial System and its Reform*, Jilin University Press, Changchun, 2004.

Zhong, G., 'Qiyejia Chengzhang Xianzhuang' [The Situation of Entrepreneurs in China], *Chinese Economic Times*, 16 April 2003.

Zhou, J., and Song, R., *Legal Protection of Foreign Investment in China*, 2005, http:// www.chinafiw.com [accessed 20 May 2006].

Zhu, J., 'Liability of Outside Directors and Corporate Governance', *Perspective*, Vol. 3, No. 3, 2002.

Zhu, Z.Q., 'The Booming Chinese Insurance Market', *Shanghai Securities*, 2002, http://stock.qd.sd.cn [accessed 30 May 2003].

Endnotes

1 *New York Times*, 12 March 2006.
2 This view is not only that of the author. The Victorian Manufacturing Minister, Andre Haermeyer, has stated that cheap Chinese manufacturing will be 'a tsunami that will rip through the nation's manufacturing industry and rip it apart'. Reported by Graham Cooke, *Canberra Sunday Times*, 28 January 2007.
3 For example, the then CEO of Ford, William Clay Ford Jr, visited Australia in October 2006, shortly after Ford cut back production by 20 per cent at its plant in Broadmeadows. He stated that he was 'confident that Australian car manufacturing has a future' but that future was as an 'intellectual capital for Asia' (Andrew Trounson, reporting in the *Weekend Australian*, 28/29 October 2006). He added that the key to continued Australian production was, however, continuing government subsidies.
4 Reported by Graham Cooke, *Canberra Sunday Times*, 28 January 2007.
5 Steven Gunn, CEO of Blundstone boots, commented in a radio interview reported in the *Canberra Sunday Times* that there are no longer Australians 'knocking at our door wanting to sell us new technology [because] they aren't there'. Graham Cooke, *Canberra Sunday Times*, 28 January 2007.
6 The maximum permitted movement is 0.3 per cent per trading day. Of course, due to the normal forces of currency supply and demand, it would be extremely unlikely to move at its maximum allowable rate each and every day. Over one year, since the yuan was allowed to float in this limited way, it has increased in value by just 1.8 per cent against the US dollar.
7 China's monthly trade surplus with the US reached as high as US$24.4 billion in October 2006.
8 Reported in *New York Times*, 19 December 2006.
9 Ibid.
10 Zhou Xiaochuan, governor of the People's Bank of China, in an announcement to mark the beginning of 2007, confirmed that the bank would continue to pursue a 'stable currency policy', which was code for stating that there would be no moves in the foreseeable future to change China's exchange rate policy.
11 Quoted by the *New York Times*, 18 September 2006.
12 M. Auffhammer, 'China's Market for Cars', *International Area Studies Program*, Department of Agricultural and Resource Economics, University of California — Berkeley, 2006.
13 B. Yates, *The Decline and Fall of the American Automobile Industry*, Empire Books, New York, 1983, p. 162.
14 There are numerous sources for a history of the Australian motor vehicle industry. They include P. Stubbs, *The Australian Motor Industry: A Study in Protection and Growth*, Cheshire, Melbourne, 1972, and S. Cheney, *From Horse to Horsepower*, Rigby, Adelaide, 1965.
15 It was not successful, probably because it was too expensive, and only around 20 cars were made.
16 P. Luck, *Australian Icons: Things That Make Us What We Are*, William Heinemann Australia, Melbourne, 1992, pp. 110–11.
17 Ibid.

18 Ibid.

19 Leyland had dropped out after the economic disaster of the Australian-designed P76, and Volkswagen had reduced its operations.

20 According to the Federal Chamber of Automotive Industries.

21 Australian Bureau of Statistics, *2005 Yearbook*, reference 1301.0 — Material Contributed by the Automotive Research and Trade Section, Australian Government Department of Industry, Tourism and Resources (September 2004).

22 Quoted by Terry Cook, *The Economist*, 22 September 2005.

23 Quoted in *The Weekend Australian*, 27/28 January 2007, p. 34.

24 Ibid.

25 Ibid.

26 Ibid.

27 R. Callick, China correspondent, *Australian Financial Review*, 8 April 2006.

28 Quoted in *The Australian*, 24 August 2006, report by Michelle Wiese Bockmann.

29 Quoted in J. Mann, *Beijing Jeep: The Short Unhappy Romance of American Business in China*, Simon & Schuster, New York, 1989, p. 306.

30 Ibid.

31 US State Department report of July 1989.

32 Mann, *Beijing Jeep*, p. 306.

33 Ibid., p. 297.

34 Ibid., p. 311.

35 Estimate from the national base price (US) of a 2007 Jeep Grand Cherokee Laredo, four-door, six-cylinder.

36 Reported in *The Australian*, 23 January 2007.

37 In Australia in August 2006, sales of a new model Commodore made Holden the number one seller over Toyota, but car sales for that month were down 5 per cent compared with the same month in the previous year, and over a full year, sales of large cars fell by 27 per cent. According to statistics of the Federal Chamber of Automotive Industries, this figure meant that large cars comprised just 14 per cent of all vehicle sales, down from 17.5 per cent in the previous year.

38 The Redbook listing of the resale values of various models forecasts that for the three years 2006–08, buyers of small cars could expect higher resale values than buyers of large cars like the Holden Commodore or Ford Falcon.

39 Based on a *Boston Globe* survey, 1 January through 31 May 2006, of vehicles with a domestic-parts-content rating of 75 per cent or more (the minimum federal standard for a car to be labelled domestic).

40 Quoted in the *Sydney Morning Herald*, 29 August 2006, report by Verity Edwards.

41 K. Odaka (ed.), *The Motor Vehicle Industry in Asia*, Singapore University Press, Singapore, 1983.

42 J.B. Schnapp et al., *Corporate Strategies of the Automotive Manufacturers*, Lexington Books, Lexington, 1979, p. 83.

43 Ibid.

44 M. Dunne, president of consultants Auto Resources Asia, quoted in the *Australian Financial Review*, 8 April 2006.

45 J. Wormald, principal of automotive strategic consultants Autopolis, adding that in his opinion, Australia represented an ideal test market for China's makers. Quoted in the *Australian Financial Review*, 8 April 2006.

46 B. Yates, *The Decline and Fall of the American Automobile Industry*, Empire Books, New York, 1983, p. 162.

47 R.L. Shook, *Honda: An American Success Story*, Prentice-Hall, New York, 1988, p. 25.

48 Ibid., p. 29.

49 Ibid.

50 Ibid., p. 33.

51 Yates, *Decline and Fall*, p. 161.

52 Yates, p. 161.

53 Note that automotive industry statistics are often a compilation, not just of apples and oranges, but of grapes and pineapples as well. There are also differences about how much the orchards are comparable.

There are statistics for sales and statistics for production, statistics that include cars, also light trucks (sometimes these include SUVs) and minivans/people-movers, and statistics for total 'vehicles' — but that category excludes motorcycles. Wherever statistics are quoted in this book, every effort is made to ensure that comparable figures are used.

54 Reported in the *New York Times*, 24 April 2007.

55 It is interesting, however, to speculate whether in 2007 Toyota may be tempted into the king of all mergers — joining forces with the struggling Ford Motor Company to form by far the largest auto making conglomerate in the world. There is also interest in speculating on a merger between GM and Chrysler, although GM's ability to absorb its rival may not be as robust as Toyota's.

56 By 2005, the Big Three's share of the US car market had fallen to 55 per cent, down from over 60 per cent a decade earlier.

57 Reported in *The Guardian*, 27 January 2006.

58 Ibid.

59 This procedure involves what is called a Chapter 11 filing. The move enables a hard-pressed company to change work conditions (provided a court approves) and avoid the 'nuclear option' of a financial meltdown that would be disastrous for all parties concerned.

60 D. Teather, writing in *The Guardian*, 21 November 2005.

61 Quoted by Andrew Clark, reporting in *The Guardian*, 19 August 2006.

62 Reported in *New York Times*, 15 September 2006.

63 Andrew Clark, writing in *The Guardian*, 17 February 2007.

64 Data from the UK Office for National Statistics, September 2006.

65 G. Gow in *The Guardian*, 2 March 2006.

66 Ibid.

67 *The Guardian*, 17 May 2006.

68 T. Woodley in *The Independent*, 19 April 2006.

69 As reported by Richard Spencer in the *Daily Telegraph* (UK), 5 February 2007.

70 Tony Woodley, of the UK Transport and General Workers Union, *The Guardian*, 3 May 2005.

71 In 2005, VW lost a total of €88 million in its Asian operations.

72 Gow, Guardian, 2 March 2006.

73 Some of these vehicles will be very basic, and hence low-cost, and may appeal to some export markets in South-East Asia and Africa. Tata has plans to develop a basic passenger car to retail for around US$2,200.

74 In 1948, the Occupation Authority had decreed that the *zaibatsu* should be dissolved, but later permitted them to continue after being reformed. Some *zaibatsu* developed close ties to US corporations.

75 Generally, in Western countries, there was not such a large number of suppliers.

76 The case of Mazda being bailed out during its year of crisis in 1975 raises the hypothetical question about whether Australia's financial giants would act in a similar fashion to ensure that major Australian car makers did not go bankrupt.

77 Productivity is measured in terms of production value per labour time in hours.

78 The Americans did, however, introduce ground-breaking emission control legislation in the form of the so-called 'Muskie Act' of 1970.

79 Toyota Automotive, *Annual Report 2005*.

80 G. Hudson, *Europe and China*, Edward Arnold & Co., London, 1931, p. 28.

81 Ibid., p. 51.

82 J. Gernet, *A History of Chinese Civilization*, Cambridge University Press, Cambridge, 1985, p. 17.

83 C. Mackerras and A. Yorke, *The Cambridge Handbook of Contemporary China*, Cambridge University Press, Cambridge, 1991, p. 156.

84 See P. Jin, *Hequ Hecong: Dangdai Zhongguo De Guo You Qiye Wenti* [Where to Go: Problems of the State-Owned Enterprises in Contemporary China], China Jinri Publishing House, Beijing, 1997.

85 Although some suggest it was a copy of a Stalinist design. To the author, it looks near identical to the MB 220 of that era.

86 J. Becker, *The Hungry Ghosts: Mao's Secret Famine*, Free Press, London, 1996.

87 M. Locket, 'China's Special Economic Zones: The Cultural and Managerial Challenges', *Journal of General Management*, Vol. 12, No. 3, 1987, pp. 21–31.

Endnotes

88 There are numerous commentaries on China's recent reforms. The author has referred especially to C. Mackerras, P. Taneja and G. Young, *China Since 1978: Reform, Modernization and Socialism With Chinese Characteristics*, Longman Cheshire, Melbourne, 1994.

89 Noted in Mackerras and Yorke, *Cambridge Handbook*, p. 156.

90 Y. Chen, *Zhongguo Guoyou Qiye: Lishi, Gaige, Qianjin* [State-Owned Enterprises in China: History, Reform, and Prospects], Sanlian Publishing House, Shanghai, 2001.

91 Mackerras, Taneja and Young, *China Since 1978*, p. 80.

92 E. Friedman, 'Globalization, Legitimacy and Post-Communism in China: A Nationalist Potential for Democracy, Prosperity and Peace', in H. Tien and Y. Chu (eds), *China Under Jiang Zemin*, Lynne Rienner, Colorado, 2000, p. 234.

93 Most of the high level of savings of ordinary people has been directed into SOEs.

94 China State Statistical Bureau, 1997.

95 M. Blecher, 'Sounds of Silence and Distant Thunder: The Crisis of Economic and Political Administration', in D. Goodman and G. Segal (eds), *China in the Nineties: Crisis Management and Beyond*, Clarendon Press, Oxford, 1991, pp. 48–49.

96 G. Jiannjong, *A Comment on Reform of State-Owned Enterprises in China: Why 'Grasp the Big and Set Free the Small* [online], 2000, accessed at http://www.dsis.org.tw.

97 National Bureau of Statistics, China Statistical Yearbook, China Statistics Press, Beijing, 2002.

98 Y. Huang, quoted in *The Australian*, 26 August 2006.

99 Y. Li, 'Gongping Yu Xiaolu' [Fairness and Efficiency], *China Human Resource Development*, Vol. 129, No. 3, 2001.

100 L. Song, 'Entry to the WTO and the Domestic Private Economy', in R. Garnaut and L. Song (eds), *China 2002: WTO Entry and World Recession*, Asia Pacific Press, Canberra, 2002.

101 W. Mei, 'Competition, Ownership Diversification and Industrial Growth', in Garnaut and Song, *China 2002*, Asia Pacific Press, Canberra, 2002.

102 Song, 'Entry to the WTO'.

103 However, car manufacturers faced a downturn in sales around this time.

104 AFP report, 1 April 2006.

105 The population of the coastal provinces of China alone was approximately 400 million in 2006.

106 Statistic quoted in R. Terrill, *The New Chinese Empire and What it Means for the World*, UNSW Press, Sydney, 2003, p. 157.

107 Friedman, 'Globalization', p. 234.

108 R. Garnaut, *The Origins of Successful Economic Reform in China*, paper presented at the Tenth Anniversary of the China Center for Economic Research, Peking University, Beijing, 16–17 September 2004.

109 Reported by Martin Crutsinger for Associated Press, 2 February 2007.

110 R. Garnaut (head of the China Economy and Business Program, Australian National University), Y. Huang (Asia economist with Citigroup Global Markets), also N. Lardy (Institute for International Economics in Washington, DC) — papers available in *The Turning Point in China's Economic Development*, Asia Pacific Press, Canberra. 2006.

111 Statistics from C. Fang and D. Wang, 'Employment Growth, Labour Scarcity and the Nature of China's Trade Expansion', in *The Turning Point of the Chinese Economy*, Asia Pacific Press, Canberra, 2006.

112 D. Perkins, 'The Prospects for China's Economic Reforms', in A. Barnett and R. Clough (eds), *Modernizing China: Post Mao Reform and Development*, Westview Press, Colorado, 1986, p. 42.

113 That is, a 100 per cent revaluation, although many experts lobby for a revaluation of 20 per cent or 40 per cent. These lower rates may be more palatable politically, but economists could still argue for a revaluation of no less than 100 per cent.

114 Note that US auto manufacturers also complain, with justification, that the Japanese yen is undervalued against the US dollar. This gives Japanese auto makers an unfair advantage in trading on world markets, and contributes to the Japanese amassing significant trade surpluses vis-à-vis the United States.

115 Automotive Resources Asia, a consulting firm in Shanghai.

116 Ashley Seager, writing in *The Guardian*, 19 August 2006.

117 The Economist Intelligence Unit (EIU) report, accessed at bizjournals.com, 31 March 2006.

118 'Semi-business use' means that the vehicles were used by executives for discretionary purposes. At the time, it was not always easy to make a clear distinction between 'business use' and 'private use' in the

Chinese context.

119 The production capacity to produce three-wheeled vehicles is not included in this book when car production statistics are discussed. There is an argument that it should be, but the line between the auto-rickshaw type of three-wheeler and a three-wheeled enclosed passenger vehicle is a fine one. The argument to leave them out of the statistics is based upon the fact that their engine capacity is so small. In this book, a 'car' by the author's definition is a passenger vehicle with an engine capacity larger than 600cc or so, and this excludes most three-wheelers.

120 David Thursfield, executive vice-president of Ford Motor Company, said at the opening of the Chang'an facility in Chongqing in April 2001 that in his opinion China would become one of the biggest auto producers in the world. He also predicted that China would produce 5 million cars by 2010. In fact he underestimated the abilities of the Chinese in that regard as the 5 million car mark was surpassed in 2005.

121 M. Auffhammer, 'China's Market For Cars', *International Area Studies Program*, Department of Agricultural and Resource Economics at University of California — Berkeley, 2006.

122 L. Zhang, *China-Made BMW on Sale Countrywide Today* [online], 2003, accessed at http://business.sohu.com.

123 C. Cheliang, *What's the Problem: BMW in Crisis* [online], 2005, accessed at http://auto.china.com.

124 In China, the Xiali is priced from 30,000 yuan — less than US$4,000.

125 According to Xu Changming, director of the Economic Consultative Center of the China State Information Center.

126 China Association of Automotive Industry statistics for 2004.

127 Lu Jinhua, president of the Beijing Municipal Auto Circulation Association.

128 *China Daily*, 3 April 2005.

129 *People's Daily*, 9 October 2006.

130 Zhu Min, State Information Center, Economic Forecasting Division, 'An Analysis of the Development Environment of China's Automobile Industry', *China Economic Times*, 25 November 2004.

131 B. Vlasic, 'First Chinese Cars to Hit US Shores', *Detroit News*, December 2005.

132 CBS Report of 10 January 2006.

133 Vlasic, 'First Chinese Cars'.

134 Qingdao municipal government statistics report, 2003.

135 At the time of this research, the Royaume was not available in Qingdao.

136 In China, there is little reluctance to discuss one's income.

137 *GM News*, 2005.

138 *Chinanews*, 2004.

139 All statistics, *Chinanews*, 2004.

140 Acknowledgements to Lisa Sun.

141 For example, as in other countries, more young people are living together without formal registration of marriage.

142 Y.J. Qin, 'Chinese Auto Market Distribution Approach and Distribution Channel Analyses', *ShangHai Auto*, 1999, pp. 42–46.

143 X.Y. Wu, *Auto 4S Shop Case Analysis* [online], 2005, accessed at URL: http://www.glr163.com.

144 A point noted by Wang Xia, vice-president of the Automobile Branch, China Council for Promotion of International Trade.

145 Ibid.

146 Acknowledgements to the research of Jason Yang.

147 Wu, *Auto 4S Shop Case Analysis*.

148 *HuaXi Metropolitan News*, May 2005.

149 Y. Mu, *Auto Distribution Channel is Stressed by Auto Companies* [online], 2004, accessed at http://www.southcn.com.

150 F.M. Wang, *Auto Distributors' Revolution* [online], 2005, accessed at http://auto.people.com.cn.

151 Z.B. Shao, *Changsha 4S Shops: Embarrassing Excitement* [online], 2005, accessed at http://www.jjbhn.com.

152 Acknowledgements to the research of Kevin Feng.

153 Min Hu, *The General Situation of the Automobile Market in China* [online], 2005, accessed at http://

www.sachina.cn.

154 Acknowledgements to the research of Christine Li.

155 Hu Min, General Situation.

156 Shandong Second-Hand Car Association, 2006.

157 These regulations are enforced by the city government and are called the Second-Hand Car Circulation Method.

158 Examples of these websites, as of May 2006, were sdesc.com and qdcars.com.

159 Qingdao Statistics Bureau, 2005.

160 Ibid.

161 Ibid.

162 The word 'compound' suggests a walled area, and there were walls around each compound, but there are several gates in the walls, so they are not totally enclosed.

163 According to the 2000 ranking of Standard & Poors.

164 Z.Q. Zhu, 'The Booming Chinese Insurance Market', Shanghai Securities, 2002, accessed at http://stock.qd.sd.cn.

165 Acknowledgements to the research of Steve Sun.

166 Studies include J. Child, Management in China During the Age of Reform, Cambridge University Press, Cambridge, 1994; Z. Wang and T. Satow, 'Leadership Styles and Organizational Effectiveness in Chinese-Japanese Joint Ventures', Journal of Managerial Psychology, Vol. 9, No. 4, 1994; and I. Bjoerkman and Y. Lu, 'Human Resource Management Practices in Foreign Invested Enterprises in China — What Has Been Learned?', in S. Stewart and A. Carver (eds), Advances in Chinese Industrial Studies, JAI Press, Connecticut, 1997.

167 D. Ding, Qiyejia Chengzhang Zhiadu Lun [Development of Entrepreneur System], Shanghai Economics University Press, Shanghai, 2002.

168 Q. Chen and Z. Jin, 'Cong Juren Jituan Weiji Tan Duoyuanhua Jingying', Zhongwai Guanli, Vol. 7, No. 9, 1997.

169 X. Guo, 'Entrepreneurship Construction and Economic Development in China', Shanghai Management Science, No. 2, pp. 24–25, 1999.

170 W. Zhang, Qiye Lilun yu Zhongguo Qiye Gaige [Theory of Enterprises and the Reform of Chinese Enterprises], Beijing University, Beijing, 2002.

171 M. Lu, 'The Behavior of Chinese Professional Managers and the Influence of Management Education', Management World, No. 6, 1999, pp. 152–55.

172 Y. Zhang and X. Ren, Management Barriers to Small Business Growth, Tianjin University Press, Tianjin, 2002.

173 D. Gan, Research Into Chinese Family Businesses, Chinese People's Press, Beijing, 2002.

174 N. Liang, Gongsi Zhili Jiegou: Zhongguo De Shijiang Yu Meiguo De Jingyan, Chinese People's Publishing House, Beijing, 1998.

175 X. Ren, Gaojishu Qiye Chanpin Zhanlue Guanli, Tianjin University Press, Tianjin, 2000.

176 T. Groves, Y. Hong, J. McMillan and B. Naughton, 'Autonomy and Incentives in Chinese State Enterprises', Quarterly Journal of Economics, Vol. 109, No. 1, 2005.

177 Chinese Enterprise Association, Guoqi Gaizhi Renzhong Daoyuan [Chinese SOE System Reform] [online], 2003, accessed http://www.lzisti.net.cn.

178 X.P. Chen, 'Zhongguo Qiye Mianlin de Liu Da Wenti' [The Six Big Problems that Chinese Enterprises are Facing], Management, Vol. 28, No. 3, 2001.

179 For example, Y. Li, 'Gongping Yu Xiaolu' [Fairness and Efficiency], China Human Resource Development, Vol. 129, No. 3, 2001.

180 China Society Survey Office, reported in the People's Daily, 17 May 2003.

181 Acknowledgements for the research of Cui Yan.

182 J.Y. Xie, Guyuan Liudong Guanli [Employee Turnover Management], Nankai University Press, Tianjin, 2001, p. 161.

183 The period ran from the end of Spring Festival 2002 to the beginning of Spring Festival 2003. The end of Spring Festival (which varies from year to year) is a common time for starting employment.

184 J. Wang, 'Toushi Qiye Rencai Liushi' [Analysing the Brain Drain in SOEs], Chengdu Youth Paper, 20 December 2002.

185 M. Bak and T. Jackson, 'Foreign Companies and Chinese Workers: Employee Motivation in the People's Republic of China', *Journal of Organizational Change Management*, Vol. 11, No. 4, 1998.

186 China Human Resources Commission, *Salary Survey 2002* [online], accessed at http://salary.chinahr.com.

187 Zhang, *Qiye Lilun yu Zhongguo Qiye Gaige*.

188 S. Zhao, 'Guoyou Qiye Fazhan Yu Renli Ziben Touzi' [The Development of SOEs and the Investment of Human Capital], *People's Forum*, Vol. 67, No. 3, 1998, pp. 45–51.

189 www.Motorola.com, accessed on 14 May 2004.

190 J. Child, *Management in China During the Age of Reform*, Cambridge University Press, Cambridge, 1994.

191 X.P. Chen and J.L. Farh, 'Transformational and Transactional Leader Behaviors in Chinese Organizations: Differential Effects in People's Republic of China and Taiwan', in W.H. Mobley and M. McCall (eds), *Advances in Global Leadership*, Vol. 2, 2001.

192 Y. Yang, 'Guoqi Rencai Liushi Yuanyin Fenxi' [Analysis of the Brain Drain in Chinese SOEs], *Worker's Daily*, 24 March 2003.

193 And the author then asked: 'How do you Chinese really see foreigners?' The answer: 'You're rather like a kind of clever gnome. You know lots of technical things we don't. So we want you to teach them to us — but after that, you should go back to your own place.'

194 For example, is the work of a housewife or househusband 'labour'?

195 As defined in the *Concise Oxford Dictionary*, 9th edition.

196 In any event, the vehicle has to be valued for customs purposes.

197 According to Heather Ridout of the Australian Industry Group, quoted in *The Australian*, 26 August 2006.

198 Acknowledgements to the research of David Wang.

199 National Statistics Bureau of China, 2005.

200 H. Chang, *The New Features of Foreign Investment in China*, Law Press, Beijing, 2005.

201 Compilation of Laws, 2002.

202 S. Luo and A. Wang, *China Law and Practice: WTO Mandated Legal Reform: China's Next Revolution* [online], 2001, accessed at http://www.chinalawandpractice.com.

203 Qu Tongzu, *Chinese Law and Chinese Society*, Chung Hwa Book Company, Beijing, 1984, p. 2.

204 Mabo v State of Queensland (No 2) (1992) 175 CLR 1, at 29–30 per Brennan J.

205 One such is A. Webb, 'China and the M&A Boom', *Accounting and Business*, February 2003, pp. 26–27.

206 C.W. Hill, *International Business: Competing in the Global Marketplace*, McGraw-Hill, New York, 1998.

207 Contract Law of the People's Republic of China (Adapted at the Second Session of the Ninth People's Congress on March 15, 1999), Article 2.

208 Yumei Wang, *Research Into the Law Relating to FDI in China*, Law Press, Beijing, 2002.

209 Qiang Zheng, *The Chinese Judicial System and its Reform*, Jilin University Press, Changchun, 2004.

210 L.H. Chaney and J.S. Martin, *Intercultural Business Communication*, Prentice-Hall, New York, 2002, p. 242.

211 Fei Xiaotong, *Shehuixue Wenji* [An Anthology of Sociology], Tianjin People's Publishing House, Tianjin, 1985, p. 4.

212 R. David, *International Company Law*, Quebec Law Press, Quebec, 1984.

213 Qiang Zheng, *Chinese Judicial System*.

214 Kevin Hopgood-Brown, quoted in *The Australian*, 6 February 2007.

215 Yumei Wang, *Research Into Law*.

216 D. Ding, *A Survey of the Foreign Investment Environment in Middle-Western Region* [online], 2002, accessed at http://www.yuxi.net.cn.

217 Hill, *International Business*.

218 Ibid., p. 53.

219 Article 2, Contract Law of the People's Republic of China.

220 S. Wall and B. Rees, *International Business*, Prentice-Hall, New York, 2004, p. 185.

221 Reported by Nan Yun, *A Crisis of Administrative Ability: The Jaialilai Case* [online], 2005, accessed at http://www. chinaelections.org.

222 Chang Huiying, *New Features*.

223 K. Shippey, *International Contracts*, World Trade Press, New York, 2002.

224 J. Song and H. Jiao, *An Analysis of Different Regions of Foreign Investment in China* [online], 2003, accessed at http://news.sina.com.cn.

225 Article 128, Constitution of the People's Republic of China.

226 Tianhua Law Firm No. 1999-324.

227 Shippey, *International Contracts*.

228 J. Zhou and R. Song, *Legal Protection of Foreign Investment in China* [online], 2006, accessed at http://www.chinafiw.com.

229 Z. Zhan, *Law Disputes Related to Foreign Invested Enterprises* [online], 2005, accessed at http://www.chinaelections.org.

230 Tianhua Law Firm No.2002-2630.

231 Compilation of Laws, p. 776.

232 W. Huang, *Warnings: Localized Money Laundering is Legalizing Corruption in China* [online], 2001, accessed at http://news.163.com.

233 Ibid.

234 For example, in He Qinglian, *China's Pitfall*, 1998, and in *The Economist*, 15 February 2002.

235 A. Hu, *Great Transformations in China: Challenges and Opportunities*, Center for China Studies, Beijing, 2000.

236 H.Y. Guo, 'Economic Perspectives on Anti-Money Laundering', *China Finance*, Vol. 3, 2003, p. 26.

237 Z. Cao, *China's Annual Report on the Economy in 2002*, Lanzhou University Press, Lanzhou, 2003.

238 A. Hu and Y. Guo, *Public Corruption*, Qinghua University, 2001, quoted in *The Economist*, 15 February 2002.

239 D. Ignatius, 'Weather the "Red Storm"', *Washington Post*, 19 April 2006.

240 Ibid.

241 C. Tierney, 'Chinese Car Maker Ambitious, Controversial — GM Has Accused Chery Automobile Co. of Copying Chevy Design, Plans to Sue', *Detroit News*, July 2006.

242 Ibid.

243 For example, G. Rhys of the Center for Automotive Industry Research, Cardiff University, quoted in *The Economist*, 8 September 2005.

244 N. Ching, *New York Times*, 12 March 2006.

245 Ibid.

246 C. Tierney, 'Chinese Car Maker Ambitious, Controversial — GM Has Accused Chery Automobile Co. of Copying Chevy Design, Plans to Sue', *Detroit News*, July 2006.

Index